Latin American Psychology:

A Guide to Research and Training

by

Gerardo Marin
University of San Francisco

Steven Kennedy
Barry Campbell Boyce
American Psychological Association

American Psychological Association
Washington, DC 20036

Published by the American Psychological Association, Inc.
1200 Seventeenth Street, N.W., Washington, DC 20036

Printed in the United States of America.

Copies may be ordered from:

Order Department
American Psychological Association
P.O. Box 2710
Hyattsville, MD 20784

Library of Congress Cataloging-in-Publication Data

Marin, Gerardo.
  Latin American psychology.

  Bibliography: p.
    1. Psychology—Research—Latin America—Directories.
2. Psychology—Study and teaching—Latin America—
Directories. 3. Psychology—Latin America—Societies, etc.
—Directories. 4. Psychology—Latin America—Bibliography.
I. Kennedy, Steven, 1952-   . II. Boyce, Barry
Campbell, 1956-   . III. Title. [DNLM: 1. Psychology
—education—Latin America—directories. 2. Psychology—
Latin America—directories. 3. Research—Latin America—
directories. 4. Societies, Scientific—Latin America—
directories. BF 30 M3371]
BF76.5.M32 1987   150.7'08   87-17409

ISBN 0-912704-84-5

Table of Contents

Acknowledgments

We wish to thank all of the individuals who so graciously provided us with information regarding their institution or country; we could not have compiled this work without their generous donations of time and effort.   Together with the directors of the various institutions and editors of the different journals, the following individuals deserve special acknowledgment for their comments, criticisms, and assistance in obtaining the information contained in this book.   We are particularly thankful for the friendship they have shown us and hope that this guide will further enhance collaborative efforts across the Americas--helping to close the gaps in information and understanding that we so often rightly deplore.

Reynaldo Alarcon (Peru)
Ermida Albizu (Puerto Rico)
Mariana Alvim (Brazil)
Ruben Ardila (Colombia)
Osvaldo Avelluto (Argentina)
Angela M.B. Biaggio (Brazil)
Amalio Blanco (Spain)
Madeleine Bourelly Laroche (Haiti)
Abelardo Brenes (Costa Rica)
Victor Colotla (Mexico)
Walter Cornejo (Peru)
Nuria Cortada de Kohan (Argentina)
Elizabeth De Windt (Dominican Republic)
Jose A. Dela Coletta (Brazil)
Gustavo Ekroth (Uruguay)
Elisa Fernandez (Guatemala)
Otto Gilbert (Guatemala)

Margarita Guzman Rico (Colombia)
Federico Leon (Peru)
Roberto Lerner (Peru)
Ignacio Martin-Baro (El Salvador)
Jorge Molina (Mexico)
Gladys Naranjo (Ecuador)
Alfonso Orantes (Venezuela)
Lourdes Quintanilla (Mexico)
Carmen I. Rivera (Puerto Rico)
Eduardo Rivera Medina (Puerto Rico)
Aroldo Rodriques (Brazil)
Jose Miguel Salazar (Venezuela)
Nelson Serrano (Ecuador)
Harry C. Triandis (U.S.A.)
Julio Villegas (Chile)
Jaime Whitford (Nicaragua)

Gerardo Marin
Steven Kennedy
Barry Campbell Boyce

Acknowledgement

1

Introduction

This guide is the result of our concern that most U.S. psychologists know little about psychology outside the United States. Because of the size and vigor of the psychological enterprise in our universities, clinics, and research centers, we often neglect developments in the field taking place in the rest of the world. Even well-intentioned researchers and professionals encounter difficulties when trying to obtain up-to-date information about psychology in other countries. By providing accurate and current information on Latin American psychology, this book will help U.S. psychologists make contact with colleagues in Central and South American countries, and will assist those throughout the world who wish to know more about Latin American psychology--its status, characteristics, and bibliography.

Psychology is by no means immune from the rapid changes occurring throughout Latin America. On the contrary, this process of change is mirrored in the rapid evolution of psychology as a science and as a profession in most countries of the region. Rosenzweig (1982) has estimated that there are well over 45,000 psychologists in Latin America, with approximately 120 psychologists per million inhabitants (a rate below that of the United States and Canada, Western Europe, and Australia/New Zealand but well above that of the socialist countries and the rest of the Third World). Of course, numbers do not tell the whole story. The political and socioeconomic changes in the region have forced psychologists to prove their usefulness in a changing society. These pressures have produced exciting developments in the traditional areas as well as in community, health, environmental, and social psychology.

Previous efforts at providing the type of information included in this guide have been worldwide in scale. Foremost among them is the volume edited for APA and the International Union of Psychological Sciences (IUPsyS) by Ross, Alexander, and Basowitz in 1966. More recent efforts have been produced by Sexton and Misiak (1976), Wolman (1979), and Gilgen (in press). Focusing specifically on Latin America, two especially prominent articles appeared in the Annual Review of Psychology (i.e., Ardila, 1982; Diaz-Guerrero, 1984), and other articles have appeared in various journals and book collections. Ardila (1986) has just filled a large gap in the literature with a discursive historical treatment of the development of psychology throughout the region. Unfortunately, much of the global information is outdated and lacks depth, while the specialized pieces are by definition limited in geographic or topical scope.

We hope this guide will help those interested in obtaining and using information on psychology in Latin America.

Collecting the Information

The information included in the guide was obtained in two phases. We relied first on personal contacts with knowledgeable psychologists in the various countries, on published reports and data bases, and on responses to initial queries sent to institutions known to be particularly active or prominent on the Pan American scene. Initial contacts were also made with well-known psychologists in the various countries and with individuals involved in the governance of the Interamerican Society of Psychology (SIP). These contacts provided us with an outline of psychology in the various countries and with sources of information to be contacted in the following phase.

Among the personal and institutional files and databases we consulted, the Hispanic division of the Library of Congress and the Columbus Memorial Library at the Organization of American States were especially helpful. We also searched APA's PsycINFO database and the files of Spanish-Language Psychology for bibliographic references.

In a second phase we wrote to all university departments, research centers, journals, and publications identified by any of the above procedures in order to get more detailed information. We sent a short questionnaire to all of the institutions (with three follow-ups). The results of these efforts make up the body of this book.

Because of space limitations we abstracted, edited, and rewrote all of the information we received. We naturally tried to be as accurate as possible, but in any effort of this nature one can expect errors of interpretation or unintended inaccuracies. We hope that readers will be understanding in this respect and will use the information contained here as a springboard for their own searches and information-gathering efforts.

Organization of This Guide

The Guide is divided into ten chapters, including this introduction: Chapter 2 contains a general overview of the standing of the science and profession of psychology in the countries of Latin America; Chapter 3 consists of a nonevaluative catalog of university training in psychology in the region, with an overview of the various training models; Chapter 4 lists centers and institutes that perform psychological research in Latin America; Chapter 5 lists international, regional, and national associations of psychologists, both academic and professional, by country; Chapter 6 contains listings of psychological journals published within Latin America or with a Latin America orientation; Chapter 7 provides information on approximately 50 publishers and distributors of tests in Spanish available in the region; Chapter 8 discusses grants and other funds available in the United States for support of research in Latin America or exchange with Latin America; Chapter 9 consists of a bibliography on Latin American psychology publications; and Chapter 10 contains annotated listings of general resources on work, study, and research in Latin American psychology.

References

Ardila, R. (1982). Psychology in Latin America today. In M.R. Rosenzweig & L.W. Porter (eds.). _Annual Review of Psychology_ Vol. 33. Palo Alto, CA: Annual Reviews, pp. 103-122.

Ardila, R. (1986). La psicologia en America Latina; pasado, presente y futuro. Bogota, Colombia: Siglo veintiuno de colombia.

Diaz-Guerrero, R. (1984). Contemporary psychology in Mexico. in M.R. Rosenzweig and L.W. Porter (eds.). _Annual Review of Psychology_ Vol. 35. Palo Alto, CA: Annual Reviews, pp. 83-112.

Gilgen, A. & Gilgen, C. (eds.) (1987). International Handbook of Psychology. Westport, CT: Greenwood Press.

Rozenzweig, M.R. (1982). Trends in development and status of psychology: An international perspective. _International Journal of Psychology_, _17_, pp. 117-140.

Ross, S., Alexander, I.E., & Basowitz, H. (eds.) (1966). _International opportunities for advanced training and research in psychology_. Washington, DC: American Psychological Association.

Sexton, V.S., & Misiak, H. (1976). _Psychology around the world_. Monterey, CA: Brooks/Cole.

Wolman, B.B. (1979). _International directory of psychology_. New York: Plenum.

2

General Background on Latin American Psychology

This introduction provides an overview of the standing of the science and profession of psychology in the more than 20 countries that make up Latin America. Although a number of salient trends are common to all nations of the region, large variations also exist between and within countries. This chapter provides a brief review of some significant characteristics of Latin American psychology, highlighting key differences between psychology as it exists in the United States and as it is found in the Spanish- and Portuguese-speaking countries of the Americas. To contain the focus of our undertaking, English-, French-, and Dutch-speaking countries and territories have been excluded.

Historical Development

Without too much exaggeration, the psychological profession in Latin America can be traced to 1566 in Mexico, where Bernardino Alvarez established the Hospital de San Hipolito, the first hospital in the Americas dedicated to serving patients with psychological problems (Ardila, 1970). Treatment at San Hipolito--and at a number of other mental hospitals opened at the time of the Spanish domination--bore little resemblance to the science-based clinical practice familiar to modern day practitioners.

The scientific developments in psychology occurring at the beginning of the 20th century in Europe and the United States were also felt in Latin America. Horacio Pinero established a psychological laboratory in Buenos Aires in 1898. Eighteen years later a second laboratory was established in Mexico by Enrique C. Aragon (Ardila, 1982). Together with this early interest in psychological research, there appeared a number of psychological treatises written by Catholic missionaries and physicians. These early beginnings reflect the three key sources of influence in the development of Latin American psychology: the scientific, the philosophical, and the psychiatric.

For some unknown reason the early laboratories did not have the influence that they did in Europe or in the United States, and the concern of many of the early psychologists was more closely allied with philosophical and psychiatric concerns. To this extent, academic psychology continued to be perceived, and pursued, as a branch of philosophy, while professional psychologists served as assistants to psychiatrists or in other paramedical roles. This approach to psychology shaped the profession in most countries for many years and became very difficult to modify as social needs and scientific achievements demanded a change.

During the early years of the 20th century, a number of influential Europeans migrated to Latin America, where they became deeply involved in developing a psychology that reflected their own experiences in Europe. In addition to those mentioned above, psychological laboratories were founded in other cities (e.g., Rio de Janeiro, Bogota, Lima) by migrating psychologists escaping political and social upheaval in Europe. Two related traditions came to Latin America by way of European migration. These were psychoanalytical theories and psychometry as a professional activity.

In an important article published in 1941, Beebe-Center and McFarland argued that South American psychology at that time was primarily a philosophical endeavor with a psychoanalytic orientation. Professional activity was scarce; the authors were able to identify only 100 psychologists in the entire continent. Most of these were in Argentina, Brazil, and Mexico.

Ten years later important changes had been set in motion. Professional identification and development were increasingly considered to be important goals for psychologists. In December 1951, the Interamerican Society of Psychology (SIP) was founded in Mexico City with the goal of providing psychologists and other behavioral scientists with a means of communicating among themselves in order to further the development of the profession. Most of SIP's early members were psychiatrists and social scientists. The organization also included a handful of Latin American psychologists trained by the early European immigrants, and was rounded out with a number of U.S. psychologists. In 1953 the first Interamerican Congress of Psychology was held in Santo Domingo (Dominican Republic) with the patronage of then dictator Rafael Trujillo. The first congress was attended by about 60 psychologists, who started a tradition that continues on a biannual basis. Twenty interamerican congresses of psychology have been held to date, the latest being convened in Caracas (1985), Quito (1983), Santo Domingo (1981), and Lima (1979). Attendance at the congresses has numbered in the thousands in recent years, while membership in the Society has grown to close to two thousand psychologists. A number of other activities (journal, newsletter, seminars, task forces) are now sponsored by the Society.

In 1962 psychology was legally recognized as a profession in Brazil, setting in motion similar processes in other countries by identifying psychologists as independent professionals and setting standards for their training. The Brazilian law (which forms the basis for the laws of most other countries where psychology has been regulated by law) defines the activities of psychologists as: (a) diagnosis; (b) professional orientation and selection; (c) educational orientation; and (d) solution of adjustment problems. The last provision has been recognized as a euphemism for "therapy" that was less threatening to psychiatrists.

From the outset, difficulties with psychiatrists have been one of the most commonly encountered experiences in the development of Latin American psychology. In many countries, psychologists were originally perceived as psychiatrists' assistants whose primary role was to apply psychodiagnostic procedures. Training for psychologists thus concentrated on psychometrics and testing and was controlled directly or indirectly by psychiatrists. As the numbers of psychologists increased, and as experiences from Europe and the United States became better known (through the literature, travel, and study abroad), claims for independence were heard from organizations of professional psychologists that had recently been established in many countries, and from schools of psychology headed and staffed by psychologists rather than by psychiatrists, psychoanalysts, or philosophers.

The end of the 1960s saw a budding profession striving for recognition under the influence of developments in psychology in the United States. A trickle of Latin American psychologists trained in the United States, Europe, and, later, in the Soviet Union, began to flow back to the region with methods and knowledge that quickly changed the characteristics of Latin American psychology. Social psychology, behaviorism, and the applied analysis of behavior became a significant professional and scientific orientation in Mexico, Colombia, Brazil, and Venezuela. These newly trained psychologists not only started laboratories but also brought new ideas about training and the scope of professional activity. Two international psychological journals began publication: the Revista Interamericana de Psicologia/Interamerican Journal of Psychology (1967) published by the Interamerican Society of Psychology, and the Revista Latinoamericana de Psicologia (1969) founded by Ruben Ardila in Colombia. Books and textbooks written by Latin American psychologists began to appear in significant numbers (many of them published by Editorial Trillas of Mexico), and research became more frequent and of better quality.

In the 1970s and 1980s, we have seen an explosion in the development of psychology in Latin America. Psychologists now number in the thousands in many countries. Rosenzweig (1982) presents figures derived from calculations made by member associations of the IUPsyS that illustrate dramatically the growth of the profession: Argentina was considered to have over 5,000 psychologists in 1979; Brazil had over 21,000 in 1980; Mexico had over 10,000 in 1979; and over 2,000 psychologists were identified in 1979 in Venezuela. Training programs also blossomed in most countries. We have been able to identify close to 300 different programs (see Chapter 3). The number of journals has increased to close to 80 publications that appear with varying degrees of regularity and success. Most countries now have a number of professional and scientific associations. Congresses or conventions are held in most countries on a periodic basis, and other international associations have been created to serve specific areas of psychology (e.g., social psychology, behavioral analysis) or geographical concerns (e.g., Central America). Textbooks are now more easily available and in many cases are written by Latin Americans. Research is much more frequent and in many cases receives international recognition.

One commonly noted characteristic of psychology in Latin America in the 1980s is the preponderance of applied concerns over more academic or scientific preoccupations. This fact manifests itself in the large number of clinical psychologists to be found in the region, in the relatively low number of basic research projects being conducted by Latin American psychologists, in the success of publications directed at presenting professional techniques, and in the overwhelming acceptance of professional topics during congresses and workshops. This applied emphasis reflects the fact that few academics have the opportunity to dedicate their professional endeavors solely to research. Most Latin American faculty psychologists hold a second or third position outside the university—usually in applied settings. Another important explanation for this phenomenon is the fact that psychologists have become aware of the contributions they can make to the development of their nations, and in many cases have reached positions of importance in the government. This concern for the utility of scientific knowledge is one of the key characteristics of Latin American psychology, where abstract concepts are often met with impatience or intolerance unless an application of them can be discerned.

Legal Status

As mentioned above, Brazil was the first country in the region to regulate by law the profession of psychology. The process is similar overall to the process of licensing in the United States, except that in Brazil, as elsewhere in Latin America, the power to grant the legal title of "psychologist" and to define the scope of psychologists' activities resides with the central government. To date only a handful of countries have regulated psychological practice (e.g., Brazil, Mexico, Colombia, Cuba, Venezuela). In most cases the regulations require psychologists to register, to carry a license, and to belong to a professional association (in many cases called a colegio) that regulates professional practice and sets professional ethical standards. Most of these regulations also govern the country's training institutions by mandating the types of courses that must be offered and determining the treatment to be accorded foreign-trained psychologists. In most cases psychologists who did not receive their training in the country must apply for a review of their credentials to be carried out by a local academic institution. Examination or additional training may also be required.

As is true in the United States, these licensing requirements usually apply only to individuals engaged in private practice or working for industry. However, some statutes also set minimum standards for academic practice. For example, the Colombian law defines psychology as a science and profession whose practitioners use psychological techniques and methods in meeting individual and social problems, carrying out basic and applied research, and teaching. Other activities proper to the psychologist include diagnosis, treatment, psychological and professional orientation, group or individual behavior modification, and prevention of illness. Training must take place in one of the institutions officially recognized by the government, and visiting psychologists from abroad must obtain a one-year license in order to practice or teach at a university. The law also defines proper ethical conduct, forbids psychologists from prescribing medications, and suggests the need for interdisciplinary consultation. To this, Brazilian law adds the supervision of professionals and students, consulting, and serving as an expert witness (Ginsberg, 1983).

Training

As noted in a later chapter, the training of psychologists in Latin America varies in length and orientation. Most programs require between 4 and 5 years of intensive (20 or more hours per week of classroom instruction) and fairly comprehensive training. The program of study allows for little variation and provides few possibilities for transferring or "changing majors." In most universities students are screened using admissions tests that assess aptitude and achievement (like the SAT), as well as personality, motivation, and even psychopathology. As is true in the United States, psychology is a popular major and some of the most capable students enter the field. Most students are women.

Students are expected to master basic theories and to become proficient in various therapeutic techniques. Testing receives significant attention in most programs since traditionally it is one area in which psychologists have found employment and are frequently asked to perform professional duties. Students usually develop a thorough understanding of psychometric theory as well as practical experience in the use of projective and objective tests. Most programs have begun to offer an eclectic understanding of psychology; psychoanalytic thought is not as dominant as it was just a few years ago.

Most training programs place significant emphasis on practical knowledge and experience. It is not uncommon for students to have research or volunteer work assigned to them as part of their course requirements. Students commonly work in groups, even when researching and writing a required thesis. In some countries, textbooks are extremely expensive, with the result that many students must share copies. Emphasis is therefore placed in the transmission of knowledge through lectures. Thanks to the strong programs of a number of publishing houses, classic textbooks and new books produced by Latin American psychologists are beginning to appear in Spanish and Portuguese throughout Latin America.

A significant number of training programs require students to dedicate a semester or more to supervised practical experience, usually in one of the classic areas of application of psychology (clinical, industrial, educational). In some countries (e.g., Mexico), this experience is mandated by law as part of the volunteer service required of all professionals-in-training.

Most programs also require a thesis to be presented upon completion of the academic training. The thesis is usually written in groups of two or more students, and may be a comprehensive review of the literature or a report on research carried out under the supervision of a faculty member. The final product is typically reviewed by a committee of faculty members, and students are expected to make an oral defense of the thesis.

Training usually occurs in "Departments of Psychology" located within a school or faculty of philosophy or of arts. The workings of a typical department are fairly similar to those found in a psychology department in the United States in terms of decision-making channels, academic independence, etc. In a few countries (e.g., Mexico, Colombia, Ecuador, Chile, and Brazil), psychology has achieved the status of a separate school or faculty within a given university. This distinction makes for greater autonomy in teaching and decision-making and is a recognition of the popularity and perceived importance assigned to psychology in these universities. This change is significant for a science that was first taught as an independent profession in 1946 (Ardila, 1982).

The professional qualification that most students receive after four or five years of postsecondary training is most commonly the title of "Licenciado" or "Psicologo," although a variety of other names are used. In all cases this is a terminal degree in the sense that graduates are expected to and entitled to perform all types of professional activities. Recently a few universities have started graduate-level programs (e.g., in Mexico, Brazil, Venezuela, Colombia, and Puerto Rico) where after one, two, or more years, students receive the degree of "Magister" or a doctoral degree. These programs were established to respond to a need for better trained faculty once a critical mass of professionals with advanced degrees had been formed.

Most university faculty members are also employed in private practice or in industrial and related settings, reflecting the low pay scales for psychologists in Latin America and the limited scope of professional activity available in a new profession still working to be fully recognized by society. (It is not uncommon for a full professor to earn just $300 per month.) Full-time faculty is less common, although great strides are being made in this direction.

Professional Practice

A large number of psychologists have a private clinical practice either as an adjunct to other activities (academic, industrial, school) or as their primary professional activity. Psychologists may now provide direct mental health services to the public independent of psychiatric supervision, although the same was not true of Latin American psychology just a few years ago. Theoretical orientations reflect the richness found in psychology worldwide, and in many cases Latin Americans are equally comfortable with psychoanalytically oriented therapies as with more behaviorally oriented procedures.

With the recognition of psychological disabilities and of mental retardation as an important societal problem, psychological services are becoming more and more common within the systems of socialized medicine now found in most Latin American countries. This has opened new areas of employment for psychologists as part of the social security systems as well as within the health services cooperatives that have recently been created. These developments have made possible the provision of psychological services at low rates (often free to individuals covered under social security or the cooperatives) and have opened up a large number of employment opportunities for psychologists. The system of third-party reimbursement differs from that found in the United States since all salaried employees in most countries of the region are registered as members of the social security system. In other countries, medicine and allied professions are socialized and available free of charge (e.g., in Cuba). In most countries with some form of national health coverage, private services continue to be available to those who choose to pay for them.

The level of employment of psychologists varies from country to country depending on the availability of psychologists, the level of development of the profession, and prevailing economic conditions. In some cases, psychologists have had no problem finding employment after graduation (e.g., in Venezuela before the devaluation of the bolivar and the economic woes brought about by mounting debt and depressed oil prices). In others, psychologists are underemployed (working part-time as psychologists and part-time in an unrelated occupation) or are unemployed. Next to the overall economic conditions of a country, the oversupply of psychologists is the factor most often cited as the reason for current or future unemployment among psychologists. The problem is particularly serious in small countries with large numbers of training programs, where many psychologists are obliged to move to other professions or occupations. The personal costs of such dilemmas can be very great. By contrast, in Cuba the professional training of psychologists is centrally planned. Graduates are assigned a job after being trained at government expense at one of the two programs that train psychologists.

Research

Basic and applied research is performed in most countries by professionals as well as by students. Unfortunately, the level of production of scientific research is not as high as might be expected given the large number of psychologists in Latin America. A number of explanations have been provided for this phenomenon. Ardila (1982) argues that scientific research is not a cultural value in Latin America. Others (e.g., Biaggio & Benko, 1975) suggest more convincingly that political and philosophical ideologies interfere with the performance of experimental research as it is known in the United States and in Europe. Still others (e.g., Marin, 1978; Salazar,1979; Sanchez & Wiesenfeld, 1982) argue that the social and political conditions of Latin America require that all efforts be devoted to applied research--research directed at solving the problems of developing nations. A final, more practical, explanation often found in the writings of Latin American psychologists is that support for research is lacking (research funding, appropriate libraries, and properly equipped laboratories).

Whatever the explanation, the fact is that, indeed, comparatively little basic or applied research is performed. Nevertheless, a number of Latin American laboratories and programs do conduct research that is world renowned. Such work is sometimes done under the auspices of interdisciplinary institutions (e.g., the important work on nutrition and child development carried out at the INCAP in Guatemala). In other places (e.g., Mexico, Venezuela, Argentina, and Brazil), independent or university-affiliated laboratories have been created to perform basic and applied research. (See Chapter 4 for a description of these laboratories).

Inadequate funding of research is a serious limitation in Latin America, just as it is in many developed countries. Where there is difficulty satisfying the basic needs of the population, it is not surprising to find that research is given short shrift. Nevertheless most countries of the region have a government institution similar to the National Science Foundation (NSF) in the United States where psychologists can obtain funding for their projects. As a matter of fact, many of these institutions have bilateral programs with NSF that fund collaborative projects between scientists in the United States and Latin America. Additional funding is at times available from European, Japanese, and U.S. foundations (see Chapter 10).

Problems in obtaining equipment and in setting up laboratories are also to be expected in developing countries that must depend on imported goods to meet these requirements. Most psychology departments now have an instructional laboratory furnished with imported equipment, although some departments do use domestically produced machines. Unfortunately, such instructional equipment is frequently not appropriate for advanced research. Computers are generally available in Latin American universities, although they are in great demand and in many cases psychologists are not expected to use them, since they were installed for the benefit of engineers and physical scientists. Few packaged programs for statistical analysis are available and access to mainframe computers is limited. Microcomputers are beginning to be more common in some countries and their use in psychology is increasing. Unfortunately, the high cost of such imported equipment places it outside the reach of the typical university professor.

Limitations notwithstanding, research is currently conducted in all areas of psychology. Ardila (1982) presented a short review of some current trends and many of the citations in chapter 8 will give the reader an idea of what is being researched in Latin America at the moment. As mentioned above, there is a strong emphasis on applied research and on findings that are applicable to the solution of social problems. The results of these projects are often presented at national and international congresses and, less frequently, are published in psychological journals. Foremost among the scientific meetings are those sponsored by the Interamerican Society of Psychology and held biannually in sites throughout Latin America. Other regional meetings are devoted to social psychology and behavioral analysis. These attract fewer participants but are often the forum for the presentation of significant findings. National conventions or congresses are also held in most countries on a yearly basis.

Although there are a large number of journals (see Chapter 6 for a listing) publication of research findings is less common. Since there is no "publish-or-perish" ethic in most countries, psychologists may not experience pressures to publish (which would be difficult in any case given the large number of professional and scientific commitments of Latin American academics). Nevertheless, the number and quality of published research is increasing. The American Psychological Association's (APA) PsycINFO database has recently expanded its coverage of Latin American publications, and summaries are now available through Psychological Abstracts or on-line through APA's various distributed information services.

Concluding Comment

As can be gleaned from the above comments, psychology in Latin America is in a state of growth and rapid change. In many cases this growth and change is somewhat chaotic (e.g., in the lack of legal recognition of the profession or in the growth of training programs in excess of demand for psychological services). But in most cases, the last few years have brought a sense of challenge and excitement seldom found in the history of our science/profession. The social conditions of developing countries have demanded of psychologists ingenuity and creativity in conceiving applications that were seldom envisioned by the creators of our basic theories or the researchers who identified our principles of behavior. Furthermore, the mixing of cultural traditions that takes place in nations continuously in contact with East and West has produced a challenging eclecticism in psychological theorizing that mixes European, North American, and Marxist traditions and orientations in epistemology and psychology. The end result is a science and a profession in a state of change that claims an ever larger role in the shaping of a young and troubled society. Readers interested in further study should consult the extensive bibliography that forms chapters 8 and 9.

References

Ardila, R. (1970). Landmarks in the history of Latin American psychology. Journal of the History of the Behavioral Sciences, 6, 140-146.

Ardila, R. (1982). Psychology in Latin America today. Annual review of Psychology, 33, 103-122

Beebe-Center, J.G., & McFarland, R.A. (1941). Psychology in South America. Psychological Bulletin, 38, 627-667

Biaggio, A.M.B., & Benko, A. (1975). American and European influences on Brazilian psychology. Paper presented at the convention of the American Psychological Association, Chicago.

Ginsberg, A. (1983). Psychology as a profession in Brazil: An example of full legal recognition. International Journal of Psychology, 18, 572-573.

Marin, G. (1978). La psicologia social y el desarrollo de la America Latina. _Boletin de AVEPSO_, _1(3)_, 1-13.

Rosenzweig, M.R. (1982). Trends in development and status of psychology: An international perspective. _International Journal of Psychology_, _17_, 117-140.

Salazar, J.M. (1979). Dependencia o cooperacion? La aplicacion de la psicologia social en latinoamerica. _Psicologia_, _6_, 45-50.

Sanchez, E., & Wiesenfeld, E. (1982). La psicologia social aplicada: Algunas consideraciones. _Boletin de AVEPSO_, _5(3)_, 7-15.

3

Undergraduate and Graduate Training

This chapter forms a sort of non-evaluative catalogue of undergraduate and graduate training in psychology in Latin America. As might be expected, the pattern of training varies from one country to the other, with concomitant variations in the courses taught, degree requirements, and so forth.

The chapter is divided into three sections. Following a brief overview of training in psychology in Latin America, a number of specific programs are highlighted. We offer information (current as of early 1987) on staff, student characteristics, program characteristics, and graduation requirements, and on the level of collaborative relationships with colleagues in other countries. Included in this section are those programs that answered our request for detailed information (four follow-up letters were sent to each of the departments listed here). The information is based on replies to our questionnaire, and no effort was made to establish the accuracy of the information provided to us. Finally, the reader will find a list of additional training programs.

Overview

Training in psychology in Latin America is almost as varied as the history and geography of the nations of the region. As we noted in the overview provided in the previous chapter, universities in most countries offer a four- or five-year professional program that qualifies the student to perform professional activities upon graduation (i.e., psychotherapy, testing, behavior modification, consulting, and university teaching). In other countries a one- or two-year masters-level graduate program leading to the degree of Magister or Maestria is offered. Mexico, Puerto Rico, and Brazil are foremost among the few countries that provide doctoral-level training requiring three to five years of graduate work. Most programs place special emphasis on applied issues although the comparatively rare masters and doctoral programs have a heavy academic orientation.

Just as the programs vary, so does the significance of the degrees. Most institutions grant the degree of "psicologo" (psychologist) after the initial four- to five-year training. In other countries (e.g., El Salvador, Guatemala), the degree of "licenciado" (licentiate) is awarded to those same individuals. In a few countries (Ecuador, for one), the degree of "doctor" is awarded upon the completion of only five years of class work and a limited amount of research. This degree is different from the doctorates awarded in countries such as Brazil, Mexico, and Puerto Rico that require more training (8 to 10 years) as well as a great deal of independent research. Degree equivalence, a thorny and largely unresolved issue in Latin America, becomes even more difficult when one wishes to establish equivalence with degrees granted in the United States. Nevertheless, a number of psychologists of the region argue effectively that the training provided during the initial five years of university study is equivalent if not superior to the training received by a masters-level psychologist in the United States.

Taking all variations into account, it is possible to define a Latin American model of training that includes: (a) five years of undergraduate courses with a high concentration in psychological topics (ranging from introductory overview courses to advanced classes in psychotherapeutic techniques and statistics); (b) a practicum (6 to 12 months) in the course of which the student performs supervised professional work in clinical, educational, industrial, or another area of psychology; and (c) a research project (ranging in complexity from a review of the literature to significant contributions to the discipline that have been published in refereed U.S. journals). This model of training is in place in most countries in Latin America and serves the needs of a rapidly developing profession. In some universities the student is obliged to become knowledgeable in two, three, or more areas of psychology (usually chosen from among, clinical, educational, or industrial) while others allow for the student to choose only one area of proficiency.

Teaching is typically performed by indigenously trained professionals who very often graduated from the university in which they teach. Universities in some countries (e.g., Mexico, Brazil, Venezuela, Colombia, and Chile) have a significant number of psychologists who have received graduate training in Europe, the United States, or, more recently, the Soviet Union. Few Latin American countries boast full-time faculties at their universities, although this pattern of employment is now becoming more and more common. For psychologists in most countries, teaching is an ancillary occupation to be combined with private practice or regular full-time employment at a clinic, school, hospital, or company. While some programs are primarily oriented toward one of the central theories of psychology (psychoanalysis, behaviorism), most schools have eclectic orientations with faculty members who expose students to a variety of orientations. The discussion of the theoretical implications of findings and ideas is more common in Latin American classrooms than in the United States, and students--and faculty--are usually knowledgeable in various theories in social science (including Marxism and neo-Marxism). As with most university students in Latin America, psychology students are more politically attuned than their counterparts in the United States and many expect their profession to make some contribution to solving the problems of a developing society.

Students are predominantly young women with a very high level of interest and commitment to their studies. Unfortunately, textbooks are usually more expensive or otherwise more difficult to obtain than in the United States, forcing many professors to depend on lectures to transmit information. Library facilities in some areas are very limited, making it difficult for students to prepare term papers with the same breadth that we may expect elsewhere. Laboratory courses are included in most teaching programs although the facilities may at times be very limited. As a result of these limitations, and as an expression of Latin American culture, students in Latin America often study and do class projects in groups.

In short, while resources and standards vary from country to country and from one school to another, a generally recognized training program of five years duration forms the backbone of training in psychology in Latin America. Both the consistencies and variations among these programs can be assessed by a quick study of the list provided in this chapter.

The listings found below were compiled from the answers to a questionnaire sent to all teaching programs. (One should recognize that the undergraduate degree titles used by different programs admit of tremendous variation in what they represent, and likewise the meaning of doctoral and masters degrees may differ from how these terms are applied in the United States.) In most cases the information should remain current for a number of years except for the name of the program chair, which of course can change with frequency. The subsection labelled "Exchange Programs" refers to the institution's desire to establish collaborative arrangements with other institutions or individuals. When a yes follows one of the possible areas of collaboration (student exchange, research projects, or faculty exchange/visits) it indicates that the institution is interested in such exchange. Psychological areas listed under "Research" are topics that would be of interest to the institution's faculty. A blank indicates that the institution did not provide an answer to that question.

Detailed Program Descriptions

<u>Argentina</u>

ESCUELA DE PSICOLOGIA
FACULTAD DE HUMANIDADES
UNIVERSIDAD DE BELGRANO
Olleros 2230
Buenos Aires, Argentina
Phone: 772-1547-8213   Chair: Dr. Alberto Braud Larraburu

Undergraduate Training
    Degree offered: Licenciado en Psicologia
    Years required: 5   **Weekly class hours:** 15
    Thesis required: Yes   **Female/Male ratio:** 90/10
        Emphasis: Clinical, educational, industrial psychology

Graduate Training: Doctorate
    Specialty: Clinical, social

Faculty: **Full-time:** --   **Doctorate:** 24
           Part-time: --   **Master's:** 0

Exchange: **Students:** Yes   **Faculty:** Yes
           Research: Psychogerontology

DEPARTAMENTO DE PSICOLOGIA
UNIVERSIDAD CATOLICA ARGENTINA SANTA MARIA DE LOS BUENOS AIRES
Bartolome Mitre 1869
1039 Buenos Aires, Argentina
Phone: 403077   Chair: Francisco Guarna

Undergraduate Training
    Degree offered: Licenciado
    Years required: 5   **Weekly class hours:** 30
    Thesis required: Yes   **Female/Male ratio:** 90/10
        Emphasis: Clinical, industrial, and educational

Graduate Training: --
    Specialty: --

Faculty: **Full-time:** 4   **Doctorate:** 4
           Part-time: 98   **Master's:** --

Exchange: **Students:** --   **Faculty:** Yes
           Research: Clinical

FACULTAD DE FILOSOFIA Y HUMANIDADES
UNIVERSIDAD CATOLICA DE CUYO
Av. Libertador General San Martin 987 Este
San Juan 5400 Argentina
Phone: 222979   Chair: Nydia Fany Munoz de Suarez

Undergraduate Training
         Degree offered: Licenciado
         Years required: 5   Weekly class hours: --
         Thesis required: Yes   Female/Male ratio: 95/5
               Emphasis: Educational

Graduate Training: --
         Specialty: --

Faculty: Full-time: 40   Doctorate: --
           Part-time: --   Master's: --

Exchange: Students: Yes   Faculty: Yes
          Research: Educational

DEPARTMENTO DE PSICOLOGIA
FACULTAD DE HUMANIDADES Y CIENCIAS DE LA EDUCACION
UNIVERSIDAD NACIONAL DE LA PLATA
Calle 48 entre 6 y 7
6 piso
La Plata, C.P. 1900, Argentina
Phone: 3-4710 (Ext. 021)   Chair: Dr. Jose Panettieri

Undergraduate Training
         Degree offered: Professor en Psicologia, Licenciado en Psicologia
         Years required: 5, 6   Weekly class hours: 36
         Thesis required: No   Female/Male ratio: 80/20
               Emphasis: Clinical, educational, industrial, and forensic

Graduate Training: None
         Specialty: --

Faculty: Full-time: 0   Doctorate: 3
           Part-time: 12   Master's: 1

Exchange: Students: No   Faculty: Yes
          Research: Educational and clinical

DEPARTMENTO DE PSICOLOGIA
UNIVERSIDAD NACIONAL DE MAR DEL PLATA
Maipu 5225
7600 Mar Del Plata
Buenos Aires, Argentina
Phone: 46577   Chair: Horacio Nestor Santagelo

Undergraduate Training
    Degree offered: Licenciado
    Years required: 5   Weekly class hours: 26
    Thesis required: Yes   Female/Male ratio: 80/20
        Emphasis: Reopened in 1986

Graduate Training: --
    Specialty: --

Faculty: Full-time: --   Doctorate: --
        Part-time: --   Master's: --

Exchange: Students: Yes   Faculty: Yes
       Research: Yes

FACULTAD DE HUMANIDADES Y ARTES
UNIVERSIDAD NACIONAL DE ROSARIO
Entre Rio 758
2000 Rosario
Argentina
Phone: Chair: Dra. Gloria Annoni

Undergraduate Training
    Degree offered: Psicologia-Profesor de Ensenanza Media y Superior en
                Psicologia
    Years required: 6   Weekly class hours: 20
    Thesis required: No   Female/Male ratio: 80/20
        Emphasis: None

Graduate Training: Clinical and educational residency
    Specialty: --

Faculty: Full-time: 20   Doctorate: 5
        Part-time: 5   Master's: 1

Exchange: Students: Yes   Faculty: Yes
       Research: Clinical and educational

FACULTAD DE PSICOLOGIA
UNIVERSIDAD NACIONAL DE TUCUMAN
Avenida Benjamin Araoz 800
4000 S.M. Tucuman, Argentina
Phone: 222570   Chair: Olga A. Doz de Plaza

Undergraduate Training
        Degree offered: Licenciado
        Years required: 5   Weekly class hours: 30
        Thesis required: No   Female/Male ratio: 90/10
                Emphasis: Clinical, educational, industrial

Graduate Training: --
        Specialty: --

Faculty: Full-time: 3   Doctorate: 38
           Part-time: 35   Master's: 0

Exchange: Students: Yes   Faculty: Yes
          Research: Yes

FACULTAD DE ANTROPOLOGIA Y PSICOLOGIA
UNIVERSIDAD DEL NORTE SANTO TOMAS DE AQUINO
Casilla de Correo 3, Suc. 2
Tucuman, Argentina
Phone: 251441   Chair: Alfredo Sachetti

Undergraduate Training
        Degree offered: Licenciado
        Years required: 5   Weekly class hours: --
        Thesis required: Yes   Female/Male ratio: 80/20
                Emphasis: Developmental anthropology, criminology, psychogenetics,
                          military psychology, psychology and theology

Graduate Training: --
        Specialty: --

Faculty: Full-time: 1   Doctorate: 6
           Part-time: 36   Master's: --

Exchange: Students: Yes   Faculty: Yes
          Research: Yes

FACULTAD DE PSICOLOGIA
UNIVERSIDAD DEL SALVADOR
Hipolito Yrigoyen 2441
Capital Federal (C.P. 1089)
Buenos Aires, Argentina
Phone: 48-2785   Chair: Dr. Saul Miguel Rodriguez Amenabar

Undergraduate Training
        Degree offered: Licenciado en Psicologia
        Years required: 5   Weekly class hours: 20
        Thesis required: No   Female/Male ratio: 80/20
              Emphasis: industrial, clinical, forensic

Graduate Training: Dr. en Psicologia
        Specialty: Clinical, industrial

Faculty: Full-time: 3   Doctorate: 14
           Part-time: 40   Master's: 0

Exchange: Students: Yes   Faculty: Yes
          Research: Yes

Bolivia

DEPARTAMENTO DE PSICOLOGIA
UNIVERSIDAD CATOLICA BOLIVIANA
Av. 14 de Septiembre 4807
Esq. calle No. 2 (OBRAJES)
Cajon Postal No. 4805
La Paz, Bolivia
Phone: 783283; 783289; 783244; 783286   Chair: Dr. Rene Calderon Jemio

Undergraduate Training
        Degree offered: Licenciado en Psicologia
        Years required: 5   Weekly class hours: 30
        Thesis required: Yes   Female/Male ratio: 65/35
              Emphasis: Clinical, experimental, educational, social

Graduate Training: Yes
        Specialty: --

Faculty: Full-time: 6   Doctorate: 5
           Part-time: 20   Master's: 15

Exchange: Students: Yes   Faculty: Yes
          Research: Clinical, experimental, educational, social

Brazil

DEPARTAMENTO DE PSICOLOGIA
CENTRO DE ENSINO SUPERIOR DE JUIZ DE FORA
Rua Halfeld 1179
Caixa Postal 105
36100 Juiz de Fora MG Brazil
Phone: 211 8683   Chair: Leopoldo Krieger

Undergraduate Training
        Degree offered: Psicologo
        Years required: 5   Weekly class hours: 30
        Thesis required: No   Female/Male ratio: 83/7
            Emphasis: Clinical, industrial, educational

Graduate Training: --
        Specialty: --

Faculty: Full-time: 2   Doctorate: 2
           Part-time: 25   Master's: 6

Exchange: Students: Yes   Faculty: No
          Research: Clinical

DEPARTMENTO DE PSICOLOGIA
FACULDADE DE CIENCIAS HUMANAS DE OLINDA
Largo da Misericordia s/n
53000 Olinda PE Brazil
Phone: 429-2679; 429-2922   Chair: Jose Adailson De Medeiros

Undergraduate Training
        Degree offered: Licenciado, or Psychologo
        Years required: 5.5   Weekly class hours: 20
        Thesis required: No   Female/Male ratio: 80/20
            Emphasis: Clinical, industrial, educational

Graduate Training: None
        Specialty: --

Faculty: Full-time: 0   Doctorate: 0
           Part-time: All   Master's: 10%

Exchange: Students: No   Faculty: No
          Research: No

DEPARTAMENTO DE PSICOLOGIA
FACULDADE DE FILOSOFIA, CIENCIAS E LETRAS DE SANTOS
Rua Euclides da Cunha 247
11100 Santos SP Brazil
Phone: 375484   Chair: Luiz Celso Manco

Undergraduate Training
        Degree offered: Psicologo
        Years required: 5   Weekly class hours: --
        Thesis required: No   Female/Male ratio: 90/10
                Emphasis: Industrial/organizational, clinical, educational

Graduate Training: --
        Specialty: --

Faculty: Full-time: 0   Doctorate: 2
               Part-time: 32   Master's: 5

Exchange: Students: --   Faculty: --
              Research: Psychohygiene

FACULDADE DE FILOSOFIA, CIENCIAS E LETRAS
FACULDADES FRANCISCANAS
Rus Alexandre Rodrigues Barbosa 45
Itatiba
Sao Paulo SP Brazil
Phone: 435-1262   Chair: Jose Norberto Comune

Undergraduate Training
        Degree offered: Psicologo
        Years required: 5   Weekly class hours: 25
        Thesis required: --   Female/Male ratio: 80/20
                Emphasis: Educational, industrial, clinical, and community

Graduate Training: --
        Specialty: --

Faculty: Full-time: --   Doctorate: --
               Part-time: --   Master's: --

Exchange: Students: Yes   Faculty: Yes
              Research: Educational, experimental analysis of behavior

DEPARTMENTO DE PSICOLOGIA
FACULDADE DE HUMANIDADES PEDRO II
Rua Pirauba s/n
Sao Cristovao
Rio de Janeiro, Brazil
Phone: 580-6426   **Chair:** Antonio Jose Chediak

Undergraduate Training
        Degree offered: Bacharel em Psicologia, Licenciado em Psicologia, or
                        Psicologo
        Years required: 5   **Weekly class hours:** 30
        Thesis required: No   **Female/Male ratio:** 90/10
                Emphasis: None

Graduate Training: Yes
        Specialty: --

Faculty: **Full-time:** 0   **Doctorate:** 1
              Part-time: 23   **Master's:** 18

Exchange: **Students:** Yes   **Faculty:** Yes
              Research: Yes

FACULDADE DE PSICOLOGIA
F.M.U. FACULDADES METROPOLITAS UNIDAS
Av. Santo Amaro 1239
04505 Sao Paulo SP Brazil
Phone: 11-240-4499   **Chair:** Celeste Das Gracas Leite Guimaraes
                                         Cassaniga

Undergraduate Training
        Degree offered: Psicologo
        Years required: 5   **Weekly class hours:** 30
        Thesis required: Yes   **Female/Male ratio:** 75/25
                Emphasis: Clinical, industrial, educational, social welfare

Graduate Training: Yes
        Specialty: Judicial, Developmental

Faculty: **Full-time:** 0   **Doctorate:** 35
              Part-time: 120   **Master's:** 85

Exchange: **Students:** Yes   **Faculty:** Yes
              Research: Yes

DEPARTMENTO DE PSICOLOGIA
FACULDADE SALESIANA DE FILOSOFIA, CIENCIAS E LETRAS
Rua Don Bosco 284
12600 Lorena SP Brazil
Phone: 522033   Chair: Nivaldo Luiz Pessinatti

Undergraduate Training
      Degree offered: Licenciado, or Psicologo
      Years required: 5   Weekly class hours: 30
      Thesis required: No   Female/Male ratio: 90/10
          Emphasis: Person-centered counseling

Graduate Training: --
      Specialty: --

Faculty: Full-time: 1   Doctorate: --
          Part-time: 43   Master's: 4

Exchange: Students: Yes   Faculty: Yes
          Research: Yes

DEPARTMENTO DE CIENCIAS PSICOLOGIAS
FACULTAD DE FILOSOFIA
FACULDADES SAO MARCOS
Av. Nazare 900
Ipiranga
04262 Sao Paulo SP Brazil
Phone: 274-5711   Chair: Profa. Leila Caran Costa Correa

Undergraduate Training
      Degree offered: Bacharel
      Years required: 4   Weekly class hours: 20
      Thesis required: No   Female/Male ratio: 90/10
          Emphasis: Educational, clinical, industrial, organizational

Graduate Training: Yes
      Specialty: Psychopedagogy

Faculty: Full-time: 0   Doctorate: 2
          Part-time: 46   Master's: 8

Exchange: Students: --   Faculty: No
          Research: Clinical, educational, industrial

DEPARTMENTO DE PSICOLOGIA
FACULTAD DE FILOSOFIA, CIENCIAS E LETRAS
Av. Francisco Rodriques Filho 1233
Sao Paulo, Brazil
Phone: 469-5822   Chair: Dilson Del Bem

Undergraduate Training
    Degree offered: Licenciado, Bacharel e Psicologo
    Years required: 5   **Weekly class hours:** 24
    Thesis required: Yes   **Female/Male ratio:** 90/10
        Emphasis: Industrial, educational, clinical

Graduate Training: None
    Specialty: --

Faculty: **Full-time:** 4   **Doctorate:** 1
           Part-time: 16   **Master's:** 12

Exchange: **Students:** --   **Faculty:** --
           Research: --

DEPARTMENTO DE PSICOLOGIA
FACULTAD DE DOM. AQUINO DE FILOSOFIA, CIENCIAS E LETRAS
FACULDADES UNIDAS CATOLICAS DE MATO GROSSO
Avenida Mato Grosso
FUCMT - 14 de Julio 2840
79100 Campo Grande MS Brazil
Phone: (67) 382-4261   Chair: Guillermo Morales Velasquez

Undergraduate Training
    Degree offered: Licenciatura plena en Psicologia
    Years required: 4-5   **Weekly class hours:** 40
    Thesis required: No   **Female/Male ratio:** 85/15
        Emphasis: Educational and organizational for 5-year students;
                teaching of psychology for 4-year students

Graduate Training: Yes
    Specialty: --

Faculty: **Full-time:** 0   **Doctorate:** 0
           Part-time: 22   **Master's:** 4

Exchange: **Students:** Yes   **Faculty:** Yes
           Research: Adolescence, values and family

DEPARTAMENTO DE PSICOLOGIA
FUNDACAO EDUCACIONAL DE BAURU
Avenida Engenheiro Luiz Edmundo Coube s/n
17033 Bauru SP Brazil
Phone: 23-2111   Chair: Celso Zonta

Undergraduate Training
        Degree offered: Psicologo
        Years required: 5   Weekly class hours: 30
        Thesis required: --   Female/Male ratio: 95/5
            Emphasis: Organizational, educational, community, social, clinical

Graduate Training: --
        Specialty: --

Faculty: Full-time: 3   Doctorate: 2
          Part-time: 18   Master's: 4

Exchange: Students: Yes   Faculty: Yes
          Research: Rehabilatation, social, clinical

INSTITUTO SUPERIOR DE ESTUDOS E PESQUISAS PSICOSSOCIAIS
FUNDACAO GETULIO VARGAS
Praia de Botafogo 190
Sala 1108
Botafogo
22250 Rio de Janeiro RJ Brazil
Phone: 551-1542 ramal 269   Chair: Antonio Gomes Penna

Undergraduate Training
        Degree offered: --
        Years required: --   Weekly class hours: 20
        Thesis required: --   Female/Male ratio: 70/30
        Emphasis: --

Graduate Training: Mestre, Doutor
        Specialty: Social, cognitive, personality

Faculty: Full-time: 8   Doctorate: 19
          Part-time: 13   Master's: 2

Exchange: Students: Yes (graduate only)   Faculty: No
          Research: No

FACULDADE DE CIENCIAS HUMANAS
FUNDACAO MINEIRA DE EDUCACAO E CULTURA
Rua Aimores 2679
30000 Belo Horizonte MG Brazil
Phone: 337-9855   **Chair:** Antonio de Padua Nunes Thomazi

Undergraduate Training
    Degree offered: Bacharel
    Years required: 5   **Weekly class hours:** 22
    Thesis required: No   **Female/Male ratio:** 95/5
        Emphasis: Clinical, educational, industrial

Graduate Training: --
    Specialty: --

Faculty: **Full-time:** 5   **Doctorate:** --
        Part-time: 12   **Master's:** 17

Exchange: **Students:** No   **Faculty:** No
        Research: Aesthetics, mental health, popular education

DEPARTAMENTO DE PSICOLOGIA
FUNDACAO UNIVERSIDADE ESTADUAL DE LONDRINA
Campus Universitario
Caixa Postal 6001
86100 Londrina Brazil
Phone: 27-5151   **Chair:** Sebastiao Ovidio Goncalves

Undergraduate Training
    Degree offered: Psicologo
    Years required: 5   **Weekly class hours:** 32
    Thesis required: --   **Female/Male ratio:** 92/8
        Emphasis: Educational, organizational, clinical

Graduate Training: --
    Specialty: --

Faculty: **Full-time:** 29   **Doctorate:** 2
        Part-time: 16   **Master's:** 18

Exchange: **Students:** --   **Faculty:** --
        Research: Yes

INSTITUTO UNIFICADO PAULISTA
Rua Luis Goes 2211
Mirandopolis
04043 Sao Paulo, Brazil
Phone: 578-6455   Chair: Dr. Yugo Okida

Undergraduate Training
    Degree offered: Psicologo
    Years required: 5   **Weekly class hours:** 30
    Thesis required: No   **Female/Male ratio:** 80/20
        Emphasis: Clinical, educational, industrial

Graduate Training: None
    Specialty: --

Faculty: Full-time: 0   **Doctorate:** 4
         Part-time: 95   **Master's:** 10

Exchange: Students: --   **Faculty:** Yes
        Research: Yes

INSTITUTO DE PSICOLOGIA
PONTIFICIA UNIVERSIDADE CATOLICA
Rua Marechal Deodoro
1117 Campinas
13100 Sao Paulo, Brazil
Phone: 27001 ext. 40   Chair: Diane Tosello Laloni

Undergraduate Training
    Degree offered: Psicologo
    Years required: 5   **Weekly class hours:** 30
    Thesis required: No   **Female/Male ratio:** 90/10
        Emphasis: Clinical, educational

Graduate Training: Mestre
    Specialty: Clinical

Faculty: Full-time: 10   **Doctorate:** 6
         Part-time: 90   **Master's:** 25

Exchange: Students: Yes   **Faculty:** Yes
        Research: Yes

DEPARTAMENTO DE PSICOLOGIA
PONTIFICIA UNIVERSIDADE CATOLICA DO PARANA
Rua Imaculada Conceicao 1155
Prado Velho
Caixa Postal 670
80210 Curitiba PR Brazil
Phone: (041) 223-0922 ext. 177   Chair: Marita Bertassoni da Silva

Undergraduate Training
        Degree offered: Psicologo
        Years required: 5   Weekly class hours: 30
        Thesis required: No   Female/Male ratio: 90/10
            Emphasis: Clinical, educational, organizational

Graduate Training: Yes
        Specialty: Social

Faculty: Full-time: --   Doctorate: 1
          Part-time: 43   Master's: 41

Exchange: Students: No   Faculty: Yes
          Research: Yes

DEPARTAMENTO DE PSICOLOGIA
PONTIFICIA UNIVERSIDADE CATOLICA, RIO DE JANEIRO
Rua Marques de Sao Vicente 225
22453 Rio de Janeiro RJ Brazil
Phone: 274-9922 ext. 318   Chair: Bernard Range

Undergraduate Training
        Degree offered: Psicologo
        Years required: 5   Weekly class hours: 24
        Thesis required: Yes   Female/Male ratio: 95/5
            Emphasis: --

Graduate Training: Masters, Doctorate
        Specialty: Clinical

Faculty: Full-time: 14   Doctorate: 14
          Part-time: 19   Master's: 18

Exchange: Students: --   Faculty: Yes
          Research: Depression, religiosity, language

DEPARTAMENTO DE PSICOLOGIA
UNIVERSIDADE DE BrazilIA
70910 Brasilia, Brazil
Phone: 274-0022   Chair: Alvaro Tamayo

Undergraduate Training
        Degree offered: Psicologo
        Years required: 5   **Weekly class hours:** 30
        Thesis required: No   **Female/Male ratio:** 90/10
                Emphasis: Clinical, organizational, educational

Graduate Training: Masters
        Specialty: Social, personality, learning and developmental

Faculty: Full-time: 25   Doctorate: 14
               Part-time: 1   Master's: 12

Exchange: Students: Yes   Faculty: Yes
              Research: Yes

DEPARTAMENTO DE PSICOLOGIA
UNIVERSIDADE CATOLICA DE GOIAS
Av. Universitaria 1440
S. Universitario
Caixa 86
74000 Goiana GO Brazil
Phone: 225-1188 ramal 224   Chair: Maria Das Gracas Gomes Monteiro

Undergraduate Training
        Degree offered: Licenciado
        Years required: 5-6   **Weekly class hours:** 40
        Thesis required: --   **Female/Male ratio:** 90/10
                Emphasis: --

Graduate Training: --
        Specialty: --

Faculty: Full-time: 26   Doctorate: 3
               Part-time: 13   Master's: 7

Exchange: Students: No   Faculty: Yes
              Research: Yes

DEPARTAMENTO DE PSICOLOGIA
UNIVERSIDADE CATOLICA DE PELOTAS
Rua Felix de Cunha 412
Pelotas Rio Grande do Sul, Brazil
Phone: --   Chair: Emilia Maria Vaz Fernandes

Undergraduate Training
      Degree offered: Licenciado
      Years required: 5   **Weekly class hours:** 30
      Thesis required: Yes   **Female/Male ratio:** 90/10
           Emphasis: Clinical

Graduate Training: --
      Specialty: --

Faculty: **Full-time:** 5   **Doctorate:** --
          Part-time: 35   **Master's:** 4

Exchange: **Students:** Yes   **Faculty:** Yes
          Research: Community, educational, social

DEPARTAMENTO DE PSICOLOGIA
UNIVERSIDADE CATOLICA DE PERNAMBUCO
Rua do Principe 526
Pernambuco, Recife, Brazil
Phone: 231-3288   Chair: Vincenzo Di Matteo

Undergraduate Training
      Degree offered: Psicologo
      Years required: 5   **Weekly class hours:** 20
      Thesis required: --   **Female/Male ratio:** 80/20
           Emphasis: Clinical, industrial, educational

Graduate Training: --
      Specialty: --

Faculty: **Full-time:** --   **Doctorate:** --
          Part-time: --   **Master's:** --

Exchange: **Students:** Yes   **Faculty:** Yes
          Research: Yes

DEPARTAMENTO DE PSICOLOGO
UNIVERSIDADE DE CAIXAS DO SUL
R. Francisco G. Vargas 1130
C.P. 1352
Caixas Do Sul RS Brazil
Phone: 222-4133   Chair: Luis Antonio Rizzon

Undergraduate Training
  Degree offered: Bacharel
  Years required: 5   Weekly class hours: 38
  Thesis required: No   Female/Male ratio: 99/1
    Emphasis: Clinical, educational, community, industrial

Graduate Training: None
  Specialty: --

Faculty: Full-time: 4   Doctorate: 0
    Part-time: 25   Master's: 4

Exchange: Students: No   Faculty: Yes
    Research: --

INSTITUTO DE LETRAS, HISTORIA E PSICOLOGIA
UNIVERSIDAD ESTADUAL PAULISTA
Av. D. Antonio s/n
Caixa Postal 335
19800 Assis SP Brazil
Phone: 222933   Chair: Antonio Quelce Salgado

Undergraduate Training
  Degree offered: Licenciado, Psicologo
  Years required: 4, 5   Weekly class hours: 30
  Thesis required: No   Female/Male ratio: 80/20
    Emphasis: Clinical, industrial, educational

Graduate Training: --
  Specialty: --

Faculty: Full-time: 2   Doctorate: 11
    Part-time: 45   Master's: 18

Exchange: Students: --   Faculty: Yes
    Research: Social, educational

INSTITUTO DE PSICOLOGIA
UNIVERSIDADE DO ESTADO DO RIO DE JANEIRO
Rua Sao Francisco Xavier 524
20550 Rio de Janeiro RJ Brazil
Phone: 284-0347   Chair: Celso Pereira de Sa

Undergraduate Training
      Degree offered: Psicologo
      Years required: 5   Weekly class hours: 30
      Thesis required: No   Female/Male ratio: 70/30
          Emphasis: None

Graduate Training: Especialista
      Specialty: Clinical

Faculty: Full-time: 8   Doctorate: 6
         Part-time: 37   Master's: 23

Exchange: Students: Yes   Faculty: Yes
         Research: Social

DEPARTAMENTO DE PSICOLOGIA
UNIVERSIDADE FEDERAL DO CEARA
Av. Da Universidade 2762
60000 Fortaleza, Ceara, Brazil
Phone: 223-5032   Chair: --

Undergraduate Training
      Degree offered: Psicologo
      Years required: 5   Weekly class hours: --
      Thesis required: Yes   Female/Male ratio: 90/10
          Emphasis: Clinical, industrial, educational, social, experimental

Graduate Training: --
      Specialty: --

Faculty: Full-time: 29   Doctorate: 1
         Part-time: 4   Master's: 15

Exchange: Students: Yes   Faculty: Yes
         Research: Yes

DEPARTAMENTO DE CIENCIAS SOCIAIS APLICADAS
FACULTAD DE CENTRO UNIVERSITARIO DE CORUMBA
UNIVERSIDADE FEDERAL DE MATO GROSSO DO SUL
Av. Rio Branco 1270
Caixa Postal 452
79300 Corumba MS Brazil
Phone: (67) 231-2616   Chair: Wilson Ferreira de Melo

Undergraduate Training
        Degree offered: Psicologo
        Years required: 5   Weekly class hours: 36
        Thesis required: No   Female/Male ratio: 95/5
                Emphasis: Clinical, educational, organizational

Graduate Training: None
        Specialty: --

Faculty: Full-time: 8   Doctorate: 4
          Part-time: 0   Master's: 4

Exchange: Students: Yes   Faculty: Yes
          Research: Administration, psychology and accounting

UNIVERSIDADE FEDERAL DE MATO GROSSO DO SUL
Centro Universitario de Corumba
Caixa Postal 252
79300 Corumba MS Brazil
Phone: (67) 231-1626   Chair: Gisela A. L. Alexandre

Undergraduate Training
        Degree offered: Licenciado e Graduado
        Years required: 5   Weekly class hours: 20
        Thesis required: No   Female/Male ratio: 90/10
                Emphasis: Clinical, educational, industrial

Graduate Training: None
        Specialty: --

Faculty: Full-time: 8   Doctorate: 0
          Part-time: 0   Master's: 3

Exchange: Students: Yes   Faculty: Yes
          Research: Yes

CURSO DE PSICOLOGIA
UNIVERSIDADE FEDERAL DE MATO GROSSO DO SUL
Rua Frei Mariano 483
79300 Corumba MS Brazil
Phone: 231-4877   Chair: Mathilde Monaco Moreira

Undergraduate Training
        Degree offered: Licenciado
        Years required: 5   Weekly class hours: 30
        Thesis required: No   Female/Male ratio: 91/9
             Emphasis: --

Graduate Training: --
        Specialty: --

Faculty: Full-time: 7   Doctorate: --
          Part-time: 2   Master's: 3

Exchange: Students: Yes   Faculty: Yes
          Research: Yes

DEPARTAMENTO DE PSICOLOGIA
FACULTAD DE FILOSOFIA E CIENCIAS HUMANAS
UNIVERSIDADE FEDERAL DE MINAS GERAIS
Rua Carangola 288
2 andar
30000 Belo Horizonte MG Brazil
Phone: (31) 223-2133 ext. 21   Chair: Regina Helena de Freitas Campos

Undergraduate Training
        Degree offered: Psicologo
        Years required: 5   Weekly class hours: 25
        Thesis required: No   Female/Male ratio: 80/20
             Emphasis: Clinical, educational, industrial, community

Graduate Training: Especialista
        Specialty: Psychoanalysis

Faculty: Full-time: 75   Doctorate: 11
          Part-time: 11   Master's: 17

Exchange: Students: Yes   Faculty: Yes
          Research: Social, cognitive

DEPARTAMENTO DE PSICOLOGIA
UNIVERSIDADE FEDERAL DO PARA
66000 Belem, Para, Brazil
Phone: 228-2088   Chair: Cileila Maria da Rocha

Undergraduate Training
        Degree offered: Psicologo
        Years required: 5   Weekly class hours: --
        Thesis required: Yes, monograph   Female/Male ratio: 90/10
                Emphasis: Psychotherapy, experimental analysis of behavior, basic
                          research, vocational orientation

Graduate Training: --
        Specialty: --

Faculty: Full-time: 33   Doctorate: 5
          Part-time: 1   Master's: 7

Exchange: Students: --   Faculty: --
          Research: --

DEPARTAMENTO DE PSICOLOGIA
UNIVERSIDADE FEDERAL DE PARAIBA
CCHLA/UFPB
58000 Joao Pessoa PB Brazil
Phone: (83) 224-7200 Ext. 2337   Chair: Lucy De Oliveira Chianca

Undergraduate Training
        Degree offered: Formacao de Psicologo
        Years required: 5   Weekly class hours: 20
        Thesis required: Optional   Female/Male ratio: 85/15
                Emphasis: Clinical, educational, organizational

Graduate Training: Masters
        Specialty: Social

Faculty: Full-time: 48   Doctorate: 7
          Part-time: 1   Master's: 25

Exchange: Students: Yes   Faculty: Yes
          Research: --

DEPARTAMENTO DE PSICOLOGIA
UNIVERSIDADE FEDERAL DE PERNAMBUCO
Edificio do Institutos Basicos
9 andar
Cidade Unversitaria
50000 Recife PE Brazil
Phone: 271-2048   Chair: Francisco Bernardo Mora Trespalacios

Undergraduate Training
     Degree offered: Psicologo
     Years required: 5   **Weekly class hours:** 40
     Thesis required: No   **Female/Male ratio:** 90/10
          Emphasis: Clinical, industrial, educational

Graduate Training: Masters
     Specialty: Cognitive

Faculty: **Full-time:** 42   **Doctorate:** 10
          Part-time: 4   **Master's:** 18

Exchange: Students: Yes   **Faculty:** Yes
          Research: Cognitive, clinical, educational, industrial

DEPARTAMENTO DE PSICOLOGIA
UNIVERSIDADE FEDERAL DO PARANA
Travessa Bufrem 140
80000 Curitiba PR Brazil
Phone: 264-2522   Chair: Luiz Andre Kossobudz

Undergraduate Training
     Degree offered: Psicologo
     Years required: 5   **Weekly class hours:** 35
     Thesis required: --   **Female/Male ratio:** 80/20
          Emphasis: Educational, organizational, clinical

Graduate Training: --
     Specialty: --

Faculty: **Full-time:** 25   **Doctorate:** 2
          Part-time: 3   **Master's:** 7

Exchange: Students: --   **Faculty:** Yes
          Research: Yes

INSTITUTO DE PSICOLOGIA
UNIVERSIDADE FEDERAL DO RIO DE JANEIRO
Av. Pasteur 250 - fundos
Pavilhao Nilton Campos
Praia Vermelha
22290 Rio de Janeiro RJ Brazil
Phone: 295-3398/295-8045/295-4548   Chair: Marion Merlone Dos Santos
                                                  Penna

Undergraduate Training
        Degree offered: Psicologo
        Years required: 5   Weekly class hours: 40
        Thesis required: Yes   Female/Male ratio: 90/10
            Emphasis: Educational, clinical, industrial, community

Graduate Training: Doctorate, Masters
        Specialty: Clinical, educational

Faculty: Full-time: 48   Doctorate: 12
           Part-time: 6   Master's: 30

Exchange: Students: --   Faculty: yes
          Research: Basic, applied

INSTITUTO DE PSICOLOGIA
UNIVERSIDADE FEDERAL DO RIO DE JANEIRO - Brazil
106 - Rua Pompen Loureno. Apto. 901
Copacabana
22061 Rio de Janeiro, Brazil
Phone: 236-1317   Chair: Marion Merione do Santos-Penna

Undergraduate Training
        Degree offered: Psicologo, or Bacharel em Psicologia
        Years required: 5   Weekly class hours: 50
        Thesis required: Yes   Female/Male ratio: 90/10
            Emphasis: None

Graduate Training: Doctorate, Masters
        Specialty: Developmental, social, personality

Faculty: Full-time: 40   Doctorate: 10
           Part-time: 10   Master's: 5

Exchange: Students: Yes   Faculty: Yes
          Research: Cognitive, social, developmental

DEPARTAMENTO DE PSICOLOGIA
CENTRO DE CIENCIAS HUMANAS LETRAS E ARTES
UNVERSIDADE FEDERAL DO RIO GRANDE DO NORTE
Campus Universitario
Lagoa Nova s/n
59000 Natal RN Brazil
Phone: 231-1213 and 231-1266 ext. 475

Chair: Rosa de Fatima Torres Lima

Undergraduate Training
    Degree offered: Bachelor in Psychology, Psychologist
    Years required: 5   **Weekly class hours:** 25
    Thesis required: Optional   **Female/Male ratio:** 90/10
        Emphasis: Clinical, organizational, educational

Graduate Training: --
    Specialty: --

Faculty: **Full-time:** 36   **Doctorate:** 2
         Part-time: 0   **Master's:** 12

Exchange: **Students:** Yes   **Faculty:** Yes
         Research: Educational, social, clinical, industrial

DEPARTAMENTO DE PSICOLOGIA
CENTRO DE CIENCIAS HUMANAS
UNIVERSIDADE FEDERAL DE SANTA CATARINA
Campus Universitario, Trindade
Caixa Postal 476
59000 Florianopolis, Santa Catarina
Brazil
Phone: 33 92 83   **Chair:** Clelia Maria Nascimento-Schulze

Undergraduate Training
    Degree offered: Bachelor in Psychology
    Years required: 5   **Weekly class hours:** 25
    Thesis required: No   **Female/Male ratio:** 80/20
        Emphasis: None

Graduate Training: None
    Specialty: --

Faculty: **Full-time:** 40   **Doctorate:** 5
         Part-time: 1   **Master's:** 15

Exchange: **Students:** Yes   **Faculty:** Yes
         Research: Social, cognitive social

DEPARTAMENTO DE PSICOLOGIA
UNIVERSIDADE FEDERAL DE UBERLANDIA
Campus Umuarama
Caixa Postal 593
Uberlandia MG Brazil
Phone: 232-2000, Ext. 235   Chair: Luzia Marivalda Barreiro Da Costa

Undergraduate Training
        Degree offered: Licenciado, Psicologo
        Years required: 5   Weekly class hours: 40
        Thesis required: No   Female/Male ratio: 92/8
            Emphasis: None

Graduate Training: None
        Specialty: --

Faculty: Full-time: 42   Doctorate: 4
            Part-time: 0   Master's: 16

Exchange: Students: --   Faculty: Yes
            Research: Social, Industrial, Educational, Clinical

DEPARTAMENTO DE PSICOLOGIA
UNIVERSIDADE GAMA FILHO
Rua Manuel Vitorino 625
Piedade
Rio de Janeiro 13 RJ Brazil
Phone: 269-7273, Ext. 479   Chair: Italo Albizatti

Undergraduate Training
        Degree offered: Licenciado, Psicologo
        Years required: 5   Weekly class hours: 30
        Thesis required: --   Female/Male ratio: 98/2
            Emphasis: --

Graduate Training: Mestre
            Specialty: Social, educational (10 hours per week in classes)

Faculty: Full-time: --   Doctorate: 10
            Part-time: 119   Master's: 46

Exchange: Students: Yes   Faculty: Yes
            Research: Social, experimental

DEPARTAMENTO DE PSICOLOGIA
UNIVERSIDADE DE MOGI DAS CRUZES
Av. Dr. Candido Xavier de Almeida Souza 200
Mogi Das Cruzes
08700 Sao Paulo, Brazil
Phone: 469-5333   Chair: Olgierd Ligeza-Stamirowski

Undergraduate Training
        Degree offered: Bacharel em Psicologia, Psicologo
        Years required: 4, 5   Weekly class hours: 24
        Thesis required: Yes   Female/Male ratio: 70/30
                Emphasis: Clinical, educational, organizational, industrial,
                          community

Graduate Training: None
        Specialty: --

Faculty: Full-time: 5   Doctorate: 5
          Part-time: 28   Master's: 17

Exchange: Students: Yes   Faculty: Yes
          Research: Organizational

DEPARTAMENTO DE PSICOLOGIA
UNVERSIDADE DO SAGRADO CORACAO
Rua Irma Arminda No. 10-50
Bauru SP Brazil
Phone: 23-2311   Chair: Marisabel Leite

Undergraduate Training
        Degree offered: --
        Years required: --   Weekly class hours: --
        Thesis required: --   Female/Male ratio: 95/5
                Emphasis: Organizational, educational, clinical

Graduate Training: --
        Specialty: --

Faculty: Full-time: 4   Doctorate: 1
          Part-time: 4   Master's: 3

Exchange: Students: Yes   Faculty: Yes
          Research: Organizational

CENTRO DE CIENCIAS HUMANAS E SOCIAIS
UNIVERSIDADE SANTA URSULA
Rua Fernando Ferrari 75
Botafogo
22231 Rio de Janeiro RJ Brazil
Phone: 551-5542   Chair: Silvio A. De Miranda Valverde

Undergraduate Training
  Degree offered: Licenciado
  Years required: 5   Weekly class hours: 28
  Thesis required: --   Female/Male ratio: 90/10
    Emphasis: --

Graduate Training: --
  Specialty: --

Faculty: Full-time: --   Doctorate: 3
    Part-time: 69   Master's: 29

Exchange: Students: Yes   Faculty: Yes
    Research: Social

INSTITUTO DE PSICOLOGIA
UNIVERSIDADE DE SAO PAULO
Av. Prof. Melio Moraes 1721
Butanta
05508 Sao Paulo SP Brazil
Phone: 211-2965   Chair: Arrigo Leonardo Angelini

Undergraduate Training
  Degree offered: Psicologo
  Years required: 5   Weekly class hours: 15
  Thesis required: --   Female/Male ratio: 70/30
    Emphasis: Educational, social, industrial, experimental, clinical

Graduate Training: Doutor, Mestre
  Specialty: Experimental, clinical, social, educational (5 hours per
    week in classes)

Faculty: Full-time: 70   Doctorate: 50
    Part-time: 26   Master's: 30

Exchange: Students: Yes   Faculty: Yes
    Research: Social, developmental

DEPARTAMENTO DE PSICOLOGIA
UNIVERSIDADE DE TAUBATE
Rua XV de Novembre, 996
Taubate
12000 Sao Paulo, Brazil
Phone: PBX: 32-7555, ext 138, 139   **Chair:** Antonio Cristina Peluso de
                                              Azevedo Mouassab

Undergraduate Training
        Degree offered: Psychologist
        Years required: 5   **Weekly class hours:** 25
        Thesis required: No   **Female/Male ratio:** 80/20
                Emphasis: Educational, clinical, industrial

Graduate Training: None
        Specialty: --

Faculty: **Full-time:** 0   **Doctorate:** 1
               Part-time: 22   **Master's:** 10

Exchange: **Students:** Yes   **Faculty:** No
               Research: Clinical, educational, industrial

DEPARTAMENTO DE PSICOLOGIA
UNIVERSIDADE FEDERAL DE RIO GRANDE DO SUL
90000 Porto Alegre RS Brazil
Phone: 24-4752   **Chair:** Claudio Simon Hutz

Undergraduate Training
        Degree offered: Psicologo
        Years required: 5   **Weekly class hours:** 24
        Thesis required: No   **Female/Male ratio:** 60/40
                Emphasis: Clinical, educational, organizational

Graduate Training: Especialista (since 1984; 10 hours per week in classes)
        Specialty: Developmental

Faculty: **Full-time:** 22   **Doctorate:** 3
               Part-time: 5   **Master's:** 18

Exchange: **Students:** Yes   **Faculty:** Yes
               Research: Yes

Chile

ESCUELA DE PSICOLOGIA
PONTIFICIA UNIVERSIDAD CATOLICA DE CHILE
Casilla 6177
Santiago 22 Chile
Phone: 555-0058 ext. 4636   **Chair:** Hugo Bustamante

Undergraduate Training
    Degree offered: Psicologo
    Years required: 5   **Weekly class hours:** --
    Thesis required: Yes   **Female/Male ratio:** 70/30
        Emphasis: Clinical, educational, organizational

Graduate Training: --
    Specialty: --

Faculty: **Full-time:** 21   **Doctorate:** 6
          Part-time: 49   **Master's:** 3

Exchange: **Students:** No   **Faculty:** Yes
         Research: --

ESCUELA DE PSICOLOGIA
UNIVERSIDAD CENTRAL
Carmencita 59 Las Condes
Santiago, Chile
Phone: 583116   **Chair:** Pablo Marassi Linzi

Undergraduate Training
    Degree offered: Bachelor in Psychology, Psychologist
    Years required: 6   **Weekly class hours:** 32
    Thesis required: Yes   **Female/Male ratio:** 60/40
        Emphasis: None

Graduate Training: None
    Specialty: --

Faculty: **Full-time:** 0   **Doctorate:** 4
          Part-time: 30   **Master's:** 2

Exchange: **Students:** Yes   **Faculty:** Yes
         Research: Social, developmental, clinical, educational

DEPARTAMENTO DE FILOSOFIA Y CIENCIAS DE LA EDUCACION
FACULTAD DE EDUCACION, HUMANIDADES Y ARTES
UNIVERSIDAD DE CONCEPCION
Casilla 82-C
Concepcion, Chile
Phone: 34985 ext. 2323   Chair: --

Undergraduate Training
      Degree offered: Psicologo
      Years required: 5   Weekly class hours: 18
      Thesis required: Yes   Female/Male ratio: 60/40
          Emphasis: Clinical, educational, industrial

Graduate Training: None
      Specialty: --

Faculty: Full-time: 5   Doctorate: 0
        Part-time: 1   Master's: 1

Exchange: Students: --   Faculty: Yes
         Research: Yes

FACULTAD DE CIENCIAS HUMANAS
UNIVERSIDAD DIEGO PORTALES
Ejercito 260
Santiago, Chile
Phone: 98275 and 97019   Chair: Domingo Asun Salazar

Undergraduate Training
      Degree offered: Bachelor in Psychology, Psychologist
      Years required: 6   Weekly class hours: --
      Thesis required: No   Female/Male ratio: 75/25
          Emphasis: None

Graduate Training: --
      Specialty: --

Faculty: Full-time: 8   Doctorate: 5
        Part-time: 44   Master's: 12

Exchange: Students: Yes   Faculty: Yes
         Research: Basic sciences, methodology, human rights, education,
             youth, women and poverty

DEPARTAMENTO DE PSICOLOGIA
FACULTAD DE EDUCACION Y HUMANIDADES
UNIVERSIDAD DE LA FRONTERA
Avenida Francisco Salazar No. 01145
Casilla: 54-D
Temuco, Chile
Phone: 37776 ext. 300   Chair: Alfredo Keller Aldunate

Undergraduate Training
        Degree offered: Psychologist, Licenciado en Psicologia
        Years required: 6   Weekly class hours: 36
        Thesis required: No   Female/Male ratio: 60/40
                Emphasis: Clinical, educational, socio-economical

Graduate Training: None
        Specialty: --

Faculty: Full-time: 12   Doctorate: 0
            Part-time: 4   Master's: 0

Exchange: Students: Yes   Faculty: Yes
          Research: Basic, clinical, social, educational

Colombia

DEPARTAMENTO DE PSICOLOGIA
FACULTAD DE CIENCIAS HUMANAS
FUNDACION INSTITUTO UNIVERSITARIO DE CIENCIAS Y TECNOLOGIA KONRAD LORENZ
Calle 77 No. 11-63
Bogota DE Colombia
Phone: 248-6790   Chair: Juan Alberto Aragon B.

Undergraduate Training
        Degree offered: Psicologo
        Years required: 5   Weekly class hours: 24
        Thesis required: Yes   Female/Male ratio: 75/25
                Emphasis: Clinical, educational, organizational

Graduate Training: None
        Specialty: --

Faculty: Full-time: 5   Doctorate: 3
            Part-time: 39   Master's: 20

Exchange: Students: Yes   Faculty: Yes
          Research: Yes

DEPARTAMENTO DE PSICOLOGIA
FUNDACION UNIVERSIDAD DEL NORTE
Apartado Aereo 1569
Barranquilla, Colombia
Phone: 345364 and 454077   Chair: Beatriz Anaya de Torres

Undergraduate Training
        Degree offered: Psicologo
        Years required: 5   **Weekly class hours:** 25
        Thesis required: Yes   **Female/Male ratio:** 91/9
                Emphasis: Industrial, clinical, social, educational

Graduate Training: None
        Specialty: --

Faculty: **Full-time:** 12   **Doctorate:** 4
              Part-time: 18   **Master's:** 14

Exchange: **Students:** Yes   **Faculty:** Yes
              Research: Yes

FACULTAD DE PSICOLOGIA
FUNDACION UNIVERSITARIA DE MANIZALES
Apartado Aereo 868
Manizales, Colombia
Phone: 414508   Chair: Jorge Octavio Prieto Tellez

Undergraduate Training
        Degree offered: Psicologo
        Years required: 5   **Weekly class hours:** 28
        Thesis required: Yes   **Female/Male ratio:** 85/5
                Emphasis: --

Graduate Training: --
        Specialty: --

Faculty: **Full-time:** 8   **Doctorate:** 0
              Part-time: 8   **Master's:** 0

Exchange: **Students:** --   **Faculty:** --
              Research: --

DEPARTAMENTO DE PSICOLOGIA
FACULTAD DE CIENCIAS SOCIALES
UNIVERSIDAD DE ANTIOQUIA
Apartado Aereo 1226
Medellin Colombia
Phone: 233 740   Chair: Luis Fernando Palacio R.

Undergraduate Training
        Degree offered: Sicologo Clinico
        Years required: 5   Weekly class hours: 20
        Thesis required: Yes   Female/Male ratio: --
             Emphasis: Clinical

Graduate Training: None
        Specialty: --

Faculty: Full-time: 19   Doctorate: 1
               Part-time: 8   Master's: 9

Exchange: Students: Yes   Faculty: Yes
             Research: Clinical, neuropsychology, psychoanalysis

FACULTAD DE PSICOLOGIA
UNIVERSIDAD CATOLICA DE COLOMBIA
Carrera 15, No. 47-31
Apartado Aereo 029832
Bogota, Colombia
Phone: 269-8348   Chair: Jose Antonio Sanchez-Gonzalez

Undergraduate Training
        Degree offered: Psicologo
        Years required: 5.5   Weekly class hours: 23
        Thesis required: Yes   Female/Male ratio: 80/20
             Emphasis: Clinical, educational, industrial/organizational, law

Graduate Training: --
        Specialty: --

Faculty: Full-time: 18   Doctorate: 4
               Part-time: 92   Master's: 12

Exchange: Students: Yes   Faculty: Yes
             Research: Developmental, testing, social, health

ESCUELA DE PSICOLOGIA
UNIVERSIDAD INCCA DE COLOMBIA
Carrera 13, No. 24-15
Apartado Aereo 14817
Bogota, Colombia
Phone: 241-3361   **Chair:** Jaime Bueno Henao

Undergraduate Training
      Degree offered: Psicologo
      Years required: 5   **Weekly class hours:** 30
      Thesis required: Yes   **Female/Male ratio:** 90/10
           Emphasis: Clinical, educational, industrial, social community

Graduate Training: None
      Specialty: --

Faculty: **Full-time:** 13   **Doctorate:** 10
           Part-time: 35   **Master's:** 15

Exchange: **Students:** --   **Faculty:** --
           Research: --

DEPARTAMENTO DE PSICOLOGIA
UNIVERSIDAD DE LOS ANDES
Carrera 10, No. 18-A-10
Apartado Aereo 4976
Bogota DE Colombia
Phone: 283-9942   **Chair:** Telmo Eduardo Pena

Undergraduate Training
      Degree offered: Psicologo
      Years required: 5   **Weekly class hours:** --
      Thesis required: Yes   **Female/Male ratio:** 85/15
           Emphasis: Clinical, educational, organizational

Graduate Training: Specialist
      Specialty: Clinical, management of human resources (3 hours per week in
            classes)

Faculty: **Full-time:** 11   **Doctorate:** 8
           Part-time: 16   **Master's:** 8

Exchange: **Students:** Yes   **Faculty:** Yes
           Research: Social, clinical

PROGRAMA DE PSICOLOGIA
UNIVERSIDAD METROPOLITANA PARA LA EDUCACION SUPERIOR
Apartado Aereo 50576
Barranquilla, Colombia
Phone: 450155   Chair: Luis Chamartin

Undergraduate Training
        Degree offered: Psicologo
        Years required: 5   Weekly class hours: --
        Thesis required: --   Female/Male ratio: 90/10
               Emphasis: Clinical

Graduate Training: --
        Specialty: --

Faculty: Full-time: 23   Doctorate: 1
              Part-time: 19   Master's: 2

Exchange: Students: Yes   Faculty: Yes
              Research: Clinical

DEPARTAMENTO DE PSICOLOGIA
UNIVERSIDAD NACIONAL DE COLOMBIA
Ciudad Universitaria
Bogota DE Colombia
Phone: 244-0859   Chair: Jorge Enrique Bossa

Undergraduate Training
        Degree offered: Psicologo
        Years required: 5   Weekly class hours: --
        Thesis required: Yes   Female/Male ratio: 63/37
               Emphasis: --

Graduate Training: -
        Specialty: --

Faculty: Full-time: 19   Doctorate: 5
              Part-time: 11   Master's: 7

Exchange: Students: No   Faculty: Yes
              Research: Social, clinical, educational, industrial

FACULTAD DE PSICOLOGIA
UNIVERSIDAD DE SAN BUENAVENTURA
Apartado Aereo 7370
Medellin, Colombia
Phone: 314600   Chair: Gustavo Perez Gomez

Undergraduate Training
      Degree offered: Psicologo
      Years required: 5   **Weekly class hours:** 28
      Thesis required: Yes   **Female/Male ratio:** 80/20
            Emphasis: Clinical, industrial, sports, educational, law

Graduate Training: --
      Specialty: --

Faculty: Full-time: 7   Doctorate: 3
           Part-time: 4   Master's: 14

Exchange: Students: Yes   **Faculty:** Yes
          Research: Social, organizational

FACULTAD DE PSICOLOGIA
UNIVERSIDAD SANTO TOMAS
Carrera 9 No. 51-23
Bogota, Colombia
Phone: 248-0482 and 235-7312   Chair: Jorge E. Vergel Villamizar

Undergraduate Training
      Degree offered: Psychologist
      Years required: 5   **Weekly class hours:** 24
      Thesis required: Yes   **Female/Male ratio:** 92/8
            Emphasis: Clinical, educational, industrial

Graduate Training: Yes
      Specialty: Clinical, family

Faculty: Full-time: 18   Doctorate: --
           Part-time: 66   Master's: --

Exchange: Students: Yes   **Faculty:** Yes
          Research: Yes

DEPARTAMENTO DE PSICOLOGIA
FACULTAD DE EDUCACION
UNIVERSIDAD DEL VALLE
Apartado Aereo 2188
Cali, Colombia
Phone: 393041   Chair: Floralba Cano

Undergraduate Training
    Degree offered: Psychologist
    Years required: 5   Weekly class hours: 23
    Thesis required: Yes   Female/Male ratio: 65/35
        Emphasis: Clinical, educational, organizational, environmental

Graduate Training: Yes
    Specialty: Child psychology: clinical-educational, psycholinguistics,
        organizational

Faculty: Full-time: 15   Doctorate: 7
      Part-time: 9   Master's: 8

Exchange: Students: Yes   Faculty: Yes
    Research: Cognitive development, mathematics, consumer psychology,
      social distance

Costa Rica

ESCUELA DE PSICOLOGIA
UNIVERSIDAD DE COSTA RICA
San Jose, Costa Rica
Phone: 531265   Chair: Daniel Flores Mora

Undergraduate Training
    Degree offered: Licenciado
    Years required: 5   Weekly class hours: 20
    Thesis required: Yes   Female/Male ratio: 80/20
      Emphasis: --

Graduate Training: Master of Science
    Specialty: Research

Faculty: Full-time: 20   Doctorate: 18
      Part-time: 80   Master's: 10

Exchange: Students: Yes   Faculty: Yes
    Research: Social, clinical, educational, industrial

Cuba

FACULTAD DE PSICOLOGIA
UNIVERSIDAD CENTRAL DE LAS VILLAS
Carretera Caibarien-Remedios
Casa #8 Central Marcelo
Salado Caibarien
Villa Clara, Cuba
Phone: 3-4541   Chair: Digna Heredero Baute

Undergraduate Training
      Degree offered: Licenciado en Psicologia
      Years required: 5   Weekly class hours: 36
      Thesis required: Yes   Female/Male ratio: 75/25
            Emphasis: Clinical, educational, social, industrial

Graduate Training: Yes
      Specialty: Social, clinical

Faculty: Full-time: 19   Doctorate: 5
               Part-time: 6   Master's: 8

Exchange: Students: Yes   Faculty: Yes
            Research: Pathological psychic states

Dominican Republic

ESCUELA DE PSICOLOGIA
UNIVERSIDAD INTERAMERCANA
Apartado Postal 20687
Santo Domingo, Dominican Republic
Phone: 687-2529   Chair: Wilfredo Alvarez

Undergraduate Training
      Degree offered: Licenciado
      Years required: 3.5   Weekly class hours: 20
      Thesis required: Yes   Female/Male ratio: 70/30
            Emphasis: Clinical, industrial, educational, social

Graduate Training: --
      Specialty: --

Faculty: Full-time: 0   Doctorate: 2
               Part-time: 15   Master's: 7

Exchange: Students: Yes   Faculty: Yes
            Research: Social, educational

DEPARTAMENTO DE PSICOLOGIA
UNIVERSIDAD NACIONAL PEDRO HENRIQUEZ URENA
John F. Kennedy
Santo Domingo, Dominican Republic
Phone: 562-6601   Chair: Elizabeth De Windt

Undergraduate Training
    Degree offered: Licenciado
    Years required: 5   Weekly class hours: 22
    Thesis required: Yes   Female/Male ratio: 98/2
    Emphasis: --

Graduate Training: --
    Specialty: --

Faculty: Full-time: 2   Doctorate: 1
         Part-time: 5   Master's: 3

Exchange: Students: Yes   Faculty: Yes
         Research: Yes

FACULTAD DE HUMANIDADES
UNIVERSIDAD TECNOLOGICA DE SANTIAGO (UTESA)
21423, Maximo Gomez, esquina Jose Contreras
Santo Domingo, Dominican Republic
Phone: 689-6566, 689-0695   Chair: Dr. Enmanuel Silvestre

Undergraduate Training
    Degree offered: Bachelor in Psychology
    Years required: 4   Weekly class hours: 25
    Thesis required: Yes   Female/Male ratio: 80/20
    Emphasis: Clinical, educational, social, industrial

Graduate Training: Yes
    Specialty: Clinical

Faculty: Full-time: 16   Doctorate: 11
         Part-time: 25   Master's: 9

Exchange: Students: Yes   Faculty: Yes
         Research: Social, measurement

Ecuador

FACULTAD DE CIENCIAS PSICOLOGIAS
UNIVERSIDAD DE GUAYAQUIL
Apartado Postal 471
Guayaquil, Ecuador
Phone: 392729   Chair: Solon Villavicencio

Undergraduate Training
    Degree offered: Psicologo
    Years required: 5   Weekly class hours: 20
    Thesis required: Yes   Female/Male ratio: 80/20
        Emphasis: Clinical, educational, industrial, rehabilatation

Graduate Training: None
    Specialty: --

Faculty: Full-time: 18   Doctorate: 1
        Part-time: 43   Master's: 1

Exchange: Students: Yes   Faculty: Yes
        Research: Clinical, educational, social

ESCUELA DE PSICOLOGIA
PONTIFICIA UNIVERSIDAD CATOLICA DEL ECUADOR
Apartado 2184
Quito, Ecuador
Phone: 528522   Chair: Maria Eugenia Moscoso de Delgado

Undergraduate Training
    Degree offered: Licenciado
    Years required: 4.5   Weekly class hours: --
    Thesis required: Yes   Female/Male ratio: 90/10
        Emphasis: Clinical, educational, industrial

Graduate Training: Doctor in Psychology
    Specialty: Clinical (5 hours per week in classes)

Faculty: Full-time: 6   Doctorate: 6
        Part-time: 20   Master's: 10

Exchange: Students: --   Faculty: Yes
        Research: Yes

AREA DE PSICOLOGIA
PONTIFICIA UNIVERSIDAD CATOLICA DEL ECUADOR, CUENCA
Apartado Postal 981
Cuenca, Ecuador
Phone: 811494   Chair: Maria Jaramillo Paredes

Undergraduate Training
    Degree offered: Licenciado
    Years required: 5   **Weekly class hours:** 23
    Thesis required: Yes   **Female/Male ratio:** 70/30
        Emphasis: Educational, special education

Graduate Training: --
    Specialty: --

Faculty: Full-time: --   Doctorate: 7
              Part-time: 19   Master's: 3

Exchange: Students: --   Faculty: Yes
              Research: Learning, special education, orientation

El Salvador

DEPARTAMENTO DE PSICOLOGIA Y EDUCACION
UNIVERSIDAD CENTROAMERICANA JOSE SIMEON CANAS
Apartado (01) 168
San Salvador, El Salvador
Phone: 24-0011   Chair: Ignacio Martin-Baro

Undergraduate Training
    Degree offered: Licenciado
    Years required: 5-6   **Weekly class hours:** 20
    Thesis required: Yes   **Female/Male ratio:** 65/35
        Emphasis: --

Graduate Training: --
    Specialty: --

Faculty: Full-time: 6   Doctorate: 7
              Part-time: 17   Master's: 3

Exchange: Students: Yes   Faculty: Yes
              Research: Yes

DEPARTAMENTO DE PSICOLOGIA
FACULTAD DE CIENCIAS Y HUMANIDADES
UNIVERSIDAD DE EL SALVADOR
Ciudad Universitaria
Final 25 Avenida Norte
Apartado Postal 1383
San Salvador, El Salvador
Phone: --   Chair: Lic. Oralia Esther Roman de Rivas

Undergraduate Training
     Degree offered: Licenciado en Psicologia
     Years required: 5   **Weekly class hours:** 20
     Thesis required: Yes   **Female/Male ratio:** 67/33
          Emphasis: Clinical, educational, industrial

Graduate Training: None
     Specialty: -

Faculty: **Full-time:** 24   **Doctorate:** 0
          Part-time: 12   **Master's:** 4

Exchange: **Students:** Yes   **Faculty:** Yes
          Research: Social, clinical, educational, industrial

Guatemala

DEPARTAMENTO DE PSICOLOGIA
FACULTAD DE HUMANIDADES
UNIVERSIDAD FRANCISCO MARROQUIN
6a Avenida
0-28 Zona 10
Guatemala City, Guatemala
Phone: 316922 and 313888   Chair: Dr. Luis Alfonso Recinos Drago

Undergraduate Training
     Degree offered: Psicologo en el grado de Licenciado
     Years required: 5   **Weekly class hours:** 15
     Thesis required: Yes   **Female/Male ratio:** 100/0
          Emphasis: Clinical, industrial

Graduate Training: Masters
     Specialty: Human resources administration

Faculty: **Full-time:** 5   **Doctorate:** 6
          Part-time: 8   **Master's:** 4

Exchange: **Students:** Yes   **Faculty:** Yes
          Research: --

DEPARTAMENTO DE PSICOLOGIA
FACULTAD DE HUMANIDADES
UNIVERSIDAD RAFAEL LANDIVAR
Vista Hermosa III, Zona 16
Guatemala City, Guatemala
Phone: 692151 and 692751   **Chair:** Lic. Angel Alfredo Velasquez Trejo

Undergraduate Training
          Degree offered: Licenciado en Psicologia
          Years required: 6   **Weekly class hours:** 20
          Thesis required: Yes   **Female/Male ratio:** 80/20
                    Emphasis: Special education, learning disabilities, educational
                              orientation

Graduate Training: None
          Specialty: --

Faculty: Full-time: 3   Doctorate: 1
               Part-time: 1   Master's: 2

Exchange: Students: Yes   **Faculty:** Yes
              Research: Yes

Honduras

DEPARTAMENTO DE PSICOLOGIA
UNIVERSIDAD NACIONAL AUTONOMA DE HONDURAS
Ciudad Universitaria
Edificio 4 A
Tegucigalpa, Honduras
Phone: 326296   **Chair:** Amparo Quan de Raquel

Undergraduate Training
          Degree offered: Licenciado
          Years required: 5   **Weekly class hours:** 20
          Thesis required: Yes   **Female/Male ratio:** 90/10
                    Emphasis: Educational, clinical, industrial, social

Graduate Training: --
          Specialty: --

Faculty: Full-time: 37   Doctorate: 3
               Part-time: 3   Master's: 10

Exchange: Students: --   **Faculty:** Yes
              Research: Yes

ESCUELA DE PSICOLOGIA
CENTRO UNIVERSITARIO DE MAZATLAN
Calle Cruz #2
Apartado Postal 275
82000 Mazatlan, Mexico
Phone: 26988   Chair: Lic. Maria Elena Magallanes Rios

Undergraduate Training
         Degree offered: Bachelor in Psychology
         Years required: 4.5   **Weekly class hours:** 25
         Thesis required: Yes   **Female/Male ratio:** 75/25
                Emphasis: Educational

Graduate Training: None
         Specialty: --

Faculty: Full-time: 3   **Doctorate:** 0
            Part-time: 12   **Master's:** 2

Exchange: Students: Yes   **Faculty:** Yes
            Research: Educational, clinical, industrial

FACULTAD DE PSICOLOGIA
ESCUELA LIBRE DE PSICOLOGIA
Bolivar, Num 419
31000 Chihuahua, Chihuahua
Mexico
Phone: 127667 and 163979   Chair: Lic. Rosario Valdes De Chavez

Undergraduate Training
         Degree offered: Licenciado en Psicologia
         Years required: 4.5   **Weekly class hours:** 25
         Thesis required: Yes   **Female/Male ratio:** 95/5
                Emphasis: Clinical, educational, industrial

Graduate Training: Masters
         Specialty: Social psychology of organizations

Faculty: Full-time: 9   **Doctorate:** 0
            Part-time: 13   **Master's:** 2

Exchange: Students: --   **Faculty:** Yes
            Research: Any area

COORDINACION DE PSICOLOGIA
ESCUELA NACIONAL DE ESTUDIOS PROFESIONALES IZTACALA
Avenida de los Barrios s/n
Apartado Postal 314
54090 Tlalnepantla, Mexico
Mexico
Phone: 565-2233 ext. 133   Chair: Sergio Jara Del Rio

Undergraduate Training
      Degree offered: Licenciado
      Years required: 4   **Weekly class hours:** 32
      Thesis required: Yes   **Female/Male ratio:** 70/30
          Emphasis: Clinical, educational, social

Graduate Training: Maestria
      Specialty: Behavior modification, behavioral pharmacology, behavioral
          research methodology

Faculty: Full-time: 130   Doctorate: 0
          Part-time: 72   Master's: 10

Exchange: Students: Yes   Faculty: Yes
          Research: Developmental, clinical, social, special education

ESCUELA DE PSICOLOGIA
INSTITUTO TECNOLOGICO Y DE ESTUDIOS SUPERIORES DE OCCIDENTE
Ninos Heroes 1342-8
Guadalajara, Jalisco, Mexico
Phone: 310297, ext. 142   Chair: Anita Nielsen

Undergraduate Training
      Degree offered: Licenciado
      Years required: 4   **Weekly class hours:** 26
      Thesis required: Yes   **Female/Male ratio:** 85/15
          Emphasis: Community, social, educational, industrial

Graduate Training: --
      Specialty: --

Faculty: Full-time: 6   Doctorate: 3
          Part-time: 40   Master's: 5

Exchange: Students: Yes   Faculty: Yes
          Research: Yes

DEPARTAMENTO DE PSICOLOGIA
INSTITUTO TECNOLOGICO DE SONORA
5 De Febrero 818SUR
Apartado Postal 541
85000 CD Obregon
Sonora, Mexico
Phone: 45656   Chair: Johann A. Egli

Undergraduate Training
        Degree offered: Bachelor in Psychology
        Years required: 4   Weekly class hours: 25
        Thesis required: Yes   Female/Male ratio: 90/10
            Emphasis: Clinical, educational, industrial

Graduate Training: None
        Specialty: --

Faculty: Full-time: 5   Doctorate: 2
           Part-time: 8   Master's: 6

Exchange: Students: Yes   Faculty: Yes
            Research: Community, environmental

ESCUELA DE PSICOLOGIA
UNIVERSIDAD ANAHUAC
Apartado Postal 10-844
11000 Mexico DF Mexico
Phone: 589-2200   Chair: Rosamaria Valle de Martinez-Palomo

Undergraduate Training
        Degree offered: Licenciado
        Years required: 4.5   Weekly class hours: 5
        Thesis required: Yes   Female/Male ratio: 95/5
            Emphasis: Psychophysiology, educational, clinical, industrial

Graduate Training: Masters
        Specialty: --

Faculty: Full-time: 12   Doctorate: 10
           Part-time: 43   Master's: 15

Exchange: Students: Yes   Faculty: Yes
            Research: Developmental, attitudes, psychopathology, personality

ESCUELA DE PSICOLOGIA
UNIVERSIDAD AUTONOMA DE COAHUILA
Unidad Universitaria Campo Redondo
Edificio D
Saltillo, Coahuila, Mexico
Phone: 23528   Chair: Humberto Hinojosa Melendez

Undergraduate Training
        Degree offered: Licenciado
        Years required: 4   Weekly class hours: 22
        Thesis required: No   Female/Male ratio: 88/12
            Emphasis: --

Graduate Training: --
        Specialty: --

Faculty: Full-time: 3   Doctorate: 2
           Part-time: 26   Master's: 2

Exchange: Students: Yes   Faculty: Yes
          Research: Social, educational

ESCUELA DE PSICOLOGIA
UNIVERSIDAD AUTONOMA DEL ESTADO DE MORELOS
Av. Universidad #1001
Colonia Champila
62210 Cuernavaca, Morelos, Mexico
Phone: 172477   Chair: Psic. Fernando Iturbe Robledo

Undergraduate Training
        Degree offered: Licenciado en Psicologia
        Years required: 4   Weekly class hours: 40
        Thesis required: Yes   Female/Male ratio: 90/10
            Emphasis: None

Graduate Training: None
        Specialty: --

Faculty: Full-time: 2   Doctorate: 2
           Part-time: 20   Master's: 1

Exchange: Students: Yes   Faculty: Yes
          Research: --

FACULTAD DE PSICOLOGIA
UNIVERSIDAD AUTONOMA DE GUADALAJARA
Av. Patria #1201
Lomas Del Valle
Zapopan, Jalisco, Mexico
Phone: 415051, ext. 2266 and 2267   Chair: Lic. Psic. Gabriela Garibay
                                                Bagnis

Undergraduate Training
        Degree offered: Bachelor of Psychology
        Years required: 4.5   **Weekly class hours:** 25
        Thesis required: Yes   **Female/Male ratio:** 85/15
                Emphasis: Clinical, educational, social, industrial

Graduate Training: Masters
        Specialty: Education

Faculty: **Full-time:** 18   **Doctorate:** 5
               Part-time: 22   **Master's:** 6

Exchange: **Students:** Yes   **Faculty:** Yes
              Research: --

DEPARTAMENTO DE SOCIOLOGIA
UNIVERSIDAD AUTONOMA METROPOLITANA UNIDAD IZTAPALA
Av. Michoacan y
CDA de la Purisima 09300
Mexico DF Mexico
Phone: 6860322, ext. 331   Chair: Dr. J. Figueroa Nazuno

Undergraduate Training
        Degree offered: Licenciado en Psicologia-social
        Years required: 4   **Weekly class hours:** 20
        Thesis required: Yes   **Female/Male ratio:** 80/20
                Emphasis: Social

Graduate Training: Yes
        Specialty: Social research

Faculty: **Full-time:** 30   **Doctorate:** 6
               Part-time: 5   **Master's:** 10

Exchange: **Students:** Yes   **Faculty:** Yes
              Research: Social

COORDINACION DE PSICOLOGIA, DIVISION DE CIENCIAS SOCIALES Y HUMANIDADES
DEPARTAMENTO DE EDUCACION Y COMMUNICACION
UNIVERSIDAD AUTONOMA METROPOLITANA-XOCHIMILCO
Calz. del Hueso 1100
Col. Villa Quietud
04960 Mexico DF Mexico
Phone: 594-7833, ext. 228   **Chair:** Guillermo Delahanty M.

Undergraduate Training
    Degree offered: Licenciatura
    Years required: 4   **Weekly class hours:** 15
    Thesis required: No   **Female/Male ratio:** 70/30
        Emphasis: Social, educational

Graduate Training: None
    Specialty: --

Faculty: **Full-time:** 68   **Doctorate:** 8
        Part-time: 0   **Master's:** 28

Exchange: **Students:** Yes   **Faculty:** Yes
        Research: Yes

ESCUELA DE PSICOLOGIA
UNIVERSIDAD AUTONOMA DE SAN LUIS DE POTOSI
Carretera Central Km. 424.5
San Luis Potosi, SLP, Mexico
Phone: 41231   **Chair:** Ana Maria Esquivel

Undergraduate Training
    Degree offered: Licenciado
    Years required: 4   **Weekly class hours:** --
    Thesis required: Yes   **Female/Male ratio:** 65/35
        Emphasis: Clinical, educational

Graduate Training: --
    Specialty: --

Faculty: **Full-time:** 19   **Doctorate:** 1
        Part-time: 23   **Master's:** 4

Exchange: **Students:** Yes   **Faculty:** Yes
        Research: Intelligence measurement

FACULTAD DE PSICOLOGIA
UNIVERSIDAD AUTONOMA DE YUCATAN
Apartado Postal 1529 suc. B
97000 Merida, Yucatan, Mexico
Phone: --   Chair: Elias A. Gongora Coronado

Undergraduate Training
        Degree offered: Licenciado
        Years required: 5   Weekly class hours: Tutorials
        Thesis required: Yes, monograph   Female/Male ratio: 80/20
                Emphasis: Educational, industrial, community

Graduate Training: Masters
        Specialty: Educational

Faculty: Full-time: 7   Doctorate: --
            Part-time: 4   Master's: 8

Exchange: Students: No   Faculty: Yes
          Research: Educational, social, developmental

DEPARTAMENTO DE PSICOLOGIA
UNIVERSIDAD IBEROAMERICANA
Av. Cerro de las Torres #395
Campestre Churubusco
Mexico DF Mexico
Phone: 549-3500, ext. 103 and 183   Chair: Dr. Juan Lafarga Corona

Undergraduate Training
        Degree offered: Licenciatura en Psicologia
        Years required: 4   Weekly class hours: 40
        Thesis required: Yes   Female/Male ratio: 80/20
                Emphasis: Clinical, educational, industrial, social

Graduate Training: Doctorate, Masters
        Specialty: Industrial

Faculty: Full-time: 15   Doctorate: 20
            Part-time: 103   Master's: 30

Exchange: Students: Yes   Faculty: Yes
          Research: Community

FACULTAD DE PSICOLOGIA
UNIVERSIDAD INTERCONTINENTAL
Col. Tlalpan
Av. Insurgentes Sur 4135
14060 Mexico DF Mexico
Phone: 573-8544; ext. 144-145   Chair: Dr. Javier Romero Aquirre

Undergraduate Training
    Degree offered: Bachelor in Psychology
    Years required: 4.5   **Weekly class hours:** 26
    Thesis required: Yes   **Female/Male ratio:** 90/10
        Emphasis: Clinical, industrial, educational

Graduate Training: Doctorate
    Specialty: Psychotherapy

Faculty: Full-time: 2   Doctorate: 5
        Part-time: 23   Master's: 5

Exchange: Students: Yes   Faculty: Yes
         Research: Yes

FACULTAD DE PSICOLOGIA
UNIVERSIDAD NACIONAL AUTONOMA DE MEXICO
Ciudad Universitaria
04510 Mexico DF Mexico
Phone: 5505215
                Chair: Darvelio Castano

Undergraduate Training
    Degree offered: Licenciado
    Years required: 9 semesters   **Weekly class hours:** --
    Thesis required: Yes   **Female/Male ratio:** 70/30
        Emphasis: Clinical, social, industrial, experimental,
             psychophysiological, educational

Graduate Training: Doctorate, Masters
    Specialty: Clinical, social, general experimental (Doctorate);
           clinical, educational, social, general experimental,
           psychobiology, experimental analysis of behavior (Masters)

Faculty: Full-time: 220   Doctorate: 82
        Part-time: 345   Master's: 59

Exchange: Students: No   Faculty: Yes
         Research: Yes

DEPARTAMENTO DE PSICOLOGIA
UNIVERSIDAD DE MONTERREY
Gonzalitos #300
64020 Monterrey NL Mexico
Phone: 485292 and 469629   Chair: Carlos Diaz Esparza

Undergraduate Training
     Degree offered: Licenciado
     Years required: 4   **Weekly class hours:** 20
     Thesis required: Optional   **Female/Male ratio:** 94/6
     Emphasis: --

Graduate Training: --
     Specialty: --

Faculty: **Full-time:** 7   **Doctorate:** 2
          Part-time: 19   **Master's:** 18

Exchange: **Students:** Yes   **Faculty:** Yes
          Research: Social, clinical, educational

FACULTAD DE PSICOLOGIA
UNIVERSIDAD DEL NOROESTE
Manuel Gonzalez #219 Sur
Colonia Centro
Apartado Postal 757
Hermosillo, Sonora, Mexico
Phone: 24445 and 24446   Chair: Hector Padilla Ramos

Undergraduate Training
     Degree offered: Carta de Pasante, Psicologo, Licenciado en Psicologia
     Years required: 3.5   **Weekly class hours:** 26
     Thesis required: Yes   **Female/Male ratio:** 90/10
       Emphasis: Industrial, clinical, educational

Graduate Training: None
     Specialty: --

Faculty: **Full-time:** 1   **Doctorate:** 1
          Part-time: 2   **Master's:** 3

Exchange: **Students:** Yes   **Faculty:** Yes
          Research: Educational, social, industrial, clinical

FACULTAD DE PSICOLOGIA
UNIVERSIDAD DEL NOROESTE
Prolongoncion Avenida Hidalgo s/n
Apartado Postal 469
Tampico, Tamps., Mexico
Phone: 35831, ext. 43   Chair: Lic. Belinda E. Cuesta Cordova

Undergraduate Training
>   Degree offered: Licenciado en Psicologia
>   Years required: 4   Weekly class hours: 25
>   Thesis required: Yes   Female/Male ratio: 80/20
>   Emphasis: Industrial, clinical, educational

Graduate Training: --
>   Specialty: --

Faculty: Full-time: 6   Doctorate: 0
>   Part-time: 17   Master's: 2

Exchange: Students: Yes   Faculty: Yes
>   Research: Clinical

DEPARTAMENTO DE HUMANIDADES Y CIENCIAS SOCIALES
FACULTAD DE PSICOLOGIA
UNIVERSIDAD REGIOMONANA, A.C.
Padre Mier #575 Pte.
64000 Monterrey NL Mexico
Phone: 430767
                                         Chair: Lic. Dionisio Kladiano Benavides,
                                              Lic. Adrian Rivas Montenegro, Lic. Ma.
                                              Alejandra Favela Rodriquez

Undergraduate Training
>   Degree offered: Licenciado en Psicologia
>   Years required: 3.33   Weekly class hours: 25
>   Thesis required: Yes   Female/Male ratio: 90/10
>   Emphasis: None

Graduate Training: Masters
>   Specialty: Counseling, industrial

Faculty: Full-time: 19   Doctorate: 5
>   Part-time: 6   Master's: 8

Exchange: Students: Yes   Faculty: --
>   Research: Educational, clinical, social, industrial

ESCUELA DE PSICOLOGIA
UNIVERSIDAD SALESIANA
Calle Colegio Salesiano #35
Col. Anahuac
11320 Mexico DF Mexico
Phone: 396-2430   Chair: Ma. Elizabeth Ramirez

Undergraduate Training
      Degree offered: Bachelor
      Years required: 4.5   Weekly class hours: 28
      Thesis required: Yes   Female/Male ratio: 90/10
           Emphasis: Clinical, industrial

Graduate Training: None
      Specialty: --

Faculty: Full-time: 0   Doctorate: 0
          Part-time: 14   Master's: 10

Exchange: Students: Yes   Faculty: Yes
          Research: --

FACULTAD DE PSICOLOGIA
UNIVERSIDAD VERACRUZANA
Iturbide y Carmen Serdan
Veracruz, Veracruz
Mexico
Phone: 324959   Chair: Psic. Miriam Ruiseco Castro Dtora

Undergraduate Training
      Degree offered: Licenciado en Psicologia
      Years required: 2   Weekly class hours: 25
      Thesis required: Yes   Female/Male ratio: 77/23
           Emphasis: Clinical, industrial

Graduate Training: None
      Specialty: --

Faculty: Full-time: 0   Doctorate: 0
          Part-time: 21   Master's: 1

Exchange: Students: --   Faculty: --
          Research: --

FACULTAD DE PSICOLOGIA
UNIVERSIDAD VERACRUZANA
Benito Juarez #81
91000 Xalapa, Veracruz
Mexico
Phone: 73109   Chair: Psic. Sebastian Fiqueroa Rodriquez

Undergraduate Training
        Degree offered: Licenciado en Psicologia
        Years required: 4   Weekly class hours: 30
        Thesis required: Yes   Female/Male ratio: 76/24
               Emphasis: Industrial, clinical, educational, social, experimental

Graduate Training: None
        Specialty: --

Faculty: Full-time: 12   Doctorate: 2
              Part-time: 42   Master's: 10

Exchange: Students: --   Faculty: Yes
              Research: Teaching, academic administration

Panama

ESCUELA PSICOLOGIA
UNIVERSIDAD SANTA MARIA LA ANTIGUA
Apartado 6-1696
El Dorado
Panama 6 Panama
Phone: 607860 and 608377   Chair: Melva P. de Mon

Undergraduate Training
        Degree offered: Licenciado
        Years required: 5   Weekly class hours: 20
        Thesis required: --   Female/Male ratio: 88/12
               Emphasis: --

Graduate Training: --
        Specialty: --

Faculty: Full-time: 4   Doctorate: 5
              Part-time: 15   Master's: 8

Exchange: Students: Yes   Faculty: Yes
              Research: Social, industrial, clinical, educational, experimental

DEPARTAMENTO DE PSICOLOGIA
FACULTAD DE HUMANIDADES
UNIVERSIDAD DE PANAMA
Ciudad Universitaria Octavio Mendez Pereira
Estafeta Universitaria
Panama, Panama
Phone: 238598   Chair: Maria Elena S. De Cano

Undergraduate Training
      Degree offered: Licenciado en Psicologia
      Years required: 5   **Weekly class hours:** 40
      Thesis required: Yes   **Female/Male ratio:** 70/30
           Emphasis: Educational, clinical, social, industrial

Graduate Training: None
      Specialty: --

Faculty: **Full-time:** 25   Doctorate: 11
          Part-time: 10   Master's: 18

Exchange: **Students:** --   **Faculty:** Yes
          Research: Educational, social

Paraguay

DEPARTAMENTO DE PSICOLOGIA
UNIVERSIDAD CATOLICA DE NUESTRA SENORA DE LA ASUNCION
CC 1718
Asuncion, Paraguay
Phone: 47173 and 41044   Chair: Carlos Luis LaFuente

Undergraduate Training
      Degree offered: Licenciado
      Years required: 5   **Weekly class hours:** 18
      Thesis required: Yes   **Female/Male ratio:** 95/5
           Emphasis: Industrial, clinical, educational

Graduate Training: --
      Specialty: --

Faculty: **Full-time:** --   Doctorate: 2
          Part-time: 15   Master's: 3

Exchange: **Students:** Yes   **Faculty:** Yes
          Research: Cross-cultural, social, educational

Peru

DEPARTAMENTO DE PSICOLOGIA
INSTITUTO SUPERIOR DE PSICOLOGIA (ISSA)
Oficina Central
Av. Garcilaso 306 Of 201
Huanchac, Cusco
Cusco, Peru
Phone: **Chair:** Jorge Elias Cuarto Silva Sifuentes

Undergraduate Training
    Degree offered: Especialista
    Years required: 2   **Weekly class hours:** 30
    Thesis required: Yes   **Female/Male ratio:** 75/25
        Emphasis: Clinical, educational, experimental research, socio-
            organizational, bilingual-community

Graduate Training: --
    Specialty: --

Faculty: **Full-time:** 3   **Doctorate:** 0
        Part-time: 2   **Master's:** 0

Exchange: **Students:** Yes   **Faculty:** Yes
        Research: Educational, clinical, social

AREA DE PSICOLOGIA, DEPARTAMENTO DE HUMANIDADES
FACULTAD DE LETRAS Y CIENCIAS HUMANAS
PONTIFICIA UNIVERSIDAD CATOLICA DEL PERU
Lima, Peru
Phone: --   **Chair:** Patricia Martinez U.; Marcia De La Flor

Undergraduate Training
    Degree offered: Bachiller en Humanidades con mencion en Psicologia
    Years required: 2   **Weekly class hours:** 20
    Thesis required: Yes   **Female/Male ratio:** 70/30
        Emphasis: General Psychology

Graduate Training: Licenciado
    Specialty: Clinical, educational, social

Faculty: **Full-time:** 6   **Doctorate:** 9
        Part-time: 3   **Master's:** 1

Exchange: **Students:** Yes   **Faculty:** Yes
        Research: Yes

FACULTAD DE PSICOLOGIA
UNIVERSIDAD NACIONAL FEDERICO VILLAREAL
Av. Colonial #450
Lima, Peru
Phone: 243338   Chair: Lic. Psic. Francisco Villanueva
                                              Tapia

Undergraduate Training
        Degree offered: Bachiller, Licenciatura en Psicologia
        Years required: 6   Weekly class hours: 25
        Thesis required: Yes   Female/Male ratio: 65/35
                Emphasis: Clinical, educational, industrial, social

Graduate Training: Yes
        Specialty: Clinical

Faculty: Full-time: 40   Doctorate: 2
          Part-time: 5   Master's: 2

Exchange: Students: Yes   Faculty: Yes
          Research: Clinical, industrial, educational, social

ESCUELA DE PSICOLOGIA
FACULTAD DE LETRAS Y CIENCIAS HUMANAS
UNIVERSIDAD NACIONAL MAYOR DE SAN MARCOS
Lima, Peru
Phone: 524641   Chair: Victor Amoros Teran

Undergraduate Training
        Degree offered: Psicologo
        Years required: 6   Weekly class hours: 30
        Thesis required: Yes   Female/Male ratio: 60/40
                Emphasis: Clinical, educational, delinquency, social, industrial

Graduate Training: None
        Specialty: --

Faculty: Full-time: 20   Doctorate: 2
          Part-time: 27   Master's: 2

Exchange: Students: Yes   Faculty: Yes
          Research: Yes

DEPARTAMENTO DE PSICOLOGIA
FACULTAD DE PSICOLOGIA Y RELACIONES INDUSTRIALES Y PUBLICAS
UNIVERSIDAD NACIONAL DE SAN AGUSTIN DE AREQUIPA
Urb. San Lorenzo
Pasaje Huanco 313
Mariano Melgar
Arequipa, Peru
Phone: 216474   Chair: Belen Salvatierra de Vega

Undergraduate Training
    Degree offered: Profesional en Psicologia
    Years required: 6   **Weekly class hours:** 25
    Thesis required: Yes   **Female/Male ratio:** 63/37
        Emphasis: Clinical, educational, industrial, social

Graduate Training: None
    Specialty: --

Faculty: **Full-time:** 20   **Doctorate:** 2
         Part-time: 1   **Master's:** 1

Exchange: **Students:** Yes   **Faculty:** Yes
        Research: Psychosocial, psychotherapy, behavioral therapy

FACULTAD DE CIENCIAS Y FILOSOFIA
ESCUELA DE PSICOLOGIA
UNIVERSIDAD PERUANA CAYETANO HEREDIA
Apartado 5045 Lima
Av. Honorio Delgado # 430 Urb. Ingenieria
Lima 31
Lima, Peru
Phone: 815772 - 29; 819112   Chair: Dr. Jose Anicama G.

Undergraduate Training
    Degree offered: Licenciado en Psicologia, Bachiller en Ciencias con
                  mencion en Psicologia
    Years required: 6   **Weekly class hours:** 24
    Thesis required: Yes   **Female/Male ratio:** 85/15
        Emphasis: Clinical, educational, industrial, socio-community

Graduate Training: Masters
    Specialty: Behavior modification, technology of teaching, human
           development, community psychology, drug dependency

Faculty: **Full-time:** 6   **Doctorate:** 4
         Part-time: 15   **Master's:** 8

Exchange: **Students:** Yes   **Faculty:** Yes
        Research: All areas

DEPARTAMENTO DE PSICOLOGIA
FACULTAD DE CIENCIAS EDUCATIVAS
UNIVERSIDAD RICARDO PALMA
Av. Armendariz 349
Apartado 138
Miraflores, Peru
Phone: 453400   Chair: Dra. Gladys Feijoo Portal

Undergraduate Training
        Degree offered: Bachiller en Psicologia
        Years required: 6   **Weekly class hours:** 22
        Thesis required: Yes   **Female/Male ratio:** 70/30
              Emphasis: Clinical, educational, industrial, social

Graduate Training: None
        Specialty: --

Faculty: Full-time: 9   Doctorate: 2
              Part-time: 32   Master's: 2

Exchange: Students: Yes   Faculty: Yes
              Research: Social, educational

Puerto Rico

DEPARTAMENTO DE PSICOLOGIA
UNIVERSIDAD DE PUERTO RICO
Recinto de Rio Piedras
Rio Piedras PR 00931
Phone: 764-0000 ext. 2094   Chair: Eduardo Rivera Medina

Undergraduate Training
        Degree offered: Bachiller
        Years required: 4   **Weekly class hours:** 17
        Thesis required: No   **Female/Male ratio:** 77/23
              Emphasis: --

Graduate Training: Masters, Doctorate
        Specialty: Community social, clinical, industrial/organizational,
                academic research (14 hours per week in classes)

Faculty: Full-time: 28   Doctorate: 38
              Part-time: 20   Master's: 10

Exchange: Students: Yes   Faculty: Yes
              Research: Social, experimental (perception), industrial,
                developmental

FACULTAD DE PSICOLOGIA
UNIVERSIDAD INTERAMERICANA DE PUERTO RICO
P.O. Box 1293
Hato Rey, PR 00919
Phone: 758-8000 ext. 154   Chair: Dagmar Guardiola

Undergraduate Training
    Degree offered: Bachiller
    Years required: 4   Weekly class hours: 12
    Thesis required: No   Female/Male ratio: --
        Emphasis: General experimental, applied, social

Graduate Training: Masters
    Specialty: Educational, counseling, personnel

Faculty: Full-time: 15   Doctorate: 13
       Part-time: 21   Master's: 22

Exchange: Students: Yes   Faculty: Yes
       Research: Yes

DEPARTAMENTO DE PSICOLOGIA
UNIVERSIDAD CATOLICA DE PUERTO RICO
Estacion 6
Ponce, PR 00731
Phone: 844-4150 ext. 253   Chair: Carmen I. Rivera

Undergraduate Training
    Degree offered: Bachiller
    Years required: 4   Weekly class hours: 15
    Thesis required: No   Female/Male ratio: 70/30
        Emphasis: None

Graduate Training: None
    Specialty:

Faculty: Full-time: 5   Doctorate: 2
       Part-time: 2   Master's: 5

Exchange: Students: Yes   Faculty: Yes
       Research: Social, gerontology

DEPARTAMENTO DE CIENCIAS Y PROFESIONES DE LA CONDUCTA
UNIVERSIDAD INTERAMERICANA DE PUERTO RICO
Carr. 174 Urbanizacion Industrial Minillas
Bayamon, PR 00619
Phone: 780-4040   Chair: Nydia Sastre-Ruiz

Undergraduate Training
         Degree offered: Bachiller
         Years required: 4   Weekly class hours: 15
         Thesis required: No   Female/Male ratio: --
                Emphasis: General experimental, applied, personality, social

Graduate Training: None
         Specialty:

Faculty: Full-time: 7   Doctorate: 2
           Part-time: 23   Master's: --

Exchange: Students: --   Faculty: Yes
           Research: --

CENTRO CARIBENO DE ESTUDIOS POSTGRADUADOS
Apartado 41246 Minillas Station
Santurce, PR 00940
Phone: 725-2556   Chair: Salvador Santiago-Negron

Undergraduate Training
         Degree offered: None
         Years required: Weekly class hours:
         Thesis required: Female/Male ratio:
                Emphasis:

Graduate Training: Ph.D, Psy.D. (After 5 years of training; thesis required;
                74% women)
         Specialty: Industrial/organizational, clinical

Faculty: Full-time: 12   Doctorate: 24
           Part-time: 12   Master's: 0

Exchange: Students: Yes   Faculty: Yes
           Research: Yes

Venezuela

ESCUELA DE PSICOLOGIA
UNIVERSIDAD CATOLICA ANDRES BELLO
Urbanizacion Montalban, La Vega
Apartado 29068
Caracas 1021 Venezuela
Phone: 475110; 475111; 475112   Chair: Alvaro Ochoa

Undergraduate Training
        Degree offered: Licenciado
        Years required: 5   Weekly class hours: --
        Thesis required: Yes   Female/Male ratio: 85/15
               Emphasis: --

Graduate Training: Maestria
        Specialty: Organizational development (12 hours per week in classes)

Faculty: Full-time: 5   Doctorate: 1
          Part-time: 56   Master's: 33

Exchange: Students: Yes   Faculty: Yes
          Research: Yes

ESCUELA DE PSICOLOGIA
FACULTAD DE HUMANIDADES Y EDUCACION
UNIVERSIDAD CENTRAL DE VENEZUELA
Ciudad Universitaria
Caracas, Venezuela
Phone: 619811, ext 2155 or 2423   Chair: Prof. Miguel Padron

Undergraduate Training
        Degree offered: Licenciado en Psicologia
        Years required: 10 semesters   Weekly class hours: 24
        Thesis required: Yes   Female/Male ratio: 75/25
             Emphasis: Clinical, industrial, educational, social, psychological
                       counseling/orientation

Graduate Training: Masters
        Specialty: Experimental analysis of behavior, social, group dynamics,
                   instructional

Faculty: Full-time: 70   Doctorate: 15
          Part-time: 39   Master's: 30

Exchange: Students: --   Faculty: Yes
          Research: Yes

COORDINACION DE POSTGRADO EN PSICOLOGIA
UNIVERSIDAD SIMON BOLIVAR
Sartenejas, Baruta
A.P. 80 659
Caracas, Venezuela
Phone: 962-1101   **Chair**: Marina Gorodeckis

Undergraduate Training
        Degree offered: Magister en Psicologia
        Years required: 2   **Weekly class hours**: 4-12
        Thesis required: Yes   **Female/Male ratio**: 75/25
                Emphasis: Social, counseling, behavior modification

Graduate Training: Magister en Psicologia
        Specialty:

Faculty: **Full-time**: 15   **Doctorate**: 7
        Part-time: 1   **Master's**: 8

Exchange: **Students**: Yes   **Faculty**: Yes
        Research: Social, counseling in the area of social change

Additional Programs

Argentina

Escuela de Psicologia
Universidad Argentina John Kennedy
Solia 950
1078 Buenos Aires, Argentina

Facultad de Artes y Ciencias
Universidad Catolica de Salta
Ciudad Universitaria
CC 18 Campo Castanares
4400 Salta, Argentina

Facultad de Filosofia y Humanidades
Universidad Catolica de Cordoba
Trejo 323
5000 Cordoba, Argentina

Facultad de Psicologia
Universidad del Aconcaqua
Catamarca 147
5500 Mendoza, Argentina

Departamento de Psicologia
Universidad Nacional de San Luis
Lavalle y Mitre
5700 San Luis, Argentina

Facultad de Filosofia y Humanidades
Universidad Nacional de Cordoba
Estafeta 32, Pabellon Residencial
Ciudad Universitaria
5000 Cordoba, Argentina

Brazil

Faculdade de Psicologia de Marilia
Vila Fragata
Rua Comendador Abel Augusto Fragata, 58
17500 Marilia SP Brazil

Faculdade de Biologia e Psicologia Maria Thereza
Centro
Rua Visconde do Rio Banco 869
24000 Niteroi RJ Brazil

Departamento de Psicologia
Centro de Ciencias Humanas Letras e Artes
Universidade Federal da Paraiba
Cidade Universitaria
58000 Joao Pessoa PB Brazil

Departamento de Psicologia
Faculdade de Filosofia, Ciencias e Letras do D.F.
Centro de Ensino Unificado de Brasilia
EQN 707/9 Asa Norte
70000 Brasilia DF Brazil

Departamento de Psicologia
Centro de Estudos Superiores de Maceio
Av. Aristeu de Andrade 256 Terreo Farol
Alagoas Maceio AL Brazil

Departamento de Psicologia
Centro de Estudos Superiores de Maceio
Fundacao Educacional Jayme de Altavila
Rua Dr. Jose Bento Junior 110
57000 Maceio AL Brazil

Faculdade Dom Bosco de Filosofia, Ciencias e Letras
Fabricas
Praca Dom Helvecio 74
36300 Sao Joao Del Rei MG Brazil

Departamento de Psicologia
Faculdade de Ciencias
Vi la Falcao
Rua Campos Salles 943
17100 Bauru SP Brazil

Departamento de Psicologia
Faculdade de Ciencias
Rua Campos Salles 9-43
17100 Bauru SP Brazil

Departamento de Psicologia
Faculdade de Ciencias Humanas (FUMEC)
Rua Aimores 2679
30000 Belo Horizonte MG Brazil

Departamento de Psicologia
Faculdade de Ciencias Humanas ESUDA
Rua Corredor do Bispo 185
50000 Recife PE Brazil

Departamento de Psicologia
Faculdade de Educacao Filosofia e Ciencias e Letras Senador Flaquer
Rua Senador Flaquer 438
09000 Sto. Andre SP Brazil

Departamento de Psicologia
Faculdade de Filosofia, Ciencias, e Letras de Santo Amaro
Rio Bonito Santa Amaro
Rua Prof. Eneas de Siqueira Netto, 340
04800 Sao Paulo SP Brazil

Departamento de Psicologia
Faculdade de Filosofia, Ciencias, e Letras de Lorena
Rua Dom Bosco 284
12600 Lorena SP Brazil

Departamento de Psicologia
Faculdade de Filosofia Ciencias e Letras de Belo Horizonte
Sao Cristovao, Av. Antonio Carlos 521
30000 Belo Horizonte MG Brazil

Departamento de Psicologia
Faculdade de Filosofia, Ciencias e Letras
Centro
39800 Teofilo Otoni MG Brazil

Departamento de Psicologia
Faculdade de Filosofia, Ciencias e Letras Tuiuti
Rua Fernando Simas s/n
80000 Curitiba PR Brazil

Departamento de Psicologia
Faculdade de Filosofia, Ciencias e Letras
Rua Rangel Pestana 762
13400 Piracicaba SP Brazil

Departamento de Psicologia
Faculdade de Filosofia, Ciencias e Letras de Guarulhos
Rua Barao de Maua 600
07000 Guarulhos SP Brazil

Departamento de Psicologia
Faculdade de Filosofia, Ciencias e Letras Santa Rita de Cassia
Av. Jacana 648
02273 Sao Paulo SP Brazil

Departamento de Psicologia
Faculdade de Filosofia do Recife
Av. Conde da Boa Vista 921
50000 Recife PE Brazil

Departamento de Psicologia
Faculdade de Humanidades Pedro II
Sao Cristavao, Rua Pirauba s/n
20000 Rio de Janeiro RJ Brazil

Departamento de Psicologia
Faculdade Farias Brito
Praca Tereza Cristina 01
07000 Guarulhos SP Brazil

Departamento de Psicologia
Faculdade Integrades Celso Lisboa
Rua 24 de Majo 797
20000 Rio de Janeiro RJ Brazil

Departamento de Psicologia
Faculdade Pailistana de Ciencias e Letras
Rua Madre Cabrini 36
03071 Sao Paulo SP Brazil

Departamento de Psicologia
Faculdades Integradas de Sao Bernardo do Campo
Rudge Ramos
Rua do Sacramento 230
09720 Sao Bernardo do Campos SP Brazil

Departamento de Psicologia
Faculdades Integradas do Inst. Metodista de Ensino Superior
Rua do Sacramento 230
09700 Sao Bernardo do Campo SP Brazil

Departamento de Psicologia
Faculdades Metropolitanas Unidas
Liberdade
Rua Tangua 150
01508 Sao Paulo SP Brazil

Departamento de Psicologia
Faculdades Unidas Catolicas de Mato Grosso
Centro
Rua 13 de Maio 1442
79100 Campo Grande MG Brazil

Departamento de Psicologia
Federacao das Escolas Superiores do ABC
Rua do Sacramento 230
09700 Sao Bernardo do Campo SP Brazil

Departamento de Psicologia
Federacao das Faculdades Braz Cubas
Av. Francisco Rodriques Filho 1233
08700 Mogi das Cruzes SP Brazil

Departamento de Psicologia
Pontificia Universidade Catolica do Rio Grande do Sul
Av. Ipiranga 6681
90000 Porto Alegre RS Brazil

Departamento de Psicologia
Pontificia Universidade Catolica de Campinas
Rua Marechal Deodoro 1099
13100 Campinas SP Brazil

Departamento de Psicologia
Pontificia Universidade Catolica de Sao Paulo
Rua Monte Alegre 984
05014 Sao Paulo SP Brazil

Departamento de Psicologia
Faculdade de Ciencias Humanas
Primero Distrito Cidade
Bairro Universidade do Trabalho
Km 200-Br 381
35170 Coronel Fabriciano MG Brazil

Departamento de Psicologia
Universidad Estadual de Campinas
Cidade Universitaria Barao Geraldo
13100 Campinas SP Brazil

Departamento de Psicologia
Universidade Catolica de Petropolis
Centro
Rua Benjamin Constant 213
25600 Petropolis RJ Brazil

Departamento de Psicologia
Universidade Catolica da Minas Gerais
Av. Antonio Carlos 6627
30000 Belo Horizonte MG Brazil

Departamento de Psicologia
Universidade de Santa Ursula
Botafogo, Rua Fernando Ferrari 75
20000 Rio de Janeiro RJ Brazil

Departamento de Psicologia
Universidade de Estado de Rio de Janeiro
Maracana, Rua Turf Club 5
20000 Rio de Janeiro RJ Brazil

Departamento de Psicologia
Universidade de Uberlandia
Jardin Umuarama, s/n, Centro
38400 Uberlandia MG Brazil

Departamento de Psicologia
Universidade de Passo Fundo
Centro
Avenida Brasil, 743-1 andar
99100-Passo Fundo-RS, Brazil

Departamento de Psicologia
Universidade do Vale do Rio dos Sinos
Praca Tiradentes 35
93000 Sao Lempoldo RS Brazil

Departamento de Psicologia
Universidade Estadual Paulista
Julio de Mesquita Filho
Av. Rio Blanco
01206 Sao Paulo SP Brazil

Departamento de Psicologia
Universidade Estadual de Mato Grosso
Cidade Universitaria
79100 Campo Grande MG Brazil

Departamento de Psicologia
Universidade Federal do Rio de Janeiro Norte
Tirol
Av. Hermes da Fonseca 780
59000 Natal RN Brazil

Departamento de Psicologia
Universidade Federal Fluminense
Icarai
Rua Miquel de Frias 9
24000 Niterol RJ Brazil

Departamento de Psicologia
Universidade Federal de Sao Carlos
Via Washington Luiz, Km 235
Carto Postal 676
13560 Sao Carlos SP Brazil

Departamento de Psicologia
Universidade Federal de Santa Maria
Floriana Peixoto 1184
37100 Santa Maria Rio Grande do Sul Brazil

Departamento de Psicologia
Universidade Federal do Rio de Janeiro
Av. Brig. Trompowski s/n
20000 Rio de Janeiro RJ Brazil

Departamento de Psicologia
Universidade Federal de Bahia
Rua Augusto Viana s/n
40000 Salvador BA Brazil

Departamento de Psicologia
Universidade Metodista de Piracicaba
Centro
Rua Rangel Pestana 762
13400 Piracicaba SP Brazil

Chile

Departamento de Psicologia
Universidad de Chile
Alameda Bernardo O'Higgins 340
Santiago, Chile

Departamento de Psicologia
Universidad de Talca
Talca, Chile

Departamento de Psicologia
Universidad del Norte
Antofagasta, Chile

Departamento de Psicologia
Universidad Gabriela Mistral
Av. Ricardo Lyon 1177
Santiago, Chile

Colombia

Facultad de Psicologia
Pontificia Universidad Javeriana
Carrera 7a, No. 43-82
Bogota DE Colombia

Departamento de Psicologia
Universidad de la Sabana
Apartado Aereo 53753
Bogota DE Colombia

Departamento de Psicologia
Universidad Javeriana-Sectionnal Cali
Apartado Aereo 26239
Cali, Colombia

Cuba

Escuela de Psicologia
Universidad de La Habana
La Habana, Cuba

Ecuador

Facultad de Pedagogia y Psicologia
Universidad Catolica de Cuenca
Apartado 19-A
Cuenca, Ecuador

Facultad de Filosofia y Ciencias de la Educacion
Universidad Catolica
Apartado 4671
Guayaquil, Ecuador

Facultad de Ciencias Psicologicas
Universidad Central
Apartado de Correos 3291
Quito, Ecuador

Facultad de Filosofia y Ciencias de la Educacion
Universidad Central
Apartado de Correos 3291
Quito, Ecuador

Departamento de Psicologia
Universidad de Loja
Apartado de Correos 'S'
Loja, Ecuador

Facultad de Filosofia y Letras
Universidad Estatal de Cuenca
Apartado 168
Cuenca, Ecuador

Escuela de Psicologia
Universidad Tecnica de Esmeraldas
Apartado de Correos 179
Esmeraldas, Ecuador

Facultad de Ciencias de la Educacion
Universidad Tecnica de Babahoyo
Apartado 66
Babahoyo, Ecuador

Facultad de Ciencias Sociales y de la Educacion
Universidad Tecnica de Manabi
Apartado 82
Portoviejo, Ecuador

Escuela de Psicologia
Universidade Laica Vicente Rocafuerte
Apartado de Correos 1133
Guayaquil, Ecuador

El Salvador

Universidad Nacional de El Salvador
7 Avenida Sur No. 722
San Salvador, El Salvador

Guatemala

Escuela de Ciencias Psicologicas
Universidad de San Carlos de Guatemala
Ciudad Universitaria, zona 12
Guatemala, Guatemala

Departamento de Psicologia
Universidad del Valle de Guatemala
Guatemala, Guatemala

Haiti

Section de Psychologie
Faculte des Sciences Humaines
Port-au-Prince, Haiti

Mexico

Facultad Psicologia
Facultades Universitarias de Saltillo
Saltillo, Coahuila, Mexico

Departamento de Psicologia
Instituto Tecnologico de Sonora
R.E. Calles & Chihuahua
85000 Obregon Son, Mexico

Departamento de Psicologia
Instituto Tecnologico y de Estudios Superiores de Monterrey
Carr. Lago de Guadalupe, Km. 4
53100 Atizapan de Zaragoza, Mexico

Departamento de Psicologia
Instituto Universitario de Ciencias de La Educacion
Colonia Anahuac
Calle Colegio Salesiano 35
11320 Mexico DF Mexico

Departamento de Psicologia
UNAM Escuela Nacional de Estudios
Professionales-Zaragoza
Col. Ejercito de Oriente
Czda. I Zaragoza & J.C. Bonilla
09230 Mexico DF Mexico

Departamento de Psicologia
Universidad Autonoma de Queretaro
Centro Universitario
Cerro de las Campanas
76010 Queretaro, Qro., Mexico

Departamento de Psicologia
Universidad Autonoma de Puebla
3 Oriente 403
72270 Puebla, Pue., Mexico

Departamento de Psicologia
Universidad Autonoma de Nueva Leon
Col. Mitras Centro
Mutualismo 110 & Salvatierra
64460 Monterrey NL Mexico

Departamento de Psicologia
Universidad Autonoma del Noroeste
Col. Republica
Monclova 1561, 2do Piso
25280 Saltillo, Coah., Mexico

Departamento de Psicologia
Universidad Autonoma de Guadalajara
Av. La Patria 1202
Lomas del Valle, 3a Seccion
44100 Guadalajara, Jal., Mexico

Departamento de Psicologia
Universidad Autonoma del Estado de Mexico
Toluca, Estado de Mexico, Mexico

Departamento de Psicologia
Universidad de las Americas
Cholula, Puebla, Mexico

Departamento de Psicologia
Universidad Femenina de Mexico
Av. Constituyentes No. 151
Mexico DF Mexico

Departamento de Psicologia
Universidad Veracruzana
Juarez 81
91000 Xalapa, Veracruzana, Mexico

Paraguay

Departamento de Psicologia
Universidad de Cristo Rey
Asuncion, Paraguay

Peru

Departamento de Investigacion
Escuela de Administracion de Negocios para Graduados (ESAN)
Casilla Postal 1846
Lima 100, Peru

Departamento de Psicologia
Universidad Femenina del Sagrado Corazon
Av. Los Frutales s/n, La Molina
Lima, Peru

Facultad de Psicologia
Universidad Nacional Federico Villareal
Av. Colonial 450, Apartado 1518
Lima, Peru

Facultad de Sociologia & Psicologia
Universidad Nacional Hermilio Valdizan
Dos de Mayo 680
Huanuco, Peru

Facultad de Psicologia
Universidad Particular Ricardo Palma
Av. Arequipa 5198
Miraflores, Lima, Peru

Departamento de Psicologia
Universidad Particular Inca Garcilaso de la Vega
Av. Arequipa 3610
San Isidoro, Lima, Peru

Departamento de Psicologia
Universidad Peruana Cayetano Heredia
Apartado 5045
Av. Honorio Delgado 932
Lima, Peru

Puerto Rico

Departamento de Ciencias Sociales y Psicologia
Recinto de San German
Universidad Interamericana de Puerto Rico
San German, PR 00753

Departamento de Ciencias Sociales y Psicologia
Recinto Universitario de Mayaguez
Mayaguez, PR 00708

Departamento de Psicologia
Universidad Central de Bayamon
Apartado 1725
Bayamon, PR 00620-1725

Departamento de Ciencias Sociales y Psicologia
Universidad de Turabo
Apartado 1091
Caguas, PR 00625-1091

Departamento de Psicologia
Universidad Interamericana de Puerto Rico
Colegio Regional de Ponce
Apartado 309
Ponce, PR 00733

Departamento de Psicologia
Universidad Interamericana de Sagrado Corazon
Box 12383 Loiza Station
Santurce, PR 00914-1383

Uruguay

Instituto de Psicologia
Universidad de la Republica
Oriental del Uruguay
Avenida 18 de Julio 1824
Montevideo, Uruguay

Venezuela

Escuela de Psicologia
Universidad Rafael Urdaneta
Apartado 614
Maracaibo, Zulia
Venezuela

4

Research Centers

This chapter presents a listing of research centers and institutes that perform psychological research in Latin America. Some of the centers listed below are engaged in interdisciplinary research; therefore, psychological research may not be their primary emphasis. Most places are staffed by well-trained researchers who welcome inquiries regarding their work and the possibilities for collaborative research.

A number of the research centers listed below are not connected with universities or government institutions and therefore depend on grants and other sources of income for their continued existence. As is true in the United States, funding priorities vary, resulting in changes in research plans and occasionally forcing a center to close. Consequently, our data are neither definitive nor exhaustive. A few of the centers listed below consider training, outreach, and clinical activities to be integral parts of their mandate. In that sense it is not unusual to find basic and applied research being conducted alongside clinical practice and seminars, workshops, or courses for professionals and the public.

This list was compiled from a number of sources. UNESCO's listings were consulted as well as those available at the Library of Congress and the Columbus Memorial Library of the Organization of American States. In addition, psychologists in the countries of the region were asked to provide us with the names of institutions where significant studies in psychology were conducted. The listing below begins, first, with those research centers that provided us with information on their activities. Following this, additional centers and their addresses are listed by country.

Detailed Center Descriptions

Asociacion Argentina de Investigaciones Psicologicas
Av. Cabildo 3050
1429 Buenos Aires, Argentina
Phone: 701-9853
Director: Raul Serroni-Coppello

A research institution dedicated to understanding the "thermodynamics of psychological issues." "Methodological and epistemological reductionism" is also of interest to the members of the association.

Centro de Estudios del Desarrollo Humano y Social
Fundacion Bariloche
Casilla de Correo 138
8400 San Carlos de Bariloche, Prov. de Rio Negro, Argentina
Phone: 48017
Director: Carlos A. Mallman; Oscar Nudler

An institution associated with the United Nations University that conducts
interdisciplinary research and training in the field of human and social
development. Topics studied in the past have included human needs applied to
life stages; epistemological and cultural assumptions related to development;
and promotion of democratic participation. Over 600 publications have been
made of the center's research activities, some of them related to psychological
concerns, i.e., epistemology, human development, and motivation.

Centro de Educacion, Terapia e Investigacion en Sexualidad
Darregueyra 2247 Depto. B
1425 Buenos Aires, Argentina
Phone: 773-7391
Director: Laura S. Caldiz and Leon Roberto Gindin

An educational, therapeutic, and research center focusing on sexuality.
Among the research projects currently underway are a study of sexuality among
the physically incapacitated and adolescent pregnancy.

Centro de Extension Psicoanalitica
Centro Cultural Gral. San Martin
Sarmiento 1551
1042 Buenos Aires, Argentina
Phone: --
Director: Roberto Harari (Coordinator)

Studies the works of Freud and Lacan, conducts workshops, and presents
conferences on Freud's contributions to an understanding of daily life.

Centro de Investigacion Medico Psicologica de la Comunicacion
Beruti 3858 1D
1425 Buenos Aires, Argentina
Phone: 718683
Director: Miguel A. Matterazzi

Conducts research on drug abuse and family psychosis and provides
treatment at the individual and group level. The center also has workshops on
drug abuse, prevention, psycho-cinema, and Lacan's theories.

Circulo Freudiano
Cangallo 3939/3941
1198 Buenos Aires, Argentina
Phone: 983-1914
Director: Jorge A. Kury

Emphasizes the study of Freudian pyschoanalysis. Holds workshops and meetings directed at analyzing and better understanding Freud's works.

Laboratorio de Investigaciones Sensoriales
Facultad de Medicina, Universidad de Buenos Aires
CC53
1453 Buenos Aires, Argentina
Phone: --
Director: Dra. Miguelina Guirao

    This is an interdisciplinary center dedicated to perceptual and sensory communication research mainly in the areas of hearing and speech, vision, and chemical senses. The laboratory provides training for Argentine and foreign graduate students in science, engineering, and humanities.

Mayeutica
San Luis 2461
1056 Buenos Aires, Argentina
Phone: 470405
Director: Edgardo Feinsilber (President)

    Conducts workshops and training in psychoanalytic theory and its intersection with Lacan's thought. It offers graduate-level training in psychoanalysis and publishes a number of booklets detailing the results of its activities.

Departamento de Educacao
Fundacao Joaquim Nabuco
Av. 17 de Agosto 2187
50000 Recife Pernambuco, Brazil
Phone: 268-2000
Director: Mariela Graziela Peregrino

    Conducts psychological research of relevance to education, particularly as it effects rural areas of developing countries and of Brazil. Among topics recently studied are: pre-school education; sexual understanding of school-age children; modular education at the university level; and training of paraprofessionals in educational settings.

Fundacao Carlos Chagas
Av. Prof. Francisco Morato
05513 Sao Paulo SP Brazil
Phone: 211-4511
Director: --

    Conducts research on education and educational innovation. The Fundacao also publishes the journal Cadernos de Pesquisa, which reports the results of its various research projects as well as the work of other researchers.

Instituto Superior de Estudos e Pesquisas Psicossociais
Fundacao Getulio Vargas
Rua Candelaria 6
20091 Rio de Janeiro RJ Brazil
Phone: 551-1542
Director: Franco Lo Presti Seminerio

This institute (founded in 1947) forms part of the Fundacao Getulio
Vargas, a large nonprofit center for research, education, and training. The
institute, commonly known as ISOP, conducts research in a variety of areas of
psychology and also provides graduate training in psychology. Applied
research, including test development and adaptation, and information
dissemination are some of its priorities. Among the areas studied are: social
and personality psychology, learning, psychometrics, thanatology, ergonomics,
and cybernetics. For 37 years, the Institute has published the journal
Arquivos Brasileiros de Psicologia.

Centro de Psicologia Gerontologica
Apartado 52366
Bogota, Colombia
Phone: 221 97 20
Director: Elisa Dulcey

A center designed to conduct research and to serve as information
repository on gerontology and its psycholgical consequences. The Center has
conducted research, organized meetings, and produced publications on the topic.

Fundacion para el Avance de la Psicologia
Carrera 14 No. 92-67
Bogota, Colombia
Phone: --
Director: --

The Foundation is devoted to psychological research, with emphasis on
funding investigations, publications, seminars, workshops and so forth. Among
the main areas covered are experimental psychology, theoretical foundations,
history of psychology, experimental analysis of behavior, comparative animal
behavior, neuropsychology, as well as basic research in psychology. The
foundation gives financial support for research in several areas, including
publication of results and organization of scientific events in psychology.

Instituto de Investigaciones Psicologicas
Universidad de Costa Rica
Ciudad Universitaria Rodrigo Facio
San Jose, Costa Rica
Phone: 23-3714
Director: Alberdo Brenes

Founded in 1961 to promote research in psychological topics relevant to
Costa Rica, its objectives include the development of psychological tests and
the study of the psychosocial characteristics of Costa Rica. The Institute has

produced over 130 publications documenting the results of its work covering topics such as: academic performance; epidemiology of psychological disturbances; community psychology; social climate; and attitudes. Current research is related to one of four general areas: health psychology, educational psychology, social psychology, and research methodology.

Centro de Investigaciones Sociales
Facultad de Ciencias Sociales, Universidad de Puerto Rico
Reciento de Rio Piedras
Rio Piedras, PR 00931
Phone: 764-0000 ext. 2104
Director: Dra. Carmen Gautier

For over 40 years, the Center has researched the social reality of Puerto Rico and helped in the training of researchers. Many psychological topics have been part of the Center's research, including the popular culture of Puerto Rico; aging; political behavior of Puerto Ricans; the effects of divorce; women's roles; and migration. Since 1957, it has published the Revista de Ciencias Sociales, where articles on psychological topics often appear.

Instituto de Psicologia
Universidad Central de Venezuela
Apartado 47563
Caracas 1041-A DF, Venezuela
Phone: 662-4761
Director: Julia Becerra Penfold

A research center associated with the Faculty of Humanities and Education of the Universidad Central, the Institute often conducts interdisciplinary research and supports the various graduate programs in the School of Psychology (social, experimental analysis of behavior, human development, group dynamics, and instructional psychology). The Latin American Center for Psychological Information is also located at the Institute. Areas of research include social, environmental, health, and developmental psychology, basic research in operant conditioning, and a variety of topics in instructional psychology.

Laboratorio de Psicologia
Universidad de Los Andes
Apartado de Correos 411
Merida, Venezuela
Phone: 35926
Director: Oswaldo Romero

Founded in 1978 to study the relationship between psychology and education, the laboratory bases most of its work on the premise that motivational poverty (externality, low need for achievement, and poor linguistic capability) plays a role in academic performance. Other topics researched include: authoritarianism, attitudes toward the aged, behavior modification in school settings, and psycholinguistics. Over 50 publications are available detailing the results of the laboratory's projects.

Additional Centers

<u>Argentina</u>

Centro de Investigacion para la Salud Mental (CIDAM)
Acevedo 1788
1414 Buenos Aires, Argentina

Centro de Investigacion en Psicologia Psicoanalitica
Quirno Costa 1260
1425 Buenos Aires, Argentina

Centro de Psicometria Aplicada
Castro Barros 888
1217 Buenos Aires, Argentina

Centro de Estudio de la Mujer
Nicaraqua 4908
1414 Buenos Aires, Argentina

Centro de Investigacion Psicologica e Interdisciplinaria
Av. Luis Maria Campos 1377
Pta. Bja. Dto. 5
1426 Buenos Aires, Argentina

Centro de Investigacion y Asesoramiento en Psicologia
Av. Cordoba 4544
1414 Buenos Aires, Argentina

Centro de Investigacion Piagetiana para la Educacion
Verbal 51
1425 Buenos Aires, Argentina

Centro de Nerologia y Psicologia Aplicada
Medrano 46-6 Piso
1178 Buenos Aires, Argentina

Centro de Investigaciones Psicologicas; Theodor Reik
Pena 3174- P.Bja. Dto. "C"
1425 Buenos Aires, Argentina

Centro de Psicologica Aplicada (CEPEDA)
Sarmiento 2021-3 Piso Dpto. "B"
1044 Buenos Aires, Argentina

Centro de Investigaciones y Orientacion "E. Racker"
Rodriguez Pena 1674
1021 Buenos Aires, Argentina

Centro de Asistencia e Investigacion Psicologia de Buenos Aires
Marcelo T. de Alvear 1887
1122 Buenos Aires, Argentina

Centro de Investigaciones en Psicologia Analitica
Anchorena No. 1654
(1425) Buenos Aires, Argentina

Brazil

Instituto Joaquin Nabuco de Pesquisas Sociais
Av. 17 de Agosto 2187
Recife-Pernambuco, Brazil

Centro Latinoamericano de Pesquisas en Ciencias Sociais
Rua Dona Mariana 132
Botafogo, 2C-02
Rio de Janeiro, Brazil

Instituto de Planeamiento Economico e Social, Instituto de Pesquisas (INPES)
Caixa Postal 2672
20000 Rio de Janeiro, Brazil

Colombia

Programa de Desarollo Comunal (PRODECON)
Apartado Nacional No. 2042
Bogota, Colombia

Instituto de Investigaciones Tecnologicas
Av. 30 No. 52 A-77
Apartado Aereo 7031
Bogota, Colombia

Instituto Colombiano de Investigaciones Sociales
Calle 48 No. 43-22
Medellin, Colombia

Instituto Columbiano para el Fomento de la Educacion Superior
Apartado Nacional 2868
Apartado Aereo 6319
Bogota, Colombia

Centro Interamericano de Vivienda y Planeamiento
Apartado Aereo 6209
Bogota, Colombia

Instituto Colombiano de Bienestar Familiar
Apartado Aereo 91186
Bogota, Colombia

Centro de Investigaciones para el Desarollo
Oficina Regional America Latina; Apartado Aereo 53016
Bogota DF, Colombia

Centro de Investigacion e Interventoria en Comportamiento Organizacional
(CINCEL), Apartado Aereo 65021
Medellin, Colombia

Ecuador

Instituto de Investigaciones Sociales y Educativas (IISE)
Universidad Tecnica de Ambato
Facultad de Ciencias de la Educacion
Av. Colombia y Salvador (Ingahurco)
Casilla 893
Ambato, Ecuador

Centro Institucional de Estudios Superiores de Comunicacion para America
Latina (CIESPAL)
Av. Amazonas 1615
Apartado 584
Quito, Ecuador

Guatemala

Instituto de Nutricion de Centroamerica y Panama
Carretera Roosevelt
Apartado 1188
Guatemala, Guatemala

Instituto de Investigaciones y Mejoramiento Educativo
Universidad de San Carlos de Guatemala
Guatemala, Guatemala

Instituto de Investigaciones
Universidad del Valle de Guatemala
Apartado Postal 82
Guatemala, Guatemala

Mexico

Unidad de Investigacion Interdisciplinaria en Ciencias de la Salud y
Educativas (UIICSE)
Escuela Nacional de Estudios Profesionales Iztacala de la UNAM
Iztacala, Estado de Mexico, Mexico

Unidad de Investigaciones Cerebrales
Instituto Literario Cien
Universidad Autonoma del Estado de Mexico
Toluca, Estado de Mexico, Mexico

Centro de Investigaciones Biologicas
Apartado Postal 57
Catemeco, Veracruz 95870, Mexico

Centro de Investigacion y Psicologia Orginizacional y Centro de
Investigacion en Psicologia Social
Facultad de Psicologia, Universidad Veracruzana
Benito Juarez
Zona Centro
Xalapa, Veracruz, Mexico

Peru

Instituto Nacional de Salud Mental
"Honorio Delgado"
Apartado 4274
Lima, Peru

Instituto Nacional de Investigacion y Desarrollo de la Educacion (INIDE)
Jr. Van de Velde 160
Urb. San Borja
Apartado Postal 1156
Lima 100, Peru

Centro de Investigaciones Psicologicas
Universidad Nacional Federico Villareal
Av. Colonial 450
Apartado 1518
Lima, Peru

Instituto de Psicologia Aplicada para el Desarrollo Economico-Social
Apartado 274
Miraflores, Lima 18, Peru

Departamento de Investigacion
Escuela de Administracion de Negocios (ESAN)
Casilla Postal 1846
Lima 100, Peru

Instituto Peruano de Analisis y Modificacion del Comportamiento (IPAMOC)
Av. del Ejercito 585
Lima 18, Peru

5

Professional and Scientific Associations in Psychology

In this chapter we provide a listing of professional and scientific associations in psychology in the Latin American countries. It is important to note that the purpose, size, level of activities, and significance of these associations vary from country to country or even within a country. Some function as promoters and defenders of the profession while others are primarily scientific in nature. None resembles the American Psychological Association in terms of central-office resources, size of staff, publication programs, or number of members.

Associations that are members of the International Union of Psychological Sciences (IUPsyS) are indicated by an asterisk. (In some countries, the largest association may not be an IUPsyS member, while a smaller association within that country is a member of IUPsyS.) To keep the listing manageable, regional or state associations within a given country have not been included. Nevertheless, detailed information about smaller associations can usually be obtained from the major national association, listed at the beginning of each country.

International

Sociedad Interamericana de Psicologia/Interamerican Society of Psychology
Dr. Ana Alvarez, Secretary-General
P.O. Box 23174
University of Puerto Rico Station
Rio Piedras, PR 00931-3174

This society (usually known as SIP) was established in 1951 to promote communication among psychologists from North, Central, and South America and to promote the development of the behavioral sciences in the Western Hemisphere. SIP publishes the <u>Revista Interamericana de Psicologia/Interamerican Journal of Psychology</u> and holds an Interamerican Congress of Psychology every two years (21 have been held to date, with the most recent being in Lima in 1979, Santo Domingo in 1981, Quito in 1983, Caracas in 1985, Havana in 1987). The 1989 meeting will take place in Buenos Aires. Members receive a quarterly newsletter and reduced rates for other publications. Three task forces are currently part of the Society: health psychology, families, and peace. About 40 percent of the members are residents of the United States.

Associacion de Psicologos Centroamericanos
a/c Colegio de Psicologos de Honduras
Bo. La Granja, detras del Centro Medico
Tegucigalpa DC Honduras

A very recently formed association that unites psychologists working in
Central America. The association holds congresses every two years. The most
recent was held in Tegucigalpa in 1985.

Asociacion Latinoamericano de Analisis y Modificacion del Comportamiento
(ALAMOC)
President: Rafael Navarro Cueva
Av. del Ejercito 585
Lima 18 Peru
Phone: 413585

The purpose of this association is to promote behavior analysis and
modification in Latin America. Seminars are periodically held in various
countries in Latin America. The association publishes the journal
Comportamiento on an irregular basis.

Asociacion Latinoamericano de Psicologia Social (ALAPSO)
a/c Hector Capello
Unidad Institucional de Planeacion
Universidad Autonoma de Tamaulipas
Apartado Postal 186
Ciudad Victoria, Tamaulipas, Mexico

Established in 1976 in order to promote the development of social
psychology in Latin America. ALAPSO holds workshops where research results and
research methodologies are presented. The most recent was held in Mexico in
1985. The association publishes the Revista de la Asociacion Latinoamericana
de Psicologia Social on a somewhat irregular basis.

National

Argentina

Federacion de Psicologos de la Republica Argentina
Francisco Acuna de Figueroa 730
1180 Buenos Aires, Argentina
Phone: 864971

Asociacion Argentina de Psicoterpia para Graduados
Julian Alvarez 1933
1425 Buenos Aires, Argentina
Phone: 871183

Asociacion Freudiana de Estudios y Practicas Grupales
Guatemala 6077
1425 Buenos Aires, Argentina
Phone: --

Asociacion Argentina de Investigaciones Psicologicas
Av. Cabildo 3050
1429 Buenos Aires, Argentina
Phone: 709-9853

Asociacion Argentina de Psicoterpia
Cuba 1873
1428 Buenos Aires, Argentina
Phone: 784-4801

Asociacion Argentina de Psicodiagnostico de Rorschach
Pueyrredon 1192, Piso 1 Dto. 11
1118 Buenos Aires, Argentina
Phone: 821-4755

Asociacion Argentina de Psicologia de la Ninez y Adolecencia
Gurruchaga 1168
1414 Buenos Aires, Argentina
Phone: 772-9865

Asoc. Argentina de Psiquitria y Psic. de la Infancia y la Adolecencia
Salguero 1904, Piso 2 Dto. 22
1425 Buenos Aires, Argentina
Phone: 84-9932

Asociacion Argentina de Psicologia Actual
Av. Cabildo 1182
1426 Buenos Aires, Argentina
Phone: 784-5419

Asociacion de Psicopatologia de la Republica Argentina
Vicente Lopez 2273, Piso 2 Dto. 22
1425 Buenos Aires, Argentina
Phone: 824-0669

Asociacion Argentina Psicologia y Psicopatologica de Grupo
Gorritti 4257
1414 Buenos Aires, Argentina
Phone: --

Asociacion Psicoanalitica de Buenos Aires
Maure 1852/72
1426 Buenos Aires, Argentina
Phone: 771-8183

Asociacion Argentina de Psicodrama y Psicoterpia de Grupo
Av. Santa Fe 3380
1425 Buenos Aires, Argentina
Phone: 849694

Asociacion Psicoanalitica Argentina
Rodriquez Pena 1674
1021 Buenos Aires, Argentina
Phone: 443518

Sociedad Argentina de Psicologia * (inactive)
Calle Bartolome Mitre 2087 piso 2
Buenos Aires, Argentina
Phone: --

Sociedad Argentina de Psicologia Clinica
Blanco Escolada 3784
1430 Buenos Aires, Argentina
Phone: 243-7451

Brazil

Asociacao Brasileira de Psocologia *
Rua Candeleria 6, 3 andar
20091 Rio de Janeiro RJ, Brazil
Phone: --

Conselho Federal de Psicologia
Ed. Brasilia Radio Center s/1029 SRTVN
70710 Brasilia DF, Brazil
Phone: --

Associacao de Psiquiatria e Psicologia da Infancia e Adolescencia de Brasilia
Caixa Postal 132055
70349 Brasilia DF, Brazil
Phone: --

Associacao Nacional de Pesquisa e Pos-Graduacao em Psicologia
Caixa Postal 11454
05508 Sao Paulo SP, Brazil
Phone: --

Associacao de Modificao do Coportamento
Caixa Postal 19210
01000 Sao Paulo SP, Brazil
Phone: --

Sociedad de Psicologia de Sao Paulo
Caixa Postal 11454
05508 Sao Paulo SP, Brazil
Phone: --

Associacao Brasileira de Psicologia Aplicada
Rua de la Candelaria 6, 2 andar
20091 Rio de Janeiro RJ, Brazil
Phone: 211-6286

Sociedad Brasileira de Psicologia do Esporte da Atividade Fisica e da Recreacao
Pca das Nacoes Unidas 35/503
90000 Porto Alegre RS, Brazil
Phone: --

Chile

Colegio de Psicologos de Chile
Calle Normandia 1875
Santiago 29, Chile
Phone: 225-0967

Asociacion de Psicologia Clinica
Calle Normandia 1875
Santiago 29, Chile
Phone: --

Asociacion Chilena de Psicologia Social
Calle Normandia 1875
Santiago 29, Chile
Phone: --

Colombia

Federacion Colombiana de Psicologia *
Apartado Aereo 5253
Bogota DE 1, Colombia
Phone: --

Asociacion Colombiana de Analisis y Terapia de Comportamiento
Transversal 19 No. 114-14, Apartado Aereo 100924
Bogota DE, Colombia
Phone: 213-8892

Asociacion de Psicologos de la Universidad Catolica de Colombia
Secretaria de la Facultad, 5 piso, Diagonal 47 No. 15-50
Apartado Aereo 76462; Bogota DE, Colombia
Phone: 269-8308

Asociacion de Psicologos Industriales y Organizacionales
Calle 30 A No. 6-22, Oficina 1903
Bogota DE, Colombia
Phone: 269-8308

Asociacion de Psicologos Javerianos
Apartado Aereo 75044
Bogota DE, Colombia
Phone: --

Asociacion Colombiana de Psicologia y Tecnologia Educativa
Apartado Aereo 75828
Bogota DE 8, Colombia
Phone: 274-2563

Sociedad Colombiana de Psicologia
Carrera 13 No. 35-27, Oficina 203
Apartado Aereo 88754, Bogota DE, Colombia
Phone: --

Asociacion de Psicologos de la Universidad Nacional
Departamento de Psicologia, Ciudad Universitaria
Bogota DE, Colombia
Phone: --

Sociedad Colombiana de Psicologia Ocupacional
Apartado Aereo 51865
Bogota DE, Colombia
Phone: --

Asociacion Colombiana de Neuropsicologia
Apartado Aereo 17021
Bogota DE, Colombia
Phone: --

Asociacion Nortesantandereana de Psicologia
Apartado Aereo 1458
Cucuta, Colombia
Phone: --

Asociacion de Psicologos de Bolivar
Carrera 2, No. 9-65
Cartagena, Colombia
Phone: --

Asociacion de Psicologos del Tolima
Calle 35, No. 4-B-18
Ibague, Colombia
Phone: --

Asociacion de Psicologos Deportivos
Av. 68 Calle 63
"El Salitre"
Bogota, Colombia
Phone: --

Fundacion Alberto Merani para el Desarollo de la Inteligencia
Calle 39 bis, 28-77
Apartado Aereo 101531
Bogota DE, Colombia
Phone: 268-5309

Costa Rica

Colegio Profesional de Psicologos de Costa Rica
Apartado 8238
1000 San Jose, Costa Rica
Phone: --

Asociacion Costarricense de Psiquiatria y Psicologia Clinica
Apartado 380, Pavas
San Jose, Costa Rica
Phone: --

Asocaiacion Costarricense de Trabajadores en Psicologia Criminologica
Apartado 8238
1000 San Jose, Costa Rica
Phone: --

Cuba

Sociedad Cubana de Psicologia *
Facultad de Psicologia   Universidad de La Habana
La Habana, Cuba
Phone: --

Sociedad Cubana de Psicologia de La Salud
a/c Hospital Psiquiatrico de La Habana   Av. Independencia
Mazorra, La Habana, Cuba
Phone: --

Dominican Republic

Asociacion Dominicana de Psicologia *
Apartado 379-2, Centro de los Heroes
Santo Domingo, Dominican Republic
Phone: --

Guatemala

Asociacion Guatemalteca de Psicologia
IIME   Ciudad Universitaria
Guatemala 12, Guatemala
Phone: --

Colegio Profesional de Humanidades
2a Calle 3-13
Guatemala 1, Guatemala
Phone: 20740

Honduras

Colegio de Psicologos de Honduras
Bo. La Granja, detras del Centro Medico
Tegucigalpa DC, Honduras
Phone: --

Mexico

Sociedad Mexicana de Psicologia *
Rio Mixcoac 66-1001   Col. Acacias
03230 Mexico DF, Mexico
Phone: 534-8985

Sociedad Mexicana de Analisis de la Conducta
Apartado Postal 69-716
04460 Mexico 21 DF, Mexico
Phone: --

Sociedad Mexicana de Psicologia Clinica
Insurgentes Sur 682-101   Col. del Valle
Mexico DF, Mexico
Phone: --

Asociacion de Psicologos Industriales
Paseo de la Reforma Norte 704-701   Edificio Veracruz
Mexico DF, Mexico
Phone: --

Asociacion Nacional de Psicologos del Sector Publico
Amsterdam 43-504
Mexico 11 DF, Mexico
Phone: --

Nicaragua

Asociacion Nicaraguense de Psicologos *
Conapro Heroes y Martires
Managua, Nicaragua
Phone: 73643

Panama

Asociacion Panamena de Psicologos *
c/o Apartado 11065
Panama 6, Panama
Phone: --

Peru

Colegio de Psicologos del Peru
Av. Jose Pardo 455, Oficina 503, Lince, Apartado 11347
Lima 14, Peru
Phone: --

Federacion de Psicologos del Peru
Av. Jose Pardo 455, Oficina 503, Lince, Apartado 11347
Lima 14, Peru
Phone: --

Sociedad Peruana de Terapia y Modificacion de la Conducta
Avenida del Ejercito 5856
Lima 18, Peru
Phone: --

Asociacion de Psicologia Clinica
Casilla Postal 6117
Lima, Peru
Phone: 636410

Asociacion de Psicologos de Salud
Jr. Francisco Macias 2399, Urb. Elio
Lima, Peru
Phone: --

Sociedad Peruana de Analisis y Modificacion del Comportamiento
Apartado 1781
Lima, Peru
Phone: --

Asociacion Peruana de Psicologia Organizacional
Av. Arequipa 4552
Oficina 5, 2 Dto. Piso
Miraflores, Lima, Peru
Phone: --

Asociacion Peruana de Analisis Conductual Aplicado a la Educacion
Av. Larco 656
2 piso D
Miraflores, Lima, Peru
Phone: --

Asociacion Peruana de Orientacion e Integracion de la Familia
Leon Velarde 483
Lince, Lima, Peru
Phone: --

Puerto Rico

Asociacion de Psicologos de Puerto Rico
Apartado 3435
Oficina General de Correos
San Juan, Puerto Rico 00936
Phone: 751-7100

Uruguay

Sociedad de Psicologia del Uruguay *
Colonia 1342
Esc. 3
Montevideo, Uruguay
Phone: --

Venezuela

Federacion de Psicologos de Venezuela *
Apartado 62558, Chacao
Caracas, Venezuela
Phone: 222487

Asociacion Venezolana de Psicologia Social
Apartado 47101
Caracas 1041-A DF, Venezuela
Phone: --

Sociedad Venezolana de Psicologia Escolar
Apartado 47901
Caracas 1041-A DF, Venezuela
Phone: --

Sociedad Venezolana de Psicologia del Deporte
Apartado 62558
Caracas 1060-A DF, Venezuela
Phone: --

Sociedad Venezolana de Psicologia Adleriana
Apartado 68340
Caracas 1062-A DF, Venezuela
Phone: --

Sociedad Venezolana de Rorschach
Apartado 68182
Caracas 1062-A DF, Venezuela
Phone: --

Asociacion Venezolana de Psicologia Vial
Apartado 62558
Caracas 1060-A DF, Venezuela
Phone: --

6

Psychology Journals

The following is a listing of psychology journals published in Latin America. At the beginning of the chapter, the reader will find a detailed description of major journals. These journals appear in alphabetical order by country where they are printed, although most of them have an international readership. At the end of the chapter is a list of additional journals about which we could not obtain information. We have tried to include all journals that were being published in 1987, but readers should keep in mind that some journals publish on a non-periodic basis due to financial and institutional constraints. Newsletters and similar publications are excluded due to their limited circulation.

Major Journals

<u>International</u>

ACTA PSIQUIATRICA Y PSICOLOGICA DE AMERICA LATINA
Malabia 2274, 13 A
1425 Buenos Aires, Argentina
Editor: Guillermo Vidal
 Price: $50

A journal of original articles that began 1954. Probably the journal with the largest circulation (4,500) in Latin America, it is published every three months. Articles appear in Spanish or Portuguese in all areas of psychiatry and psychology. English language manuscripts are not accepted.

AVANCES EN PSICOLOGIA CLINICA LATINOAMERICANA
Apartado 52127
Bogota DE, Colombia
Editor: Ruben Ardila
 Price: $7

An annual publication started in 1982 that publishes research and general articles on clinical psychology. Articles on prevention and diagnostics are also included. Manuscripts in English are accepted for publication in Spanish.

REVISTA DE LA ASOCIACION LATINOAMERICANA DE PSICOLOGIA SOCIAL
Bosque de Avellanos 156
11700 Mexico DF, Mexico
Editor: Susan Pick de Weiss
 Price: $20

A journal started in 1981 by the Asociacion Latinoamericana de Psicologia Social (ALAPSO) Two issues per year are published on a somewhat irregular basis, containing research manuscripts, articles on the teaching of social psychology, and methodological and epistemological contributions. Originals in English are accepted for possible publication in Spanish.

REVISTA INTERAMERICANA DE PSICOLOGIA/INTERAMERICAN JOURNAL OF PSYCHOLOGY
Editorial Address: Luis M. Laosa
Educational Testing Service
Princeton, NJ 08541
Subscriptions: Dr. Ana Alvarez
P.O. Box 23174, University of Puerto Rico Station
Rio Piedras, PR 00931-3174
Editor: Luis M. Laosa
 Price: $20

A publication of the Interamerican Society of Psychology (SIP) since 1967. Two issues per year are published including primarily research articles and book reviews. Manuscripts are accepted and published in Spanish, English, or Portuguese. All manuscripts are refereed.

REVISTA LATINOAMERICANA DE PSICOLOGIA
Apartado 52127
Bogota DE, Colombia
Editor: Ruben Ardila
 Price: $15

Published quarterly since 1969, it publishes articles in all areas of psychology that are primarily empirical and that emphasize Latin American issues or concerns. Book reviews are also included in a typical issue together with news about psychology in the Americas. Manuscripts written in English are accepted for possible publication in Spanish.

Argentina

APRENDIZAJE HOY
Araoz 2642, piso 5A
1425 Buenos Aires, Argentina
Editor: Marina R. Muller
 Price: $16

Founded in 1980, this journal is published three times per year and includes research reports, essays, news, and comments of interest to educational psychologists and to educators. Articles in English are accepted for publication in Spanish.

INTERDISCIPLINARIA
Manuscripts: Maria Cristina Ratto de Sala
Cangallo 2158
1040 Buenos Aires, Argentina
Subscriptions: Fernando Garcia
Cochabamba 244
1150 Buenos Aires, Argentina
Editor: Horacio J. A. Rimoldi
 Price: $20

     Begun in 1979, this journal publishes articles in Spanish and in English
in psychology and related sciences. It is published by the Centro
Interamericano de Investigaciones Psicologicas y Ciencias Afines. Two issues
per year are published.

REVISTA IBEROAMERICANA DE SOFROLOGIA Y MEDICINA PSICOSOMATICA
Montivideo 945
1019 Buenos Aires, Argentina
Editor: --
 Price: --

     A publication started in 1959 to publish articles in psychosomatic
medicine. Five issues per year are printed and articles in English are
accepted for possible publication in Spanish. The journal was being
reorganized as of early 1985

REVISTA DE PSICOLANALISIS
Asociacion Psicoanalitica Argentina
Rodriquez Pena 1674
1021 Buenos Aires, Argentina
Editor: Andres Rascovsky
 Price: $70

     A psychoanalytic journal founded in 1943 to disseminate ideas of the
Argentine School of Psychoanalysis. Publishes six issues per year with
originals as well as translations of significant articles. Book reviews and
news about congresses are also included. Manuscripts in English are accepted
for possible publication in Spanish.

Brazil

ARQUIVOS BRASILEIROS DE PSICOLOGIA
Fundacao Getulio Vargas
Praia de Botafogo 188
22253 Rio de Janeiro RJ, Brazil
Editor: Franco Lo Presti Seminerio
 Price: Cr 13,500

     A quarterly journal published since 1949 by the Instituto Superior de
Estudios e Pesquisas Psicossociais of the Fundacao Getulio Vargas in Rio de
Janeiro. It publishes original articles in all areas of psychology. Articles

appear primarily in Portuguese with occasional articles being published in Spanish. English-language manuscripts are not accepted.

CADERNOS DE PESQUISA
Fundacao Carlos Chagas
Av. Prof. Francisco Morato 1565
05513 Sao Paulo SP, Brazil
Editor: Maria M. Malta Campos
 Price: $50

    A journal primarily devoted to educational issues. Published three times per year since 1971. English-language manuscripts are accepted.

REVISTA DAS FACULDADES FRANCISCANAS
Rua Alexandre Rodriques Barbosa 45
Itatiba
13250 Sao Paulo SP, Brazil
Editor: Frei Antonio Gasparini, OFM
 Price: $3.50 (psychology issue only)

    A journal of the Faculdades Franciscanas that dedicates one issue per year to psychological themes written by the schools's faculty.

REVISTO PSICO
Instituto de Psicologia
Pontificia Universidade Catolica de Rio Grade do Sul
Av. Ipiranga 6681
90000 Porto Alegre RG, Brazil
Editor: Neli Klix Freitas
 Price: --

    Publishes articles in all areas of psychology written primarily by faculty and students of the Pontificia Universidade Catolica de Rio Grande do Sul.

PSICOLOGIA: TEORIA E PESQUISA
Departamento de Psicologia
Universidade de Brasilia
70910 Brasilia DF, Brazil
Editor: Eunice M. L. Soriano de Alencar
 Price: $15

    A new publication that comes out three times a year dedicated to publishing theoretical and empirical articles in psychology. Literature reviews are also accepted for publication

Chile

REVISTA DE TECNOLOGIA EDUCATIVA
Casilla 16445
Santiago 9, Chile

Editor: Clifton Chadwick
Price: Free

A journal established in 1974 to publish articles related to educational technology (psychological articles are often included if they relate to education). Manuscripts in English are not accepted.

REVISTA CHILENA DE PSICOLOGIA
Normandia 1875
Santiago, Chile
Editor: Jorge Gissi
Price: $10

This journal publishes research reports in all areas of psychology particularly as they relate to Chile or Latin America. It has been published twice a year by the Chilean psychological association since 1978. Manuscripts are accepted only in Spanish.

Colombia

CUADERNOS DE PSICOLOGIA
Departamento de Psicologia
Universidad del Valle
Apartado Aereo 25360
Cali, Colombia
Editor: Mariela Orozco
Price: $6

A journal started in 1976 and published by the department of psychology of the Universidad del Valle in Cali. Publishes basic and applied research, reviews of the literature, news of interest and at times, reprints of articles originally published in other languages. The journal also publishes articles that analyze current events from a psychological perspective. English-language manuscripts are accepted for publication in Spanish. Issues are often devoted to a single theme.

PERSPECTIVAS EN PSICOLOGIA
Fundacion Universitaria de Manizales
Carrera 9
No. 19-03
Manizales, Colombia
Editor: Carlos Alberto Ospina
Price: $6

A nonperiodical journal published since 1982 by the school of psychology of the Fundacion Universitaria de Manizales. Two issues per year are usually printed that include theoretical and empirical articles in all areas of psychology, book reviews, and a section that addresses psychology's relationship with other sciences. Manuscripts in English are accepted for publication in Spanish.

REVISTA DE ANALISIS DEL COMPORTAMIENTO
Apartado Aereo 100924
Bogota DE, Colombia
Editor: Leonidas Castro
 Price: --

An interdisciplinary and international journal published twice a year
since 1983 by the Asociacion Colombiana de Analisis y Terapia del
Comportamiento. Its main purpose is to publish research, applications, and
theoretical developments in the application of behavioral analysis to all areas
of behavior. Only original manuscripts are accepted for publication but they
may be written in English, French, Portuguese, or Italian (all manuscripts
appear in Spanish).

REVISTA INTERAMERICANA DE PSICOLOGIA OCUPACIONAL
Apartado Aereo 2402
Medellin, Colombia
Editor: Fernando Toro; Hernan Cabrera
 Price: $25

A quarterly journal started in 1982 to provide an interdisciplinary outlet
for individuals interested in industrial/organizational topics. Basic and
applied research as well as book reviews are often published in the journal.
English-language manuscripts are accepted for publication in Spanish.

REVISTA DE PSICOLOGIA
Departamento de Psicologia
Universidad Nacional
Bogota, Colombia
Editor: Ramiro Alvarez
 Price: $10

A journal published by the Department of Psychology of the Universidad
Nacional on a nonperiodical basis since 1956. Usually two issues are published
every year and include original articles, book reviews, translations of
articles published elsewhere, and news about psychology at the university.
Articles in English are accepted for publication in Spanish.

Costa Rica

REVISTA COSTARICCENSE DE PSICOLOGIA
Apartado 8238
1000 San Jose, Costa Rica
Editor: Dina Krauskopf
 Price: $25

A publication of the Psychological Association of Costa Rica since 1982.
Two issues per year are printed that include articles (theoretical and
empirical), book reviews, and a section ("Polemics") directed at encouraging
discussion among psychologists. Articles in English are accepted for
publication in Spanish.

Cuba

BOLETIN DE PSICOLOGIA
Av. de la Independencia 26520
Mazorra
Ciudad de La Habana, Cuba
Editor: Noemi Perez
 Price: By exchange of publications only

   A journal put out since 1978 by the Hospital Psiquiatrico de La Habana.
Three issues per year are published in all areas of psychology. Translations
of articles originally published in languages other than Spanish appear
frequently and manuscripts in English are accepted for publication in Spanish.

REVISTA CUBANA DE PSICOLOGIA
Facultad de Psicologia
Universidad de La Habana
La Habana, Cuba
Editor: Albertina Mitjans
 Price: By exchange of publications only

   A journal published since 1984 by the School of Psychology at the
Universidad de La Habana. Publishes original articles on basic and applied
topics as well as reviews of the literature.

REVISTA DEL HOSPITAL PSIQUIATRICO DE LA HABANA
Editorial Address: Av. de la Independencia 26520
Mazorra
Ciudad de La Habana, Cuba
Subscriptions: Ediciones Cubanas
Apartado 605
La Habana, Cuba
Editor: Eduardo B. Ordaz
 Price: $15

   A primarily psychiatric journal published since 1959 by the psychiatric
hospital in Havana. This quarterly journal publishes original research
articles (in psychiatry and in psychology), clinical cases, literature reviews,
and statistics on psychiatric services at the hospital. Manuscripts in English
are not accepted.

El Salvador

BOLETIN DE PSICOLOGIA
Editorial Address: Departamento de Psicologia, Universidad Centroamericana
Apartado 668
San Salvador, El Salvador
Subscriptions: Distribuidora de Publicaciones, Universidad Centroamericana
Apartado 688
San Salvador, El Salvador
Editor: Agustin Fernandez; Ignacio Martin-Baro; Mari Camen Moran
 Price: --

A quarterly publication of the Universidad Centroamericana "Jose Simeon Canas" in San Salvador. The journal started in 1981 and publishes scientific reports as well as position papers and book reviews. Most of the authors are students or faculty of the department of psychology at the university.

Mexico

ACTA PSICOLOGIA MEXICANA
Secretaria General
Facultad de Psicologia
Ciudad Universitaria
04510 Mexico DF, Mexico
Editor: Fernando Garcia
 Price: --

A journal published by the School of Psychology of the Universidad Nacional Autonoma de Mexico since 1981. Publishes articles by faculty members of the School in all areas of psychology.

ENSENANZA E INVESTIGACION EN PSICOLOGIA
Editorial Address: Circuito Rio Chuviscar 22
Col. Paseos de Churubusco
09030 Mexico DF, Mexico
Subscriptions: Edificio 16-Despacho 503
Villa Olimpica
Mexico 22 DF, Mexico
Editor: Humberto Ponce
 Price: $10

A semiannual journal of the Consejo Nacional para la Ensenanza e Investigacion en Psicologia since 1974. Publishes original research articles, book reviews, training program descriptions, and commentary on the training of psychologists in Mexico. Manuscripts in English are accepted.

REVISTA MEXICANA DE ANALISIS DE LA CONDUCTA/MEXICAN JOURNAL OF BEHAVIORAL ANALYSIS
Apartado Postal 69-716
04460 Mexico DF, Mexico
Editor: Javier Nieto
 Price: $15

Published twice a year since 1975 to advance the study of behavior as well as other significant experimental studies. Publishes invited reviews of the literature and book reviews. Articles appear in English or Spanish.

REVISTA MEXICANA DE PSICOLOGIA
Apartado Postal 21-966
Delegacion Coyoacan
04000 Mexico DF, Mexico
Editor: Juan Lafarga
 Price: $12

Published since 1984 by the Sociedad Mexicana de Piscologia. Two issues per year are published with original research articles and reviews of the literature. Manuscripts in English are accepted.

SALUD MENTAL
Editorial Address: Instituto Mexicano de Psiquiatria
Calzada Mexico Xochimilco 101 Col. San Lorenzo Huipulco
14370 Mexico DF, Mexico
Subscriptions: Masson Editores
Apartado 18-848
Mexico DF, Mexico
Editor: Hector Perez-Rincon
 Price: $36

A publication of the Instituto de Psiquiatria begun in 1977. Eight issues are published every year that include original research articles in psychiatry and psychology as well as reviews of the literature. Manuscripts in English are accepted for possible publication in Spanish.

TRABAJO DEL PSICOANALISIS
Editorial Address:; Callejon de Colima #15B
Coyoacon
04000 Mexico DF, Mexico
Subscriptions: Apartado Postal 21098
04000 Mexico DF, Mexico
Editor: Silvia Bleichmar
 Price: $25 (surface mail) $35 (air mail)

A quarterly journal founded in 1982 to publish research and theory in psychoanalysis. News about meetings, book reviews, and translations of articles not available in Spanish are also regularly published. Only articles in Spanish are accepted for publication.

Panama

ARCHIVOS PANAMENOS DE PSICOLOGIA Y ANUARIO DEL SANATORIO LAS CUMBRES
Apartado 681
Panama 9A, Panama
Editor: Francisco Ramon de Aguilar
 Price: $5

A publication started in 1964 to include articles in psychology, psychiatry, cosmobiology, and parapsychology. Manuscripts in English are accepted for possible publication in Spanish. Published irregularly.

LA ANTIGUA
Universidad Santa Maria La Antigua
Apartado 6-1696 Estafeta El Dorado
Panama, Panama
Editor: --
 Price: --

A publication of the Universidad Santa Maria La Antigua covering all of the social sciences but with frequent articles on psychology. Other than scientific articles, this publication includes book reviews.

Peru

REVISTA ANDINA DE PSICOLOGIA
Cuzco 784
Huancayo, Peru
Editor: Walter Cornejo
 Price: $10

A new journal, begun in 1985, that publishes articles in all areas of psycholotgy particularly as they are related to those who live in the area of Los Andes. Book reviews are also published. Manuscripts written in English are accepted for possible publication in Spanish. The journal appears twice per year.

REVISTA DE PSICOLOGIA
Editorial Address: Departamento de Psicologia
Pontificia Universidad Catolica
Apartado 1761
Lima, Peru
Subscriptions: Fondo Editorial
Pontificia Universidad Catolica
Apartado 1761
Lima, Peru
Editor: Dr. Roberto Lerner
 Price: $12

A journal published by the Department of Psychology at the Pontificia Universidad Catolica in Lima since 1983. It publishes original research articles and reviews of the literature as well as professional and scientific news and book reviews. The Revista is published twice a year.

REVISTA COPSI
Consultorio Psicologico de la Universidad Nacional Mayor de San Marcos
San Carlos
Nicolas de Pierola 1245
Parque Universitario
Lima 1, Peru
Editor: David Janregni C.
 Price: 5 Intis.

Published by the counseling center of the Universidad Nacional Mayor de San Marcos in Lima, its purpose is to disseminate information on the professional role of psychologists particularly within a clinical and educational setting. Current events are often analyzed in terms of psychological principles.

Puerto Rico

REVISTA DE CIENCIAS SOCIALES
Centro de Investigaciones Sociales
Facultad de Ciencias Sociales
Universidad de Puerto Rico
Río Piedras, PR 00936
Editor: Wenceslao Serra
 Price: --

Published by the Centro de Investigaciones Sociales of the Universidad de Puerto Rico since 1957. It includes articles in all of the social sciences-- including many on psychology--on topics of relevance to Puerto Rico.

Venezuela

BOLETIN DE LA AVESPO
Apartado 47101
Los Chaguaramos
Caracas 1041-A DF, Venezuela
Editor: Ruben Loaiza
 Price: $12

A journal published three times per year by the Venezuelan Association of Social Psychology (AVESPO) since 1977. The Boletin publishes 3 or 4 articles per issue that advance the theoretical or empirical development of social psychology in Latin America. Particular emphasis is given to articles that are relevant to the social conditions of Latin America. News of interest to social psychologists is also included. Articles are refereed and are only considered if written in Spanish.

PSICOLOGIA
Escuela de Psicologia
Universidad Central de Venezuela
Ciudad Universitaria
Caracas, Venezuela
Editor: Carlos Villalba; Jose Vicente Losada; Carlos Munoz
 Price: $25

A journal started in 1974 and published by the school of psychology at the Universidad Central de Venezuela. Publishes articles in all areas of psychology including reprints of articles originally published in other languages. Four issues per year are published on a somewhat irregular basis. Manuscripts are accepted only in Spanish.

Additional Journals

Revista Argentina de Psicologia
Nueva Vision
Tucuman 3748
1189 Buenos Aires, Argentina

Revista de Psicomotricidad
Uriburu 381 6M
Buenos Aires, Argentina

Psicologia Medica
Fundacion Argentina para la Salud Mental
Aguero 1287
1425 Buenos Aires, Argentina

Psychologica: Revista Argentina de Psicologia Realista
Fundacion Arche
Rodriquez Pena 778
1020 Buenos Aires, Argentina

Klinica
Departamento de Psicologia
Faculadade de Psicologia de Itatiba
Itatiba SP, Brazil

Psicologia
Conselho Editorial da Sociedade de Estudos Psicologos
Caixa Postal 20532
01498 Sao Paulo SP Brazil

Psicologia Argumento
Editora Universitaria Champagnat
Pontificia Universidade do Parana
Rua Imaculada Conceicao
1155 Curitiba, Parana, Brazil

Revista Chilena de Psicologia Clinica
Normandia 1875
Santiago, Chile

Boletin de la Asociacion Chilena de Psicologia Social
Normandia 1875
Santiago, Chile

Perspectivas en Psicologia
Universidad Cooperativa de Manizales
Apartado Aereo 868
Manizales, Colombia

Archivos Panamenos de Psicologia
Apartado 681
Panama 9A, Panama

Revista de Psicologia Clinica
Casilla Postal 6117
Lima 1, Peru

Revista Peruana de Analisis de la Conducta
Apartado Postal 1781
Lima, Peru

Cuadernos de Psicologia
Facultad de Psicologia y Humanidades
Universidad Femenina del Sagrado Corazon
Av. los Frutales s/n
La Molina
Lima, Peru

Revista Uruguaya de Psicologia
Sociedad de Psicologia del Uruguay
25 de Mayo 535, esc. 9
Montivideo, Uruguay

Aprendizaje y Comportamiento
Apartado 66126
Caracas 106, Venezuela

7

Publishers and Distributors of Psychological Tests

To our knowledge, the status of psychological and educational testing in Latin America has never been subjected to rigorous and comprehensive scrutiny. Among the questions that might be approached in such a study are the following:

1. <u>Extent and function of testing</u>. How widespread is the use of psychological and educational testing in the region compared to levels of use in other countries? In what settings (clinic, school, industry) and for what purposes (diagnostics, forensics, job screening, counseling, placement, assessment, measurement of aptitude and achievement, etc.) are tests most commonly used?

2. <u>Controversy</u>. Are psychological and educational tests generally accepted within the region? What controversies surround their use?

3. <u>Rights and responsibilities</u>. What safeguards exist in the various countries of Latin America to protect the rights of test takers? What measures exist to ensure that tests are administered only by qualified people?

4. <u>Home-grown tests vs. imports</u>. What percentage of the psychological and educational tests circulated in the various countries of the region are produced domestically? What percentage comes from neighboring Latin American countries? What percentage from the United States?

5. <u>Standardization and validity</u>. With particular reference to translated tests, how often and how systematically are the Spanish- or Portuguese-language versions of tests standardized for the populations and uses for which they are intended?

In the United States, where psychological and educational tests are extensively used in education, industry, and the clinic, their proper use has been of concern at least since 1954, when <u>Technical Recommendations for Psychological Tests and Diagnostic Techniques</u> was published by the American Psychological Association. Since that time, a number of documents guiding the development and use of tests in the United States have appeared, the latest of which is the <u>Standards for Educational and Psychological Testing</u> (APA, 1985), produced by the Committee to Develop Standards for Educational and Psychological Testing of the APA, the American Educational Research Association (AERA), and the National Council on Measurement in Education (NCME).

In the absence of national or regional standards reflecting the role and function of testing in Latin America, test users in the countries of the region may wish to take note of some of the recommendations of the <u>Standards</u>, which can be obtained by writing to the Order Department, American Psychological Association, 1200 17th Street, NW, Washington, DC 20036, USA. The volume costs $16 for members of APA, AERA, or NCME; $23 for nonmembers.

A number of specialized publications developed in the United States are also available from APA or other sources. These include the Guidelines for Computer-Based Tests and Interpretations (1986), developed by APA's Committee on Psychological Tests and Assessment and the Committee on Professional Standards; the Uniform Guidelines on Employee Selection Procedures (1978), currently under revision by the US Equal Employment Opportunity Commission; and the Principles for the Validation and Use of Personnel Selection Procedures (1980), a policy statement of the Division of Industrial-Organizational Psychology of the American Psychological Association.

In the United States and elsewhere in the world, the issue of safeguarding the rights of test-takers and ensuring that tests are administered only by qualified users is particularly urgent. The Test User Qualifications Working Group of the Joint Committee on Testing Practices (a United States group composed of representatives of the APA, AERA, and NCME) is in the in the process of producing a technical report to aid test publishers in determining whether a prospective purchaser of a test is qualified to use that test. Within the International Test Commission (ITC), too, the question of the qualifications of persons ordering test materials across national borders is very much alive. The ITC is also concerned about the need to make expert information about tests available to present or prospective test users in developing countries, particularly where those users are administering tests developed in another country.

Numerous other resources are being prepared. The Subcommittee on Testing and Special Education of APA's Committee on Psychological Tests and Assessment is producing a report on testing and assessment for the placement of children in special education classes to be completed in 1988. A working group of the Joint Committee on Testing Practices is developing a Code of Fair Testing Practices in Education to be completed early in 1988. Lastly, the International Test Commission is working on an international handbook of assessment. Questions about the foregoing may be addressed to the Office of Scientific Affairs, American Psychological Association, 1200 17th Street, NW, Washington, DC 20036, USA.

The documents mentioned above cover many facets of test construction, evaluation, and use, and deserve the careful attention of test users. However, the section of the Standards devoted to "Testing Linguistic Minorities" (pp. 73-75) is especially pertinent to test users and test takers in Latin America, where English-language tests produced for use with U.S. populations are too often simply translated into Spanish or Portuguese without concern for further standardization and validation. Local norms may subsequently be obtained, but the validity of the new version is too often not established. We recommend that individuals planning to use a psychological or educational test available in Spanish or Portuguese take care to determine whether the version in question meets Standard 13.4 of the Standards: "When a test is translated from one language or dialect to another, its reliability and validity for the uses intended in linguistic groups to be tested should be established." Assumptions should not be made regarding a given test's equivalency, reliability, or validity for specific uses in its non-English version until the user has carefully reviewed the appropriate test manual.

The best centralized sources of information concerning tests for Spanish-speakers are the annotated bibliographies published by the Educational Testing Service's Test Collection. The Test Collection, an extensive library of 14,000 tests and other measurement devices, was established to provide information on tests and related materials to those in research, advisory services, education, and related activities. The tests are acquired from a variety of US test

125   Psychological Tests

publishers and individual test authors. Some foreign tests are also acquired, mainly from Canada, Great Britain, and Australia. The entire Test Collection file is accessible through BRS (Bibliographic Retrieval Services), a commercial vendor of databases.

The Test Collection publishes approximately 200 annotated test bibliographies in specific subject or population areas. These include three bibliographies of tests for Spanish speakers (price: $8.00 each). The annotations for each test include title, author, publication date, target population, publisher or source (in the United States), and an indication of the purpose of the instrument. A brochure listing the available bibliographies, and an order form, can be obtained by writing:

Test Collection
Educational Testing Service
Princeton, NJ 08541
Tel. (609) 734-5686.

The list of Latin American test publishers and distributors that appears below is certainly not exhaustive. It was compiled from responses to inquiries sent three times to Latin American-based publishers whose names were forwarded to us by colleagues in the region, and to 239 publishers of at least two tests each appearing in the 1983 edition of Tests in Print. The entries are organized alphabetically by country. Latin American distributors of US or other tests are listed under the name of the country in which they are based.

Inclusion of particular publishers or tests does not imply endorsement by the authors or by the American Psychological Association. Additional references to test instruments used in Latin America may be found by consulting Psychological Abstracts or the online PsycINFO database (distributed in Latin America by Dialog Information Systems, 3460 Hillview Ave., Palo Alto, CA 93404; Telephone: 800-334-2564, 415-858-3816), or, in some cases by writing psychological societies in the region (see chapter 5). Many countries around the world have councils for educational research or similar central bodies that standardize and validate tests. It may be that some Latin American countries have, or are developing, such councils. Lastly the following general references on testing are recommended to readers, although they may be difficult to find outside North America.

Goldman, B.A. (vols. 1-2), Saunders, J.L. (vol. 1 only), & Busch, J.C. (vol. 2 only) (Eds.). (1974). Directory of unpublished experimental mental measures. New York: Behavioral Publications.
Basic information on 1034 unpublished tests organized into 22 classes.
Mitchell, J.V., Jr. (Ed.). (1983). Tests in print III: an index to tests, test reviews, and the literature on specific tests. Lincoln, NE: Buros Institute of Mental Measurements.
This single-volume work provides summary information and references for 2581 tests of all types available in 1983. Fully indexed.

Mitchell, J.V., Jr. (Ed.). (1985). The ninth mental measurements yearbook. Lincoln, NE: Buros Institute of Mental Measurements.
This two-volume work provides basic information and reviews of 1409 currently available tests in all fields, as well as citations to other literature in which the tests are discussed. Indexes of titles, acronyms, subjects, publishers, names, and scores are also provided.

References

American Psychological Association. (1954). Technical recommendations for psychological tests and diagnostic techniques. Washington, DC: Author.

American Psychological Association, Committee on Professional Standards and Committee on Psychological Tests and Assessment. (1986). Guidelines for computer-based tests and interpretations. Washington, DC: Author.

American Psychological Association, Division of Industrial-Organizational Psychology. (1980). Principles for the validation and use of personnel selection procedures. (Second edition) Berkeley, CA: Author.

Equal Employment Opportunity Commission, Civil Service Commission, Department of Labor, & Department of Justice. (1978). Adoption by four agencies of uniform guidelines on employee selection procedures. Federal Register, 43(166), 38290-38315.

Standards for educational and psychological testing. (1985). Washington, DC: American Psychological Association.

Listing of Publishers and Distributors

<u>Argentina</u>

Editorial Paidos
Defensa 599, Piso 1
1065 Buenos Aires

Distributors for CPS, Inc. (USA) and J.C. Raven, Ltd. (UK), and the Verlag Hans Huber AG (Switzerland) (publisher of the Spanish edition of the Rorschach), among others.

El Ateneo
Florida 340
1005 Buenos Aires

Espasa-Calpe
Tacuari 328
1071 Buenos Aires

A branch of a Spanish company (see below).

Kapeluz
Moreno 376
1091 Buenos Aires

Material Didactico "Nicora"
Avenida San Martin 1873
1416 Buenos Aires
Tel. 594276

Specializes in educational tests (Terman Merrill, Piaget, etc.)

<u>Brazil</u>

Casa do Psicologo Livraria e Editora Ltda.
Rua Jose dos Santos Junior 197
Brooklin
04609 Sao Paulo SP, Brazil

Distributors for the Verlag Hans Huber AG (Switzerland).

CEPA
Centro Editor de Psicologia Aplicada, Ltda.
Rua Senador Dantas, 118, 9 Andar, ZC-06
Rio de Janeiro
Tel. 232-4983

Distributors for the Institute for Personality and Ability Testing, Inc. (USA) and for the Australian Council for Educational Research

Edites
Empresa Distribuidora de Testes, Ltda.
Rua Ferreira de Araujo 877
05428 Sao Paulo SP, Brazil
Tel. 212-6196

Specialists in the area of industrial psychology. With the exception of the personnel selection tests of Industrial Psychology Inc. (USA) and two other instruments adapted from US originals, all of the firm's tests are its own.

Multimedia S.A. Tecnologia Educacional
Rua Piaui 270
01241 Sao Paulo

Distributors for Consulting Psychologists Press, Inc. (USA), publisher of the Spanish-language versions of the Strong-Campbell Interest Inventory, the California Psychological Inventory, the Myers-Briggs Type Indicator, and the State-Trait Anxiety Inventory, among others.

Vetor
Editora Psicopedagogica Ltda.
Avenida Paulista 2518
01310 Sao Paulo SP

Chile

Petrinovich y Cia, Ltda.
Avenida Bernardo O'Higgins 108
Santiago

Distributors for the Verlag Hans Huber AG (Switzerland), publishers of the Spanish edition of the Rorschach and other tests.

Pontificia Universidad Catolica de Chile
J.V. Lastarria 65
Santiago 1

The Universidad Catolica has been authorized by the University of Minnesota to distribute a translation of the MMPI.

Colombia

Cincel, Ltda.
Centro de Investigacion e Interventoria en Comportamiento Organizacional
Apartado Aereo 65021
Medellin
Tel. 433187

Publisher of the Cuestionario de Motivacion para el Trabajo (CMT).

Ediciones Pedagogicas Latinoamericanas
Apartado Aereo 2632
Barranquilla

PSEA Ltda.
Carrera 11 No. 84-42 Interior 1
Apartado Aereo 53435
Bogota DE
Tel. 257-9581, 218-5245, and 218-5208

A 12-year old firm that distributes within Colombia the tests of The Psychological Corporation (USA) and TEA, SA (Spain), in addition to dozens of other tests of aptitude, personality, and intelligence (WAIS, WISC) tests for use in clinical, educational, and industrial settings.

Guatemala

Centro de Investigacion Educativa
Universidad del Valle de Guatemala
Apartado Postal 82
Guatemala City
Tel. 692563, 692776, 692827

One of the first publishers and distributors of psychometric tests in Latin America, handling Pintner, Otis, Stanford-Binet, WISC, WPPSI.

Mexico

Editorial Trillas, SA
Avenida 5 de Mayo 43-105
Mexico 1, DF

El Manual Moderno
Libreria Interacademica, SA
Avenida Sonora 206
Col. Hipodromo
Mexico 11, DF
Tel. 574-6630, 574-5636, and 584-5636

Mexican distributors for the Institute for Personality and Ability Testing, Inc. (USA); Consulting Psychologists Press (USA), publishers of the Spanish-language versions of the Strong-Campbell Interest Inventory, the California Psychological Inventory, the Myers-Briggs Type Indicator, and the State-Trait Anxiety Inventory, among others; and the Verlag Hans Huber AG (Switzerland), publisher of the Spanish version of the Rorschach.

Psicologia Evaluativa e Industrial, SC
Velazquez de Leon 71-305
06070 Mexico, DF
Tel. 592-5597 and 592-8776

Distributors for Latin America of the Spanish versions of the tests of Industrial Psychology, Inc. (USA). Mailing address: Apartado Postal 383-D, 62430 Cuernavaca, Morelos (tel. 160370).

Tecnica Psicologica
c/o Alfonso Garcia
PO Box 1697
San Ysidro, CA 92073

Distributors of the new Spanish versions of the MMPI and CPI narrative reports produced by Behaviordyne, Inc. (USA)

Peru

Distribuidora de Tests
Apartado 5254
Lima 18

Equipos y Materiales Psicologicos
Pasaje Ostolaza 127
Lince, Lima

EMPAP
Jr. Risso 137
Lima

Puerto Rico

Camera Mundi, Inc.
Amatisto 8, Villa Blanca
GPO Box 6840
Caguas, PR 00626

Distributors for Puerto Rico only of the products of the American Guidance Service (USA).

The College Board
Call Box 71101
San Juan, PR 00936-1101

Distributors of the Spanish versions of the College Board's university admissions tests and other instruments.

Spain

Espasa-Calpe, SA
Carretera de Irun, Km 12,200 (variante de Fuencarral)
Apartado 547
28049 Madrid
Telex 48850 ESPAC

A large publisher, with offices in Argentina, Colombia, and Mexico.
Publishes translations of the Lorge and Thorndike intelligence test and the
Terman and Merrill method for the Stanford Binet.

TEA Ediciones, SA
Fray Bernardino de Sahagun 24
Apartado 19007
28036 Madrid
Tel. 458-8311
Telex 22135

Large publisher of numerous Spanish tests distributed in Latin America, as
well as Spanish-language adaptations of the Wechsler Intelligence Scales (WAIS,
WISC, WPPSI), the differential Aptitude Tests, the McCarthy Scales, the Bayley
Scales of Infant Development, the Cattell Personality Questionnaires, the
Eysenck Personality Questionnaires, the Kuder Preference Tests, and many
others.

United States

Prospective test users wishing to order tests directly from the United
States are advised to consult the annotated bibliographies of Spanish-language
tests prepared by the Educational Testing Service, which were described earlier
in this chapter.

Venezuela

JESEG, SA
Avenida Este 2 con sur 21
Apartado Postal 291
Caracas 101
Tel. 571-3913

Distributes the tests of the Institute for Personality and Ability
Testing, Inc. (USA), and of the Consulting Psychologists Press (USA), publisher
of the Spanish-language versions of the Strong-Campbell Interest Inventory, the
California Psychological Inventory, the Myers-Briggs Type Indicator, and the
State-Trait Anxiety Inventory, among others.

8

Funding for International Research and Exchange

This chapter is intended for US and Latin American psychologists and students interested in finding support for individual and collaborative international exchanges within the hemisphere. The chapter will be less useful for individuals seeking ties outside the hemisphere, e.g., with colleagues and institutions in Europe, although most of the reference works we consulted will be of value to those with a wider range of geographic interest. The vast majority of the entries pertain to exchanges of academic psychologists, including those performing research in health-related fields, to the exclusion of professional psychologists working in clinics, schools, industry, etc. A short section of the chapter is devoted to international opportunities for teachers.

The chapter has its limitations. First, information on financial resources for international study does not remain current indefinitely; the scope and parameters of programs change continually, and the user of this guide is advised to verify the specific points of programs that may be of interest before making extensive plans. Second, we make no pretense of exhaustiveness; all of the sources consulted for this chapter were compiled and published in the United States, so that international funding available in and from the individual states of Latin America is certainly inadequately represented. Third, no written treatise, even one much more comprehensive than the present, can properly catalogue the opportunities for collaborative work that develop as the result of personal contact and discussion at international meetings, often among individuals who have known of each other's work through the literature in the field. For this reason individuals interested in exchange and collaboration are urged to consider joining and participating in the international and regional organizations described in an earlier chapter, or others, not necessarily hemispheric in scope, in specialty areas. The International Affairs Office at APA is a good source of information about such groups and their activities.

With these caveats, we shall proceed.

Financial assistance for international exchanges and collaborative projects can be classified according to its purpose and its source, and by the most salient of the applicable restrictions. The purposes covered include awards to individuals for study above the secondary level, for dissertation research, for postdoctoral research, and for teaching. Also covered are resources for collaborative research projects and for conferences and publications. Generally not covered here are opportunities for paid or unpaid work, such as internships or development-related work; or secondary school exchanges such as those offered by the American Field Service or through Youth for Understanding. Also not covered are the many domestic grant programs in which the potential for introducing an international or intercultural component or dimension is at least implicit (e.g., in much behavioral research funded by the US Department of Defense), or into which an international component could be built at the discretion of the principal investigators.

The sources of financial assistance described herein include intergovernmental organizations, national governments, and private institutions such as universities and foundations. In general, the sources of support based in North America appear to be more varied, due to the larger size and role of private universities and foundations; in Latin America, assistance for international study and research in psychology is most often centralized within the national ministries of health and education, or within a specialized central body such as ICETEX in Colombia. Private foundations in Latin America, while numerous as a result of their favored tax status, are generally small and quite specialized. We have not made an effort to study them, but interested readers are referred to the Foundation Center (see reference section) for assistance in locating and reviewing available surveys.

The most common restrictions specified in financial aid programs concern the field or subfield for which a given award is tenable; the citizenship of the awardee, as well as his or her level of prior education, training, or experience; requirements for cosponsorship of proposals; the duration of the award; and specific provisions concerning what may or may not be covered (e.g., international and local travel, university tuition and fees, books and research equipment, living expenses for awardee and family, conference registration fees, publication costs, etc.). In the entries that follow, space limitations dictated that we provide only the most essential information; we encourage readers to write to individual program sponsors for more detailed information (e.g., concerning deadlines for applications).

Because the material contained herein is neither exhaustive nor timeless, it is essential to discuss briefly the methods by which further information on financial support for international projects can be found. These methods may be bibliographic or institutional. The most useful bibliographic sources known to us are listed in the reference section at the end of this chapter. Most of the information that appears below was extracted from the sources listed, which in many cases provide more ample information than we were able to reproduce. Likewise, the reference section includes a number of institutions that provide information useful to those interested in support for international education and research.

Intergovernmental Organizations

Most programs administered by intergovernmental organizations require that applicants for awards be nominated by their national ministry of health, education, or science, and that they be accepted by an institution in the country in which they wish to carry out their study or research.

International Brain Research Organization
IBRO Fellowship Secretariat
Universite Pierre et Marie Curie
Laboratoire de Physiologie des Centres Nerveux
4, Place Jussieu
75230 Paris Cedex 05, France

IBRO/UNESCO Fellowships

These fellowships for postdoctoral neuroscientists cover one-year stays at participating IBRO laboratories in Brazil, Venezuela, and most of the countries of Europe. Preference appears to be given to candidates from developing countries, and to young scientists seeking to acquire new techniques in a discipline other than their primary field of research. The stipend varies but is sufficient for modest living expenses; travel costs may be borne by an IBRO/UNESCO Travel Fellowship.

Information may also be obtained by writing IBRO/UNESCO Fellowships, UNESCO House, 7 Place de Fontenoy, 75700 Paris, France.

Organization of American States
Secretariat for Development Cooperation
Seventeenth and Constitution Avenues, NW
Washington, DC 20006
Tel. (202) 789-3902

Regular Training Programs (PRA) Fellowships

These fellowships, tenable for any field and varying in length, are awarded for advanced study at the graduate level and for research in any field except the medical sciences. The grants may be used in any OAS member country outside the applicant's home country. They cover travel expenses, tuition and fees, study/research materials, and a living allowance that varies from country to country.

Applicants must be accepted by an institution in the country in which they propose to do their research. Applications are submitted to OAS through the liaison agency designated by OAS for the applicant's country, except in the United States, where applications are submitted directly.

Fellowships in Education, Science, and Culture (BECC)

The OAS General Secretariat offers these fellowships through specific announcements keyed to the three broad fields of education, science, and culture. The competition is open to permanent residents of OAS member states. Eligibility requirements are set forth in the announcements. Applications are submitted through the liaison agency designated by each member government.

Leo S. Rowe Pan American Loan Fund

The purpose of the fund is to provide interest-free loans of up to $1,500 to individuals from the Latin American and Caribbean member states of the OAS who are enrolled, or have been accepted by, an accredited US college or university for study in any field. Certain other conditions apply. Tel. (202) 789-6208.

Pan American Health Organization/
World Health Organization Regional Office for the Americas
525 Twenty-Third Street, NW
Washington, DC 20037

PAHO/WHO Fellowship Program

These fellowships for up to a year of postgraduate study in any field in the health sciences, including teaching, are tenable in any WHO member country other than the applicant's country of permanent residence. Applicants must be sponsored by the national health ministry in their country and must return home for at least three years of national service after the termination of the program of study of which the fellowship forms a part. Priorities for fields of study are defined by each member state and thus may or may not include the behavioral aspects of public health, preventive medicine, and other health sciences. Applications should be initiated through the national health ministry using WHO Form 52.

In the United States, the Human Resources and Services Administration within the Department of Health and Human Services manages the PAHO/WHO Fellowship Program on behalf of the Public Health Service, helping to select US participants in the program and to arrange programs for fellows from other countries who come to the United States. The HRSA is located at 5600 Fishers Lane, Room 16A-17, Rockville, MD 20857, tel. (301) 443-6580.

Fellowships of the Caribbean Institute on Alcoholism

Short-term training at the Caribbean Institute on Alcoholism in the US Virgin Islands is provided for professionals in the field of alcoholism treatment and prevention. Funds are provided by the health ministries of PAHO member states; the individual ministries set eligibility requirements. Not all PAHO member states provide the fellowships.

UNESCO
7, Place de Fontenoy
75700 Paris, France

UNESCO Fellowships

Senior educators concerned with drug abuse are eligible for fellowships covering visits or courses related to the fields of UNESCO's mission. Applications should be made through the National Commission for UNESCO or other body cooperating with UNESCO (usually the ministry of education or foreign affairs) in the applicant's country.

United Nations
United Nations Plaza
New York, NY 10017
(See specific addresses, below)

A number of UN agencies offer internship programs that may be of interest to certain students of psychology interested in international exchange, although the programs do not relate specifically to psychology. The names and addresses of some of these programs are provided below.

UN Ad Hoc Internship Program

This program is designed to provide young students with an opportunity to serve the United Nations for a period of two months or more, generally at UN headquarters in New York City. Information can be obtained from the Internship Coordinator, UN Office of Personnel, UN Plaza, Room 2475, New York, NY 10017.

UN Department of Public Information Graduate Student Internship Program

A four-week program of seminars, lectures, briefings, and study is offered in New York each summer (June/July) to an international group of outstanding young graduate students. A similar program is conducted for two and one-half weeks in Geneva in July/August. Application forms are available from deans of participating universities. Information on the New York program can be obtained from: DPI Graduate Student Intern Program, UN Department of Public Information, UN Plaza, Room S-1037G, New York, NY 10017. For information on the Geneva program, write: Graduate Study Program, Information Service, UN Department of Public Information, Palais des Nations, Geneva 10, CH-1211 Switzerland.

UN Development Program (UNDP) Summer Internships

UNDP internships provide on-the-job training for young graduate students in development-oriented fields. Interns spend eight to 10 weeks in a UNDP field office or at headquarters in New York. Educational and language requirements apply. Write: Chief, Recruitment Section, Summer Internship Program, Division of Personnel, UNDP, One UN Plaza, New York, NY 10017.

UN Institute for Training and Research (UNITAR) Internship Program

UNITAR accepts a small number of visiting scholars and interns for research, training, or administration. Internship periods vary from two months to one year. Applications may be sent through the UN mission in the applicant's country, or through a sponsoring university or institute. Contact: Executive Director, UNITAR, 801 UN Plaza, New York, NY 10017.

National Governments

United States Government

AGENCY FOR INTERNATIONAL DEVELOPMENT
Bureau for Science and Technology
Washington, DC 20523

AID is the US Government's development assistance arm. Psychologists and other behavioral scientists have skills that generally have been underutilized in the Agency's work in the areas of health services, population planning, manpower training, education, industry, and community development. This is probably due as much to institutional divisions between psychological studies and development studies in US universities as it is to the complexities of the AID grants and contracts process. This is not to deny that the latter process is complex; indeed, it is beyond the scope of this book. However, US psychologists interested in performing research or applying knowledge at the interface of behavioral science and development can learn more about the AID **Central Research Program** and **Joint Career Corps** by contacting the Bureau for Science and Technology at the Agency. Information on currently funded grants to universities can be obtained from the Support Division of the Office of Contract Management ("AID-Financed University Contracts and Grants," annual).

Participant Training Program

Each year more than 10,000 AID-sponsored participants receive academic or technical training in the United States. Of these, approximately 20 percent come from Latin America or the Caribbean. About half of all participants are enrolled in academic programs in US colleges and universities, primarily in graduate degree programs.

Participants are selected jointly by their government and by US personnel in the AID Mission in that country. They generally come from government, the private sector, or the academic world and are already advanced in their professions. The goal of their AID-sponsored training in the United States or a third country is typically quite specific and is intended to further the development of their country.

Latin American psychologists with expertise in any of AID's areas of interest, including health, education, and community development, may be eligible for the participant program. Information is available at AID missions or from the Office of International Training at the address above.

ALCOHOL, DRUG ABUSE, AND MENTAL HEALTH ADMINISTRATION
5600 Fishers Lane
Rockville, MD 20857

National Research Service Awards are available through ADAMHA's institutes for research on alcohol-related problems, drug abuse, or mental health/mental illness. Applicants must be US citizens or permanent residents of the United States. They must have a doctoral degree and be accepted by a sponsor at an appropriate institution. If a foreign institution is selected as the research site, applicants must present information on the exceptional resources offered by the institution.

Awards cover payment of a stipend for up to three years and, if training will occur at a foreign site, may include round-trip airfare for the fellow.

Information may be obtained from the Grants Management Office at any of the three institutes of ADAMHA: National Institute on Alcohol Abuse and Alcoholism, National Institute on Drug Abuse, and National Institute of Mental Health, all located at the ADAMHA address given above.

In 1983, NIAAA was designated as a WHO Collaborating Center for Research and Training. In this capacity, the Institute performs a variety of functions, including the exchange of scientific research and professional personnel in work-study programs and the training of personnel from developing countries. NIAAA also has an extensive program of bilateral cooperation, including a program with Mexico.

INTER-AMERICAN FOUNDATION
1515 Wilson Boulevard
Rosslyn, Virginia 22209

The Inter-American foundation, a public corporation created by the US
Congress in 1969, provides direct financial support for self-help efforts
initiated by poor people in Latin America and the Caribbean. The Foundation
makes about 200 grants a year for projects in more than 25 countries. In 1984,
the total awarded was more than $17 million. Approximately half of the
Foundation's funds are appropriate by Congress, and the remainder comes from
the Social Progress Trust Fnd of the Inter-American Development Bank. the 1986
budget was approximately $28.7 million.

Responding to proposals from non-governmental Latin American and Caribbean
organizations, the Foundation complements local resources for self-help
programs and projects that benefit and involve people of low incomes and few
opportunities. Projects should be sustainable beyond the period of the
Foundation's grant, and offer promise for demonstration, expansion, or
replication in other settings. It is expected that projects receive
counterpart support.

Organizations interested in submitting a proposal for Foundation funding
can obtain an initial reaction to their project by sending a brief letter of
inquiry outlining the project's purposes, the means proposed for achieving
them, and the amount of financial support required. All proposals and
inquiries should be sent to the address above.

Fellowship Programs

The Foundation awards approximately 50 fellowships a year to graduate
students from the United States, Latin American, and the Caribbean. The
fellowships are intended to encourage scholarly and professional attention to
development activities at the local level. Candidates must be supported by
their home institution and be accepted by an institution abroad. Other
conditions apply. Those interested should write to Elizabeth Veatch,
Fellowship Officer, at the address above, or call (703) 841-3864.

NATIONAL INSTITUTES OF HEALTH
9000 Rockville Pike
Bethesda, MD 20892
(Individual entries contain more complete addresses)

The National Institutes of Health is the principal biomedical and
behavioral research and communications agency of the United States Government.
The many bureaus, institutes, and divisions of NIH engage in a broad and
complex range of activities with other countries and with multilateral
organizations. In 1985, NIH spent a total of $73.9 million (about 1.3 percent
of its total budget) on such activities, which included the following types of
programs:

--   Research grants and contracts awarded to foreign institutions, as well as
     awards to US grantees for research having an international component.
     (About $35 million.)

-- Exchanges of scientists, including the Visiting Scientist and Guest Worker programs of the various NIH institutes, as well as several exchange programs administered by the Fogarty International Center (see below). (About $27.5 million.)

-- Collaborative projects under bilateral Science and Technology Agreements and/or bilateral Health Agreements with other countries. The Latin American nations with which the US Government has reached such agreements are Argentina, Brazil, Mexico, and Venezuela. (Almost $9 million.)

-- Support for international travel to meetings and conferences and in connection with other multilateral and bilateral activities. (About $2.5 million.)

Research Grants Division

The number of NIH research grants and contracts awarded to Latin American investigators or involving Latin American researchers, facilities, or populations is relatively small in any given year (and the number having any relation to psychology is even smaller). Nevertheless, applications from outside the United States are not discouraged. A number of factors may increase the chances that an application will be successful. These include (1) the relevance of the proposed research to the specific mission of one or more of the institutes of NIH; (2) the involvement of a collaborating institution in the United States; and (3) a demonstration that the proposed research could not as successfully or as appropriately be carried out in the United States. Interested psychologists should contact the Office of Grants Inquiries, Research Grants Division, National Institutes of Health, Westwood Building, 5333 Westbard Avenue, Bethesda, MD 20814. The telephone number is (301) 496-7441.

Similarly, US applicants for **National Research Service Awards** for postdoctoral behavioral research training who wish to pursue their training outside the United States must provide a justification of the suitability of the proposed foreign research site. Such sites generally must be seen to provide research advantages not available in the United States. The National Research Service Awards Program also provides **Senior Fellowships** for experienced scientists. Although these fellowships, too, are tenable outside the United States, the choice of the foreign site must be justified. Interested US psychologists should contact the NIH Grants Inquiries Office at the address given in the previous paragraph.

Fogarty International Center (FIC)

The John E. Fogarty International Center for Advanced Study in the Health Sciences was established in 1968 to provide a focus for NIH activities in international biomedical and behavioral research. The purposes of the Center are to:

-- Facilitate the assembly of scientists and others in the biomedical, behavioral and related fields for discussion, study, and research relating to the development of health science internationally;

-- Provide postdoctoral fellowships for research training in the United States and abroad, and promote exchanges of senior scientists between the United States and other countries;

-- Coordinate the activities of the National Institutes of Health concerned with the health sciences internationally; and

-- Receive foreign visitors to the National Institutes of Health.

The FIC discharges its responsibilities through four programs, three of which are relevant to users of this guide: Advanced Studies, International Research and Awards, and Foreign Scientists Assistance.

The goal of the **Advanced Studies Program** is to facilitate international scientific communication by providing international forums for the exchange of information and for the review and evaluation of major areas of biomedical and behavioral research of interest to NIH. This is accomplished in part through a Scholars-in-Residence Program that offers selected US and foreign scholars to devote time to research and writing.

Under the heading of **International Research and Awards** the FIC administers and fully or partially supports several types of international fellowship programs enabling foreign scientists to pursue their research interests in US laboratories, including those at NIH, and providing opportunities for US researchers to work in foreign laboratories. The fellowship programs applicable to Latin America are:

-- International Research Fellowships
-- WHO/NINCDS/FIC International Neuroscience Fellowships
-- Senior International Fellowships

The International Research Fellowship Program is probably the program of greatest potential interest to Latin American psychologists. It provides opportunities for biomedical or behavioral scientists who are in the formative stage of their career (no more than 10 years beyond the doctorate) to extend their research experience in a US laboratory. Roughly 22 percent of the 100-odd fellowships offered in 1985 were awarded to Latin American scientists. Awards include a one-year stipend and round-trip travel for the fellow only. In addition to holding a doctoral degree, applicants must have a sponsor in the United States who has agreed to host the applicant, and must be nominated by a Nominating Committee in his or her home country. Application forms may be obtained from Nominating Committees in Argentina, Bolivia, Brazil, Chile, Colombia, Costa Rica, Mexico, Peru, Uruguay, and Venezuela. A list of the Nominating Committees and their addresses may be obtained from the Fogarty Center at the address below.

The purpose of the Senior International Fellowship Program is to provide established US scientists with opportunities to conduct collaborative research in a foreign institution for up to one year. Since the program was founded in 1975, few of the nearly 500 fellows have used their fellowships in Latin America, although this option is available. Applicants must be sponsored by a US institution and invited by a foreign institution.

The **Foreign Scientists Assistance Programs** at FIC assist the bureaus, institutes, and divisions of NIH in administering the NIH Visiting Program and the NIH Guest Research Program. These programs link the NIH with other components of the Department of Health and Human Services, the Immigration and Naturalization Service of the Department of Justice, the US Information Agency, and foreign embassies and science attaches. They offer the opportunity for talented scientists throughout the world to engage in collaborative research with NIH scientists.

Under the NIH Visiting Program, foreign researchers are invited to the laboratories of NIH and cooperating institutions such as the National Institute of Mental Health by senior investigators for stays of 1 to 3 years. The program is intended to provide mutual benefits to NIH and the invited scientists. The program has separate components for scientists of varying levels of experience and seniority.

A total of 1,421 persons from 63 countries participated in the NIH Visiting Program in 1985. Potential applicants may review the NIH Scientific Directory and Annual Bibliography to identify senior investigators in their field and communicate directly with them for possible sponsorship. These publications may be obtained from the Office of Comunications, Public Inquiries, National Institutes of Health, Building 31, Room 2B10, Bethesda, MD 20205, USA.

For full information on the programs described above, contact the International Research and Awards Branch, Fogarty International Center, National Institutes of Health, Building 38A, Room 613, Bethesda, MD 20892, USA. The telephone number is (301) 496-6688.

NATIONAL RESEARCH COUNCIL
Fellowship Office
2101 Constitution Avenue, NW
Washington, DC 20418

Postdoctoral Fellowships for Minorities

Members of US minority groups, including Hispanic-Americans, who in the past have been underrepresented in academic disciplines in the United States are offered fellowships for one year of postdoctoral research tenable anywhere in the world. Applicants are expected to devote full time to a program of study and/or research.

NATIONAL SCIENCE FOUNDATION (NSF)
Division of International Programs
Directorate for Scientific, Technological, and International Affairs
1800 G Street, NW
Washington, DC 20550

Within the framework of its international cooperative science program, the National Science Foundation supports three types of activities:

-- cooperative research projects designed and conducted jointly by principal investigators from the United States and one or more foreign countries

-- research-oriented seminars or workshops to exchange information, review the current status of a specific field of science, and plan cooperative research

-- scientific visits for purposes of performing research or planning cooperative activities.

Although the behavioral and social sciences stand on a more or less equal footing with other sciences within NSF and are generally eligible for support within the cooperative science program, NSF and its counterpart agencies in various Latin American countries have agreed on program priorities that may or may not favor psychologists. In general, the cooperative science programs of NSF and its foreign counterparts have been quite underutilized by psychologists, at least over the past 10 years, leading us to believe that carefully conceived research projects in the social and behavioral sciences would stand a good chance of receiving funds.

US universities and colleges, professional societies, research institutes, and individual scientists and agencies affiliated with such organizations may apply for support. Principal investigators/project directors should be US scientists with professional experience equivalent to at least five years of postdoctoral scientific work.

In most of the programs listed below, each country pays for the costs of its participation. NSF usually provides only the supplemental support required to introduce an international element or broaden the international character of a research effort. Primary funding for a US-based effort may come from any US funding source, including the domestic research support programs of NSF.

For cooperative research and seminars, a US applicants sends a proposal to NSF at approximately the same time as the cooperating foreign scientist submits a corresponding proposal to the appropriate agency in his or her home country. In formal bilateral programs, activities typically require approval of both NSF and its foreign counterpart agency before funding can be approved.

US scientists may obtain further information about any international program, including descriptive program announcements, by writing to the particular program at the address provided above, or by contacting the appropriate program manager at (202) 357-9563. Latin American scientists should contact the appropriate agency in their home country.

Formal bilateral programs

NSF administers the following formal bilateral programs with counterpart agencies in Latin America (the agency and date of establishment of the agreement are provided in parentheses):

-- **US/Argentina Cooperative Science Program** (National Council for Scientific and Technological Research-CONICET, 1972)

-- **US/Brazil Cooperative Science Program** (National Council for Scientific and Technological Development-CNPq, 1971)

-- **US/Mexico Cooperative Science Program** (Consejo Nacional de Ciencia y Tecnologia-CONACYT, 1972)

-- **US/Venezuela Cooperative Science Program** (State Ministry for Science and Technology and National Council for Scientific and Technological Research-CONICIT, 1973)

Each of these programs includes the three components listed at the head of this entry: cooperative research grants; seminar and conference grants; and visiting scientist grants.

US/Latin America and Caribbean Cooperative Science Program

In addition to activities under the formal bilateral arrangements, NSF supports US participation in projects under less formal arrangements with countries in Latin America and the Caribbean. The general scope and content of the program is as outlined above for the bilateral programs.

Science in Developing Countries Program (SDC)

Like the programs described above, the main purpose of the SDC program is to strengthen scientific cooperation with developing countries. The SDC does this through small grants ($20,000 or less) directed primarily toward improving the scientific infrastructure of developing countries.

Grants are made to US institutions, but projects often involve activities at a foreign site, and project budgets may include partial support for developing-country counterparts. The following categories of awards are made to US institutions that sponsor SDC projects:

-- Research participation grants to support the participation of US scientists in a research project in an eligible country and/or the participation by foreign scientists in an appropriate US-based research project, with the program providing only supplemental costs related to the international collaborative component of the research;

-- Grants for research-oriented seminars, workshops, and colloquia focused on developing-country problems;

-- Dissertation improvement grants for the incremental support of developing-country graduate students who are enrolled at US universities. Among the costs covered are those for field equipment and supplies, and for travel to and from research sites. No stipend, tuition, fees, or indirect costs are provided.

UNITED STATES INFORMATION AGENCY (USIA)
Bureau of Educational and Cultural Affairs
301 Fourth Street, SW
Washington, DC 20547

The purposes of the US International Communication Agency are to give foreign peoples an understanding of US policies and of the social and cultural determinants of those policies; to encourage, aid, and sponsor the broadest possible exchange of people and ideas between the United States and other nations; to assist the US Government, as well as individual Americans and institutions, in learning about other nations and cultures; and to prepare cultural exchanges with other governments.

The agency achieves its mission through media operations such as the Voice of America, and through its network of over 200 posts in approximately 125 countries. There are approximately 32 posts housed in US embassies and consulates throughout Latin America and the Caribbean. In addition, the agency maintains approximately 15 libraries in various countries of the region, including four in Mexico and three in Brazil. It is through USIA's posts that many of the exchange activities discussed below are initiated.

The Agency's Bureau of Educational and Cultural Affairs sponsors a variety of exchange activities, including:

-- **Fulbright Scholar Programs**, administered by the Council for International Exchange of Scholars (see entry for CIES)

-- **Fulbright Teacher Exchange Program** (see special section on teaching at the end of this chapter)

-- **International Visitors Program**

-- **American Participants Program**

-- **University Affiliations Program**

International Visitors Program

Each year, USIA post chiefs invite over 3,500 foreign leaders in all fields to visit their counterparts in the United States for periods of up to 30 days. About 1,500 of these visitors come at USIA's expense, with the rest funded by their governments or institutions, or through personal funds. Planning itineraries for such visitors involves more than 100,000 US volunteers and many scores of institutions, including the American Psychological Association. Although the individual heads of USIA posts are responsible for issuing formal invitations, US institutions interested in receiving a visitor may ask USIA to consider issuing an invitation. The Agency's Academic Exchange Specialists and Academic Advisers (the latter being faculty members asked to spend a year or more working in the Academic Exchange Programs Division of USIA) can provide guidance in arranging such exchanges. The telephone number of the division is (202) 485-7360.

American Participants Program

In response to specific requests from its posts, USIA sends "American Participants" overseas for short-term speaking programs in a variety of areas, including science and social processes in the United States. Some 600 American experts take part in the program each year, many of them in the course of travel arranged for other purposes.

Prospective US participants are asked to fill out a data sheet to assist the Washington-based program development staff in making appropriate suggestions to the USIA post originating the invitation. Participants selected for the program receive the standard US Government per diem during their travel and a modest honorarium. USIA will pay for travel within the host country. In some cases, diversionary travel to other countries for similar programming, and even international travel from the United States, may be allowed.

Potential American Participants should write to the Office of Program Coordination and Development at USIA (telephone: (202) 485-2750) indicating their travel plans (if any) and professional speciality. Latin American institutions wishing to host an American Participant should make this known to the nearest USIA post.

University Affiliations Program

The University Affiliations Program provides three-year support for US universities that have developed collaborative exchange relations with a foreign university (either new affiliations or existing affiliations not previously funded by this USIA program).

Participating institutions should be prepared to assign US faculty or staff to the partner institution for teaching, lecturing, or research, maintain said person(s) on full salary; and receive visiting faculty from the partner institution. USIA funds are to be used for participant travel costs and modest supplements for maintenance expenses. Institutional overhead is not allowable.

At this point, the thematic priorities for grants involving Latin American institutions are restricted to law, history, and political science, but these guidelines may change, and an American institution seeking to form or continue an affiliation with a Latin American counterpart in the area of psychology may wish to direct an inquiry to the University Affiliations Program at the address above or call the American Republics Programs Bureau at (202) 485-7365.

Other programs

Because its mission is related to the foreign policy of the United States, USIA's programs and priorities may change more quickly than those of other agencies such as NIH or NSF. US psychologists interested in USIA support for an exchange idea would do well to contact an Academic Exchange Specialist or Academic Adviser to discuss current programs. Other USIA programs of potential interest include the **Cooperating Private Institutions Program**, which is designed to provide renewable one-year support for exchanges between US and foreign universities, associations, and other private institutions (grants range from $9,000 to $2.2 million); and the **Private Sector Program**, which provides funding for non-academic conferences if a matching grant from the private sector can be obtained.

Government of Australia

UNIVERSITY OF QUEENSLAND
St. Lucia, Brisbane
Queensland 4067, Australia
Tel. (07) 377-2842

Postdoctoral research fellowships

The purpose of these one-year fellowships, for which citizenship is unrestricted, is to permit young holders of the doctorate to study at the University of Queensland. Shorter fellowships (8 weeks) are also available for qualified members of a recognized university who are engaged in academic work that will contribute to the work of one of the departments at the University of Queensland. Both the long- and short-term fellowships cover airfare; the long-term fellowships also pay a stipend.

Government of Brazil

UNIVERSIDADE DE SAO PAULO
Divisao de Difusao Cultural
Caixa Postal 8191
01000 Sao Paulo, Brazil

Scholarships

Scholarships of ten-months' duration, sometimes renewable, are available to graduate students preparing for teaching or research work who wish to study at the University of Sao Paulo. Applicants should write to the address above for current information.

BRAZILIAN EMBASSY
Cultural Section
3006 Massachusetts Avenue, NW
Washington, DC 20008
Tel. (202) 745-2700

Fellowships for foreign graduate students

College graduates are eligible to apply for awards to enable them to conduct research or pursue a graduate degree at a Brazilian university or institution. Tuition, fees, health insurance, and a stipend are offered. Because the terms of these fellowships vary, current information should be sought from the Brazilian Embassy.

Government of Colombia

ICETEX
Division de Programacion y Control de Servicios Estudiantiles
Carrera 3a, No. 18-24
Apartado Aereo 57-35
Bogota, Colombia

ICETEX was created in the early 1950s as a government agency responsible for providing student loans, administering certain national scholarship programs, and supervising scholarship offerings of other governments for Colombian students. Student loans are available for study at Colombia universities or, especially at the graduate level, for studies abroad, in which case loans may be made to complement a foreign scholarship offered to a Colombian student. ICETEX represents a comprehensive approach to international education in which information on foreign study opportunities, monitoring of national participation in international education, and financing through grants and loans is integrated within one agency having exclusive rights in the field guaranteed by government charter.

Cultural Exchange Scholarships

ICETEX offers Cultural Exchange Scholarships to citizens of other nations to pursue graduate study at Colombian universities and research institutes.

Andres Bello Convention Scholarships

These ICETEX scholarships are available only to nationals of Bolivia, Chile, Ecuador, Peru, and Venezuela.

Both of the scholarship programs listed above cover tuition, fees, books, health insurance, living expenses, travel, and relocation for periods of up to two years.

Government of Finland

Finnish Government Scholarships

Through the Institute of International Education in New York, the Finnish Government offers short-term scholarships to specialists in various fields to strengthen their collaboration with persons or institutions in Finland.

Citizenship is unrestricted, but applicants must possess a doctoral degree and speak Finnish, Swedish, English, or German. Awards cover payment of a stipend, free tuition, and possibly travel within Finland if it is related to the research program.

Government of Mexico

MEXICAN EMBASSY
Office for Cultural Affairs
2829 Sixteenth Street, NW
Washington, DC 20009
Tel. (202) 234-6000

Cultural Exchange Program Scholarships

US university graduates fluent in Spanish are eligible for scholarships of up to two academic years for graduate study or research at a Mexican university. Awards cover tuition and fees, health insurance, a book allowance, and a monthly subsidy.

Government of Norway

ROYAL NORWEGIAN COUNCIL FOR SCIENTIFIC AND INDUSTRIAL RESEARCH
Sognaveien 72
PO Box 70, Tasen
Oslo, Norway

Research opportunities in Norway

In order to stimulate international collaboration by providing foreign scientists with opportunities to conduct research in Norway, the Council offers one-year awards to young postdoctoral scientists who have established contact with an appropriate research team in Norway. Awards cover payment of a stipend, an allowance for accompanying family, and travel costs.

United Kingdom

THE BRITISH COUNCIL
Schemes Unit - Higher Education Division - CICHE
90/91 Tottenham Court Road
London W1P ODT, England
Tel. (1) 580-6572, ext. 25

Academic Links and Interchange Scheme

The purpose of this program is to promote direct contact between departments and institutions of higher education in Britain and equivalent institutions overseas with mutual scientific or academic interests, and to encourage the development of longer-term cooperation and research.

Awards are open to the academic and research staff of universities and equivalent institutions of higher education in Latin America (as elsewhere in the world). Students are not eligible.

Priority is given to exchanges or visits which form part of, or might lead to, a program of collaboration in research, publication or teaching. Awards, which are intended primarily as a contribution towards travel expenses of visitors and are available for visits either to or from Britain, or for subsistence, may be made for any of the following activities: joint research; joint publication; curriculum/course development; planning for student exchanges; staff/faculty exchange and development. Funding will normally be provided for exploratory visits and for visits during the formative stage of a link. Funds may also be available for the design and planning of international seminars or workshops, but not for attendance at same.

Government of Venezuela

EMBASSY OF VENEZUELA
2445 Massachusetts Avenue, NW
Washington, DC 20008
Tel. (202) 797-3800

A number of public and private institutions administer student loans and grants for domestic and international purposes in Venezuela. These include:

--   EDUCREDITO, a private entity that offers educational loans to students for study in Venezuela and abroad, and administration for private sponsors of student loan and scholarship programs

--   Other private institutions, including SACUEDO, the Fundacion Indio Orinoco, and the Instituto Nacional de Hipodromos

--   Gran Mariscal de Ayacucho Foundation, the largest of several government agencies that administer scholarship programs for the Venezuelan public

--   National Council on Science and Technology (CONICIT) (see entry for US National Science Foundation, above)

Venezuela's embassies (the address of the embassy in the United States appears above) may have more information on the activities and priorities of the groups listed above.

Private Organizations

American Cancer Society
Research Department
777 Third Avenue
New York, NY 10017
Tel. (212) 371-2900

Behavioral and emotional risk factors linked to the onset and progress of cancer, and to remission and cure, have received increasing attention in recent years, as have psychological aspects of the treatment and recovery process. Therefore, although the great preponderance of research in cancer continues to have a biomedical focus, perhaps it is not unreasonable to expect that entities such as the ACS will give favorable consideration to proposals of a behavioral or psychological nature.

Research fellowships

ACS offers postdoctoral awards of 1-2 years (possibly renewable for a third year) for US citizens or permanent residents engaged in research likely to contribute to the conquest of cancer. Awards include a stipend and travel expenses to the research site, which may be in the United States or abroad. An institutional allowance may also be requested.

Eleanor Roosevelt International Cancer Fellowships

Citizenship is not restricted for these fellowships, the purpose of which is to enable experienced postdoctoral researchers from any country to work in collaboration with scientists in another country for periods of six months to one year. Applicants must have a position on the staff of a university, teaching hospital, or research laboratory, or similar institution, and must be accepted at a host institution for the proposed research period. Awards include a stipend, which may cover dependents; travel expenses for the fellow and dependents; and, upon request, an institutional allowance. Those interested should contact the International Union Against Cancer, 3 rue du Conseil-General, 1205 Geneva, Switzerland, tel. (22) 201811.

American Council of Learned Societies
228 East 45th Street
New York, NY 10017

Travel Grant Program

US or Canadian psychologists holding the doctoral degree and proposing to present papers of a social-scientific or humanistic nature at an international scholarly meeting, or to play a major official role in such a meeting, are eligible to apply for travel grants from the ACLS. The number of grants offered in a given year is fairly small.

American Psychological Association
International Affairs Office
1200 Seventeenth Street, NW
Washington, DC 20036
Tel. (202) 955-7685

Travel Grants for Interamerican Congress of Psychology

Using funds made available by the National Science Foundation, the APA conducts a travel grant program for US-resident psychologists participating in the biennial Interamerican Congress of Psychology. The criteria for these competitive grants favor those having the most substantial roles in the congress program. Once this criterion is met, the relative youth of the applicant becomes a determining factor. Some 20 to 30 awards are made, covering approximately one half of the international airfare to the congress.

Travel Grants for Foreign Graduate Students

Latin American students enrolled in psychology graduate programs in US universities and not supported by US government funds may be eligible to apply for $300 grants to enable them to attend the APA convention in August of each year. Approximately 10 grants are made each year, using funds provided by the US Information Agency under the Short-Term Enrichment Program.

Association of Universities and Colleges of Canada
Scholarship Administration Services
151 Slater Street
Ottawa, Ontario K1P 5N1, Canada
Tel. (613) 563-1236

AUCC Foreign Graduate Fellowships and Scholarships

On behalf of the Canadian government and cooperating foreign governments, including Colombia and Mexico, the AUCC administers a graduate awards program for Canadian citizens wishing to study abroad. The individual to contact at the number or address above is Michelyne Parker.

Atlantic History, Culture, and Society Program
c/o David William Cohen
Johns Hopkins University
Baltimore, MD 21218
Tel. (301) 338-7597

These fellowships are intended to support research by investigators in the humanities and social sciences whose subject is the history, culture, or society of the Atlantic region, including Latin America and the Caribbean. Interdisciplinary research is encouraged. The maximum grant is $25,000, plus up to $2,000 for relocation expenses.

The Burroughs Wellcome Fund
3030 Cornwallis Road
Research Triangle Park, NC 27709
Tel. (919) 541-9090

Wellcome Research Travel Grants

US citizens or permanent residents engaged in full-time research in an institution devoted to the health sciences may be considered for short-term travel support (2-12 weeks) for visits aimed at exchanging views and studying new techniques with non-US colleagues having similar interests.

Business and Professional Women's Foundation
Research Department
2012 Massachusetts Avenue, NW
Washington, DC 20036
Tel. (202) 293-1200

Sally Butler Memorial Fund for Latina Research

Women of Latin American descent or citizenship who are doctoral candidates or postdoctoral students in a field of importance to women may apply for research support totalling $500 to $3,000. Contact Ellen Mutari, Research Associate, at the address above.

James McKeen Cattell Fund
Box 219, Teachers College
525 West 120th Street
New York, NY 10027

Supplemental Sabbatical Awards for Psychologists

Tenured or tenure-track psychologists planning sabbatical leave for a full academic year may apply for an award to bring their income for the sabbatical period up to their normal academic year salary, with an $18,000 cap on the Cattell Fund's contribution.

Council for International Exchange of Scholars
11 Dupont Circle, NW
Washington, DC 20036-1257
Tel. (202) 939-5460

CIES was set up in 1947, soon after the passage of the Fulbright-Hays Act, which provided the initial legislative authority for the the Fulbright Exchange programs administered by CIES and a number of other organizations with funds provided by the USIA. Grants are made to US citizens and nationals of other countries for a variety of educational activities, primarily university teaching, advanced research, graduate study, and teaching in elementary and secondary schools.

Those programs relating to Latin America and administered by CIES are noted below, whether or not awards in psychology are currently offered. Other

Fulbright-funded projects are described under the entries for the Institute of International Education and the US Information Agency (University Affiliations Program), and in the special section on teacher exchange that concludes this chapter. More ample information, including program announcements, application forms, and directories of scholars participating in the current year's exchanges, are available from CIES or from the binational Fulbright commissions in seven Latin American countries (see addresses below).

Particularly useful for American scholars is the comprehensive annual booklet entitled "Fulbright Scholar Program: Research Awards and Lectureships," in which awards available to US scholars are indexed by discipline and country. For US scholars, fluent Spanish is generally required.

University Teaching and Research in the American Republics

Grantees are in residence at a Latin American or Caribbean institution for a period of 3-10 months. In addition to performing personal research, Fulbright scholars in participating South American countries (Argentina, Brazil, Chile, Colombia, Ecuador, Peru, and Uruguay) may be involved in teaching graduate courses, advising students preparing theses, and assisting in the development of new teaching and research programs. Lecturers at universities in Central America and Caribbean are more likely to be asked to teach at the undergraduate level and to help develop research programs. Fluency in Spanish or Portuguese is generally required, as is a doctoral degree.

During the 1986-87 exchange year, three US psychologists worked in institutions in Latin America (Peru, Guatemala, and Brazil). During the same period, three Latin American psychologists (one from Chile and two from Costa Rica) lectured or performed research in US universities under Fulbright sponsorship.

Because of the enormous popularity of psychology in Latin America, the CIES often has difficulty in filling all of the exchange positions offered in Latin America. US psychologists with fluency in Spanish are therefore urged to contact CIES.

American Republics Research Program

Up to 20 awards in any discipline, each for six months, are available for support of research conducted in one or more countries of the Caribbean, Mexico, or South America. A separate program exists for Central America (see below). Applications are encouraged from scholars whose projects involve collaboration with colleagues in the host country and who are willing to give occasional lectures. Awards vary from approximately $1,600 to $3,000 per month, depending on the country and the size of the scholar's family. The travel expenses of the grantee are also paid. In some countries, reimbursement of tuition costs for dependent children is also available, up to a limit of $8,000 per year.

Central American Republics Research and Lecturing Program

Fulbright program support for research and lecturing in Belize, Costa Rica, El Salvador, Guatemala, Honduras, Nicaragua, and Panama has been expanded. For research, up to 15 awards for 3-9 months in one or more countries are available. Lecturing awards are available for 6-12 months in selected fields. Benefits are comparable to those in the previous entry.

Visiting Fulbright Scholars and Occasional Lecturers

Each year over 1,200 scholars from abroad are invited to lecture and conduct research in American colleges and universities under the **Fulbright Scholar Program**. Some 1,050 of the scholars apply for grants through Fulbright commissions or US embassies in their home countries; another 150 are invited by colleges and universities in the United States to lecture in their specific fields under the **Scholar-in-Residence Program**. To acquaint the US academic community with the visiting scholars and their fields of specialization, CIES publishes an annual <u>Directory of Visiting Fulbright Scholars and Occasional Lecturers</u> which lists scholars' names, disciplines, home country, and affiliation in the United States, as well as the topics on which each scholar is prepared to lecture.

Although colleges and universities are encouraged to contact visiting scholars directly using the directory, visits may also be arranged through the CIES **Occasional Lecturer Program**, under which prospective institutions, especially those with little opportunity to receive international visitors, are assisted in selecting appropriate lecturers. Limited funds are available from CIES for travel costs.

Binational Fulbright Commissions and Foundations

Within the United States, the components of the overall Fulbright program are administered by four private and public agencies (CIES, IIE, the US Information Agency, and the US Department of Education) under the overall direction of USIA. Cooperating with USIA are binational educational commissions and foundations in more than 40 countries that have executive agreements with the United States for continuing exchange programs. Where no binational agreement exists, the US Embassy, cooperating with USIA's Office of Academic Programs, develops the Fulbright program and supervises it locally.

The binational commissions and foundations propose the annual country programs, which establish the numbers and categories of grants based on requests from local institutions; review applications of nominated Americans and arrange or confirm their academic affiliation; make travel arrangements for grantees and their families; and provide orientation services.

A list of the binational commissions in Latin America follows:

ARGENTINA   Commission for Educational Exchange Between the USA and the Argentine Republic, Avenida de Mayo 1285, Quinto Piso, Buenos Aires, tel. 384890

BRAZIL   Commission for Educational Exchange Between the USA and Brazil, Edificio Casa Thomas Jefferson, W-4 Sul, Entre Quadras 706/906, 70390 Brasilia, DF, tel. 244-1080 and 244-1270

CHILE   Commission for Educational Exchange Between the USA and Chile, Casilla 2121, Santiago, tel. 380580

COLOMBIA   Commission for Educational Exchange Between the USA and Colombia, Apartado Aereo 034240, Carrera 21, No. 39-70, Bogota, tel. 287-3995, 287-3829, and 287-3718

ECUADOR   Commission for Educational Exchange Between the USA and Ecuador, 10 De Agosto 1832 y Roca, PO Box 826-A, Quito, tel. 230119

PERU   Commission for Educational Exchange Between the USA and Peru,
            Maximo Abril 599, Lima 11, tel. 245494 and 240793

URUGUAY   Commission Between the USA and Uruguay, Paraguay 1217, Montevideo,
            tel. 914160

                    Council of International Programs (CIP)
                            1030 Euclid Avenue
                            Cleveland, Ohio 44115
                            Tel. (216) 861-5478

     CIP is a private, nonprofit organization that conducts international
exchange programs for individuals in the human service fields, including social
work, early childhood education, special education, youth work, public
administration, public health, and related areas. Since its founding in 1956,
the program has arranged for more than 6,000 professionals from 120 countries
to come to the United States for a program of "cross-cultural integration and
interaction."
     Non-US citizens from 23 to 40 years of age and having at least two years'
professional practice in their human service field are eligible for the
program. Participants spend four months in the United States in training and
work-study environments appropriate to their professions.
     CIP participants receive travel grants from USIA, Fulbright Commissions,
and their governments, as well as from other public and private sources abroad.
Some participants pay their own expenses. Room and board is provided by
American host families. Some participants may be selected for an extended
field-work program of nine months' duration.
     Americans may join CIP international programs in other countries.
Participating countries in the Americas include: Argentina, the Bahamas,
Barbados, Belize, Bolivia, Brazil, Chile, Colombia, Costa Rica, Dominica, the
Dominican Republic, Ecuador, El Salvador, Grenada, Guatemala, Haiti, Honduras,
Jamaica, Martinique, Mexico, the Netherlands Antilles, Nicaragua, Panama,
Paraguay, Peru, St. Vincent, Surinam, Trinidad and Tobago, Uruguay, and
Venezuela.

                        The Lady Davis Fellowship Trust
                                PO Box 1255
                           Jerusalem 91904, Israel

     Postdoctoral scholars in any field may apply for awards to support study,
research, or teaching at the Hebrew University or the Technion in Israel. The
one-year awards cover a stipend and travel to the host institution.

                    Eisenhower Exchange Fellowships (EEF)
                            256 South 16th Street
                          Philadelphia, PA 19102
                            Tel. (215) 546-1738

     Since its founding in 1953, EEF has brought over 700 influential men and
women from 91 countries to the United States for individually tailored programs
of professional consultations, visits, conferences, and social contacts with

counterparts in the United States. The visits typically last from 10 to 12 weeks and are fully paid.

Fellows are men and women between the ages of 35 and 50 who are leaders in fields deemed to be of paramount importance to their country's future development.

Each year, EEF invites a number of countries to participate in the program for that year. In each country selected, a binational nominating committee is formed to solicit and screen applicants. Between 20 and 30 fellowships are offered annually.

Fulbright Programs

See entries for US Information Agency (University Affiliations Program), Council for International Exchange of Scholars, and Institute of International Education, as well as the "Note on Teacher Exchanges" below.

General Electric Foundation
3135 Easton Turnpike, Building E1B
Fairfield, CT 06431
Tel. (203) 373-3216

International Understanding Program Grants

Grants of $5,000-$50,000 are made to organizations conducting international programs in the United States. Such programs may include visits to the United States by young adults from other countries, fellowships to enable foreign students to continue doctoral studies at US universities, and research and analysis of critical issues facing the countries of Latin America. The Foundation's secretary is Paul M. Ostergard.

General Service Foundation
PO Box 4012
Boulder, CO 80306
Tel. (303) 447-9541

Population Grants

The Foundation seeks proposals in the general area of population planning in Latin America, including family planning information and services, improvements in maternal and child health, reproductive health, and agricultural and economic development.

Grants are made to organizations that are tax-exempt under US law. The foundation prefers proposals that are innovative and that promise to make a significant contribution. Contact Robert W. or Marcie J. Musser at the address or phone number given above.

The Harry Frank Guggenheim Foundation
233 Broadway, Seventeenth Floor
New York, NY 10279
Tel. (212) 267-3860

Research Grants

Individuals and institutions working in the social, behavioral, or biological sciences in any country may apply for support of specific innovative projects that promise to improve our understanding of the basic causes of human dominance, aggression, and violence. Grants average $20,000 and are typically made for a one-year period.

The John Simon Guggenheim Memorial Foundation
90 Park Avenue
New York, NY 10016
Tel. (212) 687-4470

Fellowships

Individual awards are made to citizens and permanent residents of the United States and Canada, of all the other American states, of the Caribbean, and of the French, Dutch, and British possessions in the Western Hemisphere to allow them "to carry on advanced study in any field of knowledge ... under the freest possible conditions ...."
The size of the approximately 300 fellowships granted each year is tailored to the purpose and scope of the fellow's project.

Alexander Von Humboldt-Stiftung
Bad Godesberg
Auswahllabteilung
Jean-Paul Strasse 12
D-5300 Bonn 2, Federal Republic of Germany

The Humboldt Foundation makes approximately 450 grants annually to scientists of all countries wishing to perform research in any field at a German institution. Applicants must possess a doctoral degree, be new investigators, have professional experience in the health sciences for at least two of the last four years, and provide evidence of acceptance by a sponsor in a German institution.
Awards are for 6-24 months and cover payment of a stipend, with an additional allowance for family, travel expenses, and language courses.

Institute for Intercultural Studies, Inc.
c/o Sloane and Hinshaw
145 East 74th Street, Suite 1C
New York, NY 10021

Grants of up to $2,000 are made for doctoral level research which advances the knowledge of the behavior, customs, psychology, and social organizations of the various peoples and nations of the world.

Institute of International Education (IIE)
809 United Nations Plaza
New York, NY 10017

IIE administers a number of exchange programs involving US and foreign students, primarily at the graduate level. The programs are sponsored by US and foreign governments, corporations, educational institutions, and private organizations. IIE also conducts research in the field of international educational exchange and publishes a variety of guides, directories, and reports on the subject. IIE programs of relevance to US-Latin American exchangs include:

Fulbright Grants for Graduate Study Abroad

US graduate students are eligible for one-year Fulbright grants offered in over 70 countries, including many in Latin America. Interested students should consult IIE's annual booklet entitled "Fulbright and Other grants for Graduate Study Abroad" and the Fulbright Program Adviser on campus for current information. The program is administered by IIE's Study Abroad Programs Division, tel. (212) 883-8266.

Hubert H. Humphrey North-South Fellowship Program

The purpose of this program is to bring to the United States mid-career professionals from developing countries who have demonstrated leadership qualities in certain fields, including health and nutrition, planning and resource management, and public administration. Fellows are placed for one year in US graduate programs. Work-related experience is also provided.

The fellowships cover tuition and fees, international travel, and a monthly stipend of one academic year. Limited support for professional travel within the United States may also be provided.

Applications from candidates are received and processed by binational Fulbright commissions or, where no binational commission exists, by US Embassy committees.

ITT International Fellowship Program

Since 1973 funds provided by the International Telephone and Telegraph Corporation have enabled some 500 graduate students from the United States and more than 50 other countries to spend a year or more studying overseas. ITT chooses the countries that participate in the program. These presently include Argentina, Brazil, Chile, Mexico, and Venezuela.

Foreign ITT Fellows receive an award for one academic year, which may be renewed up to 21 months to complete requirements for a master's degree. The award covers airfare, tuition and fees, an allowance for books and supplies, insurance, and a monthly subsistence allowance.

Prospective fellows from participating Latin American countries should apply through the binational Fulbright commission, or other designated agency, in their country. IIE's Study Abroad Programs Division can inform prospective foreign applicants of the agency to which they should apply.

US fellows receive a one-year stipend, the amount of which varies with the cost of the program and the country of study. It covers maintenance, tuition, books, insurance, and travel. The country of study must be a participating country. US candidates enrolled in academic institutions may obtain further

information and applications from the Fulbright Program Adviser on campus.
Those not enrolled should write to the IEE Study Abroad Programs Division at
the address above.

The Latin American countries that sent or received ITT Fellows between
1973 and 1982 are (with the total number of fellowships involved): Argentina
(7), Brazil (21), Chile (12), Colombia (6), Ecuador (1), El Salvador (1),
Mexico (14), Peru (6), Puerto Rico (4), Uruguay (1), and Venezuela (8).

International Christian Youth Exchange (ICYE)
134 West 26th Street, Room 403
New York, NY 10001

ICYE Scholarships

ICYE offers scholarships to enable young persons to spend a year abroad in
a program committed to international understanding, reconciliation, and social
justice. Participants live with families, work with community organizations,
and become involved in local social issues. The Latin American countries in
which the program operates are Bolivia, Colombia, Costa Rica, and Honduras.
The cost of the program is $4,200, which covers travel, orientation, insurance,
room and board, and incidental spending money. Applicants must be 16 to 24
years of age. The director of the US program is Jim Paulson.

International Federation of University Women
c/o American Association of University Women
2401 Virginia Avenue, NW
Washington, DC 20037

Winifred Cullis Grants

Tenable in the humanities, social sciences, and natural sciences, these
grants are intended to assist women graduates to carry out research, obtain
specialized training essential to their research, or to train in new
techniques. Applicants must be members of a national federation or association
affiliated with the International Federation of University Women. The awards
are not offered every year.

International Union Against Cancer

See entry for American Cancer Society.

Japan Society for the Promotion of Science
Exchange of Persons Division
5-3-1 Kojimachi, Chiyoda-Ku
Tokyo 102, Japan
Tel. (3) 263-1721

The Society contributes to the advancement of science by inviting
scientists in all fields to Japan for cooperative research or other academic
activities. Applicants must be eminent scientists holding the doctoral degree

and must receive an invitation from a Japanese colleague in the same field, who will submit the application on behalf of the applicant.

Short-term awards cover up to four months of discussions, seminars, or lectures. Airfare and subsistence are provided, as well as an allowance for travel within Japan. About 200 such awards are made annually in all fields of science.

Long-term awards are similar in scope, but cover 6-10 months of collaborative research. About 45 such awards are made each year.

Helen Kellogg Institute for International Studies
University of Notre Dame
Notre Dame, IN 46556
Tel. (219) 239-6580

Residential Fellowships

The Institute accepts applications for residential fellowships from candidates from any country holding a PhD or equivalent degree in any discipline of the social sciences. The grants are tenable at the Institute and are based on comparable North American academic salaries, plus round-trip airfare.

The Institute selects fellows whose work will contribute to its research themes, which focus on Latin America and include: (1) alternative policies of economic development and their social consequences; (2) responses of those excluded from participation in political and economic life, including new patterns of association and changes in popular culture; (3) the social roles of religion and the Catholic Church; and (4) the processes and possibilities of democratization.

W. K. Kellogg Foundation
400 North Street
Battle Creek, MI 49017-3398
Tel. (616) 968-1611

International Health Fellowships in Latin America

Doctoral and postdoctoral fellowships are offered to the faculty and staff of Latin American and Caribbean universities and other institutions that are receiving or are being considered for funding from the Kellogg Foundation. Among the Foundation's many areas of academic interest in the health care field are: educational technology, primary health care, maternal and child health, preventive medicine, and epidemiology. Applicants should contact Karen R. Hollenbeck at the address or number above.

Partners of the Americas
1424 K Street, NW
Washington, DC 20005
Tel. (202) 628-3300

Partners of the Americas is a private, nonprofit organization that fosters and administers linkages between the people of over 40 US states and 27 Latin

American and Caribbean countries. The purpose of the links is to mobilize resources at the community level for technical and cultural projects.   Among the organization's projects are:

US-Brazilian University Linkages

A total of 35 US and Brazilian educational institutions are linked in 13 partnerships for the purpose of promoting faculty and student exchange, expanding graduate programs, performing joint research projects, improving curricula, and enlarging library and database holdings.

Travel Grants

These grants are designed to support professionals who wish to travel to their partner area to engage in specific projects for periods of at least 10 days.

Small Grants

Small grants are available for the initiation of projects that promote economic or social development in fields such as health, special education, rehabilitation, and women in development.

Training Grants

Partners of the Americas committees in Latin American or Caribbean countries may nominate professionals to receive advanced training in the partner areas of the United States. The training period may range from six months to two years and may occur in an academic, industrial, professional, or other setting. Grants cover part of the cost of transportation, tuition, living expenses, and materials.

The Rotary Foundation of Rotary International
1600 Ridge Avenue
Evanston, IL 60201
Tel. (312) 328-0100

The Rotary Foundation's graduate and undergraduate scholarships are open to students of any country wishing to spend a year studying abroad. Most applicants use the award for a full-time continuation of ongoing studies in their home country. Requirements concerning character and language ability apply.

Graduate and Undergraduate Scholarships

Candidates for graduate scholarships must be between 18 and 28, must hold a bachelor's degree or the equivalent, and may be married.

Candidates for undergraduate scholarships must be between the ages of 18 and 24 and must have completed at least two years of university study, without having yet received a bachelor's degree. Candidates may not be married.

Teacher of the Handicapped Scholarships

Candidates for these scholarships must be between the ages of 25 and 60, must have completed secondary education, and must have been employed as a full-time teacher of the mentally, physically, or educationally handicapped for at least two years. Candidates may be married.

All Rotary Foundation Scholarships include airfare to and from the place of study, some related travel expenses, tuition and fees, books and supplies, room and board, an allowance for educational travel, and, if needed and agreed to by the Foundation, funds for intensive language training. Each scholarship recipient is assigned a sponsoring Rotarian counselor and a host Rotarian counselor who provide orientation, advice, and assistance to the scholar in preparing for and accomplishing a successful year in a foreign country.

Application for a Rotary Foundation Scholarship must be made through a Rotary club either in the Rotary district in which the applicant's legal or permanent residence is located, or in the Rotary district in which he is studying or employed at the time of making application.

Alfred P. Sloan Foundation
630 Fifth Avenue
New York, NY 10111
Tel. (212) 582-0450

Sloan Research Fellowships

Promising neuroscientists under the age of 32 are eligible for two-year postdoctoral fellowships comprising a stipend, indirect costs, equipment allowance, travel, trainee support, and other activities directly related to the fellow's research.

Social Science Research Council (SSRC)
Office of Fellowships and Grants
605 Third Avenue
New York, NY 10158
Tel. (212) 661-0280

Doctoral Dissertation Research

Fellowships are offered for doctoral dissertation research in social psychology and other areas of the social sciences and humanities on topics related to cultural, social, and scientific development in Latin America and the Caribbean. Applicants must be US citizens or permanent residents, must be engaged in full-time graduate study at a U.S. university, and must have completed all requirements for the doctorate except the dissertation. Applicants should affiliate with a university, research center, or other appropriate institution to be used as a base for the required nine months of field work.

Awards are tenable for 9-18 months and typically cover stipends and transportation expenses for the fellow and dependents, health insurance, and a research allowance. Applicants may request up to six months of support for specialized preparatory training (e.g., in language skills).

Postdoctoral Research Grants

These grants are intended to support social scientists and humanists of any country for research related to cultural, economic, political, social, or scientific development in Latin America or the Caribbean. The research may involve one or more of the countries of the region, as well as countries of other regions.

Latin American scholars may present proposals for research in their own country or abroad. Support is available for periods of 2-12 months, and applications may be submitted in English, Spanish, or Portuguese. The maximum grant is $15,000. Additional funds for courses to increase competence in research or language training may be requested.

US and Canadian applicants must hold the doctorate; others must have an academic degree acceptable for a university career in their own country.

International Collaborative Research Grants

Grants are offered to pairs of scholars in the social sciences or humanities for research dealing with modern Latin American or Caribbean cultures, societies, or institutions. One scholar must be working in and be a citizen of a Latin American or Caribbean country; the other must be working in another country within or outside Latin America and the Caribbean.

The maximum award is $15,000. Applications may be submitted in English, Spanish, or Portuguese.

Seminars and Conference Grants

The SSRC Joint Committee on Latin American Studies brings together groups of scholars in seminars and conferences designed to advance social scientific and humanistic research in and on Latin America and the Caribbean. Projects may be initiated by submitting a letter of inquiry to the program staff. Preference is given to projects in which the committee can take an active intellectual role. Cost-sharing is encouraged.

The Tinker Foundation
645 Madison Avenue
New York, NY 10022
Tel. (212) 421-6858

Tinker Postdoctoral Fellowships

Citizens of the United States, Canada, Spain, Portugal, and the Spanish- and Portuguese-speaking countries of Latin America are eligible to apply for one-year postdoctoral awards of $25,000 for support of research in the social sciences or international relations. Candidates must have received their doctorates no less than three years, but no more than ten years, prior to the time of application.

Tinker Field Research Grants

Recognized centers or institutes of Latin American studies based at US universities and offering a doctoral degree are eligible to apply for Field Research Grants to support graduate students and junior faculty for brief

periods of research in Latin America. Each program receiving one of the
$15,000 grants (which must be matched by at least $5,000 from the university
that houses the recipient program) conducts a competition to select the
individual grantees.

Woodrow Wilson International Center for Scholars
Latin American Program
Smithsonian Institution Building
Washington, DC 20560
Tel. (202) 357-2841

Fellowships

The Latin American Program seeks outstanding project proposals in any
field, with particular attention given to projects examining the interplay
between cultural traditions and political institutions, the history of ideas,
and the evolution of US-Latin American relations. Fellows will devote four
months to a year in full-time research and writing at the Center. Fellowships
are intended for established scholars at the postdoctoral level.

Guest Scholars Program

The accommodations, facilities, and services of the Center and its staff
will be made available for short-term use by distinguished guest scholars by
arrangement with the director of the Center. Preference is given to scholars
working on significant international, governmental, and social problems.

Resources and References

Institutional Resources

Much of the material in this chapter was drawn from the publications of
the organizations listed below, which provide information or services useful to
individuals seeking support for individual or collaborative international
exchanges. They are valuable resources indeed. However, the most valuable and
accessible resources could not be listed in this book. They are the
international studies officers at US colleges and universities, and the
reference librarians who provide guidance (at no cost!) to the vast array of
directories, guides, compendia, and other reference works that exists to orient
the individual engaged in planning international educational or scientific
exchanges.

Up-to-date information and new leads can also be obtained by those willing
to proceed crabwise through the bureaucratic circuitry of the United States
Government (and, we presume, other governments as well). In the United States,
this is best done by telephone, and the seeker is well advised to consult one
of the available guides to the government's departments and agencies (e.g., The
Federal Yellow Book) which can usually be found in the reference section of
libraries. Of course, many of the most useful addresses and phone numbers can
be found in this chapter!

Embassies and consulates are another source of information on educational
opportunities and fellowships. See chapter 10.

Finally, notices of individual grants and fellowships appear in newspapers and periodicals such as The Chronicle of Higher Education and the APA Monitor. On the level of larger-scale grants and contracts for research and services, the US Government places requests for proposals in the Commerce Business Daily, The Federal Register, and other publications. Needless to say, the grants officers of US universities make a point of staying abreast of such information.

American Psychological Association
International Affairs Office
1200 Seventeenth Street, NW
Washington, DC 20036
(202) 955-7685

The APA International Affairs Office serves as a point of contact between the APA and colleagues and students abroad who seek professional ties in the United States or information on psychological study, research, and practice in the United States. The Office can provide information on the Association's annual convention and publications. The Office also coordinates APA's activities in the field of international human rights.

Asociacion Panamericana de Instituciones de Credito Educativo (APICE)
Calle 38 No. 8-56, Oficina 202
Apartado Aereo 17388
Bogota, Colombia

APICE is a union of educational credit organizations in Latin America. Among other activities, APICE sponsors seminars and congresses in which educational credit concerns, including international study, are addressed.

The College Board
Publications, Department C43
Box 886
New York, NY 10101

The College Board is a nonprofit organization that provides tests and other educational services, including publications, for students, schools, and colleges. The membership is composed of more than 2,600 colleges, schools, school systems, and education associations.
Among its publications of international interest are the pamphlets entitled "Financial Planning for Study in the United States," and "Entering Higher Education in the United States." A complete catalogue of publications in the area of admissions, financial aid, international education, etc., is available.

The Foundation Center
888 Seventh Avenue
New York, NY 10106
(212) 975-1120
(800) 424-9836 (toll-free number for current information)

The Foundation Center is a national service organization founded and supported by US foundations to provide a single authoritative source of information on foundation giving. The center accomplishes its purposes by publishing reference books on foundations, foundation grants, and philanthropy; disseminating information on foundations through a nationwide public information and education program, which makes use of the resources of two national libraries (in New York and Washington), two field libraries (in Cleveland and San Francisco), and a network of over 160 cooperating library collections, including one in Puerto Rico and one in Mexico City; and operating special service programs that facilitate the search for funding.

Among the special services are the Foundation Center's computer database products, such as the "Comsearch" series of computerized searches focusing on foundation giving for specific purposes, including Social Science Programs, International & Foreign Programs, Minorities, Public Health, Family Services, Medical & Professional Health Education, Physically and Mentally Disabled, Alcohol & Drug Abuse, Children & Youth, and Psychology & Behavioral Sciences. "Comsearch" products are available online (through DIALOG Information Services) or as bound reports.

Among the Foundation Center's publications are The Foundation Directory (10th edition, October 1985, $65.00), and a Supplement published in October 1986 ($35.00). The Directory contains "full facts and figures on over 4,400 of the largest US foundations" and is well indexed for easy use. Also available is Foundation Grants to Individuals (5th edition, October 1986, $18), which contains information on the giving programs of 1,041 foundations that award grants of $2,000 or more to individual applicants. Again, the book is well indexed.

The Center's cooperating collection in Mexico is located at the Biblioteca Benjamin Franklin, Londres 16, Mexico City 6, DF, tel. 591-0244. In Puerto Rico, the cooperating collection is located at the Universidad del Sagrado Corazon, MMT Guerarra Library, Correo Calle Loiza, Santurce 00914, tel. (809) 728-1515, ext. 343.

Institute of International Education
809 United Nations Plaza
New York, NY 10017
(212) 883-8200

The Institute of International Education is an excellent source of information, much of it provided free of charge. Titles of available pamphlets include, "A Guide to Scholarships, Fellowships, and Grants: A Selected Bibliography"; "Basic Facts on Foreign Study"; "Financial Resources for International Study: A Selected Bibliography"; and "Bibliography on Higher Education: A World View." In addition, IIE operates an International Education Information Center that is open daily to the interested public for research purposes.

IIE operates programs for foreign visitors under contract to the US Information Agency, and administers a number of grant and fellowship programs for US citizens and foreign nationals (see IIE entry earlier in this chapter).

IIE's annual publication, Open Doors: Report on International Educational Exchange, constitutes a census of foreign students in the United States. The Institute also publishes annual directories of study-abroad opportunities (see bibliography below). A complete catalogue of IIE publications can be obtained from the Institute's Publications and Communications Division.

Intercultural Press
PO Box 768
Yarmouth, Maine 04096
(207) 846-5168

The press describes itself as "the biggest source of mail-order books on cross-cultural training subjects." Its list includes dozens of titles in the broad area of intercultural communication and exchange, including many produced by SIETAR (see above). Many of the works cited in chapter 10 are available from the Intercultural Press.

National Association for Foreign Student Affairs
1860 Nineteenth Street, NW
Washington, DC 20009
(202) 462-4811

With 5,400 members in the United States and 50 foreign countries, NAFSA represents over 1,600 academic institutions, educational associations, local citizens' groups, and associates from foreign embassies in Washington.

NAFSA has published more than 350 books, reports, research studies, and working papers in the area of foreign student education and international educational interchange, and has organized professional workshops, seminars, and other consultations for individuals involved in international exchange.

The NAFSA Directory of Institutions and Individuals in International Educational Exchange is an excellent biennial resource. The association also makes available a free "Bibliography on Study, Work, and Travel Abroad" (1982).

NAFSA offers a variety of grants to support campus and community programs and activities that enrich the experience of foreign students in the United States, enhance the preparation and return of US students studying abroad, and improve and expand the competencies of those who work with foreign students and US students going abroad. The association currently operates four major funding programs, which are supported by the US Information Agency and the US Agency for International Development. These are described in NAFSA's pamphlet, "Funding Opportunities through the National Association for Foreign Student Affairs."

National (and International) Scholarship Research Service
122 Alto Street
San Rafael, CA 94901
(415) 456-1577

NSRS maintains a databank of over 200,000 listings for scholarships, fellowships, grants, and loans, representing over $10 billion in private-sector funding (corporations, trusts, foundations, religious groups), providing an alternative, or supplement, to government funding sources.

Prospective undergraduate or graduate students who fill out a detailed application and enclose a fee of $45 will receive a printout of sources of funding matched to the application submitted, along with lists of other organizations and publications that can provide further assistance.

Sietar International
1505 Twenty-Second Street, NW
Washington, DC 20037
(202) 296-4710

The International Society for Intercultural Education, Training and Research (SIETAR International) is an international association of individuals and institutions concerned with promoting effective intercultural interaction through conferences, workshops, and other participatory programs held in various locations throughout the world, and a variety of publications (including training manuals and reference works).

The annual SIETAR International conference features experiential workshops, formal presentations, symposia, and a variety of other programs and cultural events. Membership is open to individuals or institutions concerned with intercultural communication, cross-cultural relations, and associated fields.

Bibliography of Financial Support for International Activities

The list that follows concentrates on guides, directories, and bibliographies with an international focus. However, a number of general resources are also listed. Readers are also urged to consult the free bibliographies provided by IIE, NAFSA, and other organizations (see preceding section), and to make liberal use of the resources available in the reference sections of large libraries, which generally have available costly and comprehensive sources such as the <u>Directory of Federal Aid</u>, the <u>Catalog of Federal Domestic Assistance</u>, or the <u>Directory of Research Grants</u>. The great bulk of the information contained in this chapter was abstracted from the sources listed below.

American Psychological Association. (1987). <u>Graduate Study in Psychology and Associated Fields, 1986 (With 1987 Addendum)</u>. Washington, DC: Author.

This biennial volume contains practical information on more than 600 graduate programs in the United States and Canada. Each listing provides specific information on the programs the institution offers, including areas of study, faculty/student statistics, financial aid provisions, tuition and fees, teaching opportunities, housing facilities, degree requirements, program goals, and more.

Brown, W.T., Cassani, R., & Dembo, D. (1986). <u>The CISP International Studies Funding Book</u>. New York: Council on International and Public Affairs. (ISBN 0-939288-06-0)

The purpose of this looseleaf-format book is to provide college and university faculty and administrators with information necessary to enable them to implement programs in international/intercultural education. In addition to providing a listing of funding programs for institutions, faculty, and students, the <u>Funding Book</u> provides profiles of international studies organizations, as well as discursive and bibliographic information on current trends in international studies, funding for international programs, how to write a grant proposal, and foreign sources of support.

Fogarty International Center for Advanced Study in the Health Sciences. (1984). <u>Directory of International Opportunities in Biomedical and Behavioral Sciences</u>. Washington, DC: US Government Printing Office. (GPO 1984 461 320 4822)

This 64-page booklet is devoted to a listing of fellowships in the biomedical and behavioral sciences for US and foreign nationals.

Herring, K.L. (Ed.). (1987). <u>Guide to Research Support</u>. Washington: American Psychological Association.

Information on 180 US Federal programs and 70 nonfederal organizations that fund behavioral science research, with contact names, addresses, and telephone numbers. For each program or organization listed, the <u>Guide</u> describes the types of projects supported and analyzes grants made in previous years.

Howard, E. (Ed.). (1987). <u>Academic Year Abroad (The Learning Traveler: Vol. 1)</u>. New York: Author (ISBN 87206-149-3)

This is the sixteenth edition of IIE's annual guide to study-abroad programs sponsored or cosponsored by US colleges and universities during the academic year. This edition contains information on 1,100 programs, and includes useful information on planning for study abroad.

Institute of International Education. (1986). <u>Vacation Study Abroad (The Learning Traveler, Vol. 2)</u>. New York: Author (ISBN 87206-148-5)

The companion volume to <u>Academic Year Abroad</u>, containing information on over 1,000 summer and short-term study-abroad programs.

Institute of International Education. (1986). <u>Specialized Study Options USA, 1986-88 (Vol. 2: Professional Development)</u>. New York: Author. (ISBN 87206-141-8)

This is "a guide to short-term educational programs in the United States for foreign nationals." The chapter devoted to "Psychology, Psychiatry, and Psychotherapy" consists of just six entries, although other headings such as "Social Sciences" and "Social Research" describe opportunities that may be of interest to psychologists and students of psychology.

Laughlin, P.R. (Ed.). (1985-86). <u>Directory of Internship Programs in Professional Psychology</u>. Knoxville, Iowa: Association of Psychology Internship Centers.

The <u>Directory</u> is issued as a service to students and professional psychology training directors by the Association of Psychology Internship Centers (PO Box 574, Knoxville, Iowa 50138). The information provided is intended to serve as a guide to students and their directors of training in helping to identify those programs which are likely to meet their particular training needs. The price of the guide varies, but is around $30.

Leider, A.J. (Ed.). (1986). <u>Scholarships for International Students: A</u>
<u>Complete Guide to United States Colleges and Universities</u>. Alexandria, VA:
Octameron Press. (ISBN 0-917760-84-0)

This book was designed to assist non-US students wishing to study in the
United States. The book covers choosing and paying for a university education,
visa and immigration requirements, and US customs and lifestyle, as well as
providing data on 3,000 US institutions of higher education. Appendices
provide the names and addresses of 92 binational centers in 18 Latin American
countries that provide information about education in the United States, as
well as the addresses of the binational Fulbright commissions (see entry for
CIES in the body of this chapter), of foreign embassies in the United States,
and of the offices of the US Immigration and Naturalization Service. This
particularly useful and relatively inexpensive ($14.95) book may be obtained
from the Scholarship Research Group, 16600 Sprague Road, Suite 110, Middleburg
Heights, OH 44130, tel. (216) 243-0133 and 243-1030.

Office of International Programs, University of Minnesota. (1985). <u>Directory</u>
<u>of Financial Aids for International Activities</u>. Minneapolis: Author.

The bulk of this 330-page guide is devoted to listings of sources of
support for individuals seeking to study or perform research abroad. The same
sort of information as found in the <u>Directory of Research Grants</u> can be found
in this less expensive, and less expansive, guide. Write Office of
International Programs, University of Minnesota, 201 Nolte West, 315 Pillsbury
Drive, SE, Minneapolis, MN 55455, or call (612) 373-3793.

Oryx Press. (1987). <u>Directory of Research Grants</u>. Phoenix, AZ: Author. (ISBN
0-89774-337-7)

The <u>Directory</u> is a "tool for individuals and institutions in search of
support for research and other creative endeavors." Over 5,700 grant programs
are arranged alphabetically by grant title. Each entry includes a description,
deadline date, program number (for US Federal programs), restrictions or
requirements, addresses, telephone numbers, and funding amounts.

Sivon, E.W. (1984, rev. 1985). <u>Private Sector Funding Available to Foreign</u>
<u>Scholars and Students in the United States</u>. Washington, DC: National
Association for Foreign Student Affairs.

This 54-page booklet, available from NAFSA (address above), is intended as
"a sourcebook for foreign students and scholars already in the United States
who are seeking additional financial resources to complete their US education."
The sources listed are primarily US private, nonprofit organizations. Support
available from US government agencies and US colleges and universities is
generally not included. Indexes and bibliography. Price: $2.95.

UNESCO. (1986). <u>Study Abroad XXV: 1987-88</u>. Paris: Author. (ISBN 92-3-
002337-X)

The current edition contains over 1,300 pages of information on
international courses and scholarships in all fields. Extensively indexed.
Comprehensive listing of international organizations and educational
institutions from nearly every country in the world.

A variety of fellowships, grants, services and bibliographic resources is available for teachers wishing to spend a period of time abroad. These range from job placement services to conventional grants for short-term exchanges. We close this chapter with a sample of such services and materials.

Placement and Recruitment Services

International Schools Services
126 Alexander Street
PO Box 5910
Princeton, NJ 08540
(609) 921-9110

ISS is a private, nonprofit organization founded in 1955 to support and advance the education of expatriate children living around the world. ISS provides recruitment and other services to American and International Schools overseas that enroll children of business and diplomatic families living away from their home countries. Most of the schools are independent and governed by boards of directors drawn from the communities in which they are located. ISS serves approximately 700 such schools throughout the world. A brochure and preliminary registration form can be obtained by writing to the address above.

Office of Dependents Schools
(US) Department of Defense
2461 Eisenhower Avenue
Alexandria, VA 22331

The Office of Dependents Schools of the US Department of Defense operates approximately 270 elementary, middle, junior high, and high schools, as well as one two-year college, in 20 countries around the world. Enrollment is approximately 136,000 students, served by a staff of 11,000. The DoD overseas school system thus ranks among the largest US school systems. Teachers interested in the possibility of teaching in the DoD overseas system should contact the Office of Dependents Schools and obtain the booklet entitled Overseas Employment Opportunities for Educators.

RISE: Register for International Service in Education
Box CH
Institute of International Education
809 United Nations Plaza
New York, NY 10017
(212) 883-8241

RISE is a computer-based referral service designed to enable universities, technical institutes, research centers, government ministries, and development projects outside the United States to locate qualified educators, specialists, researchers, technicians, and consultants for education-related assignments.

Although created primarily to help developing countries locating help in development-related fields, RISE is open to prospective employers worldwide and to individuals in all fields of specialization. Those qualified to teach, consult, or conduct research at the university or other postsecondary level are invited to register. US citizenship is not required.

Grant and Exchange Programs

Center for International Education
US Department of Education
400 Maryland Avenue, SW
Washington, DC 20202-3223

The Center for Internatioanl Education is responsible for expanding the international and global dimensions of US education. Although it administers projects that fund summer seminars for teachers, as well as post- and predoctoral research, and although Central America and the Caribbean have a special status in several of its projects, all of the Center's activities are focused primarily on foreign languages and area studies, with secondary emphasis on the humanities, economics, geography, political science, and sociology. Interested individuals may wish to write the Center for a full description of its activities.

Fulbright Teacher Exchange Program
c/o Teacher Exchange Branch (E/ASX)
US Information Agency
Bureau of Educational and Cultural Affairs
301 Fourth Street, SW
Washington, DC 20547
(202) 485-2555

This competitive program enables American educators to teach in an educational system abroad, and educators from other countries to teach in schools and junior colleges in the United States. US teachers may also participate in short-term seminars offered during the summer. Annual exchanges average approximately 300 in each direction. The program primarily involves the United States, Canada, and Europe.

Peace Corps
806 Connecticut Avenue, NW
Washington, DC 20526

The Peace Corps maintains approximately 1,000 positions for teachers at all educational levels and in all subjects, with an emphasis on technical and vocational training, agriculture, and the teaching of English as a second language.

Rotary Foundation of Rotary International
1600 Ridge Avenue
Evanston, Illinois 60201

The Rotary Foundation annually awards 10 grants of $10,000 to selected higher-education faculty to enable the latter to teach for a period of 6-10 months at universities in countries other than their own, especially in developing countries. The fields taught must have international applications in the general areas of economic, political, social, or cultural studies. Application must be made to a Rotary Club in the Rotary district in which the applicant holds academic appointment. A brochure describing the program is available from the Rotary Foundation at the address above.

Bibliography

Connotillo, B.C. (Ed.) (1984). Teaching Abroad (The Learning Traveler. Vol 3). New York: Institute of International Education. (ISBN 0-87206-124-8)

Teaching Abroad describes the scope of formal teacher exchange programs, faculty needs as reported by non-US governments, and the approximate number of faculty positions available annually within US and international schools abroad. Approximately 20 pages of entries pertain to educational institutions in Latin America.

International Schools Services. (1984). The ISS Directory of Overseas Schools. Princeton, NJ: Author. (ISBN 0-913663-01-8)

A 460-page directory of US and international schools throughout the world. An appendix provides the names and addresses of associations of US schools in South America, Central America, and the Caribbean.

9

Bibliography on Latin American Psychology

A bibliography of significant articles in various languages on the history and current status of psychology in Latin America forms the body of this chapter. The publications listed here will be of interest to those who wish to know more about the development and general orientation and achievements of psychology in the region.

The bibliography is generally limited to publications that have appeared since 1970, although some earlier articles of wide historical interest are included as well. As with any bibliography, ours is not totally comprehensive, although we have tried to make it as complete as possible. Sources consulted in compiling this listing include APA's PsycINFO database, the files of the journal Spanish-Language Psychology, the catalogue of the Hispanic division of the Library of Congress, the Columbus Memorial Library of the Organization of American States, collections of a number of relevant Latin American journals, the authors' files, and references submitted to us by interested colleagues.

General

Abt, L. E. (1964). Clinical psychology in Latin America. In L. E. Abt & B. F. Rieses (Eds.), Progress in Clinical Psychology (Vol. 6). New York: Grune & Stratton.

Aiza, V. M. (1984). Corrientes actuantes en el pensamiento psicoanalitico latinoamericano. Revista de Psicoanalisis, 61, 609-624.

Alarcon, A. M. (1976). Hacia una identidad de la psiquiatria latinoamericana. Boletin de la Oficina Sanitaria Panamericana, 81, 109-121.

Alvarez, A. M. (1981). El I Seminario Internacional de Psicologia en la Comunidad (Cuba). Revista Latinoamericana de Psicologia, 13, 293-296.

Alvarez Cuadros, R. (1984). Relexiones informales acerca de la actividad del psicologo. Revista Interamericana de Psicologia Ocupacional, 13, 55-58.

Angelini, A (1979). The role of the Interamerican Society of Psychology in the development of psychology in Latin America. Revista Interamericana de Psicologia/Interamerican Journal of Psychology, 13, 5-25.

Ardila, R. (1968). Psychology in Latin America. American Psychologist, 23, 567-574.

Ardila, R. (1969). Desarollo de la psicologia latinoamericana. Revista Latinoamericana de Psicologia, 1, 63-74.

Ardila, R. (1970). Jose Ingenieros, psychologist. Journal of the History of the Behavioral Sciences, 6, 41-47.

Ardila, R. (1970). La psychologie Latino-americaine. Bulletin de Psychologie, 23, 410-415.

Ardila, R. (1970). Landmarks in the history of Latin American Psychology. Journal of the History of Behavioral Sciences, 6, 1401-1446.

Ardila, R. (1971). Acontecimientos importantes en la historia de la psicologia latinoamericana. Revista Interamericana de Psicologia/Interamerican Journal of Psychology, 5, 1-11.

Ardila, R. (1971). La psicologia en America Latina. Revista de Psicologia General y Aplicada, 26, 359-369.

Ardila, R. (1971). Professional problems of psychology in Latin America. Revista Interamericana de Psicologia/Interamerican Journal of Psychology, 5, 53-57.

Ardila, R. (1973). The Interamerican Society of Psychology. American Psychologist, 28, 1137-1138.

Ardila, R. (1973). La situacion de la psicologia en 1973. Razon y Fabula, 31, 3-12.

Ardila, R. (Ed.). (1974). El analisis experimental del comportamiento: La contribucion latinoamericana. Mexico: Trillas.

Ardila, R. (1975). The XV Interamerican Congress of Psychology. International Journal of Psychology, 10, 89-90.

Ardila, R. (1975). The first Latin American Conference on Training in Latin America. International Journal of Psychology, 10, 149-158.

Ardila, R. (1976). Educational psychology in Latin America. In C. D. Catterall (Ed.), Psychology in the schools in international perspective, Vol 1. Columbus: International School Psychology Steering Committee.

Ardila, R. (1976) Latin America. In V. S. Sexton & H. Misiak (Eds.), Psychology around the world. Monterey, CA: Brooks/Cole.

Ardila, R. (1977) Latin America: Psychology. In B. B. Wolman (Ed.), International encyclopedia of psychiatry, psychology, psychoanalysis and neurology. (Vol. 6, pp. 353-355). New York: Aescuplaius Publishers.

Ardila, R. (1977) La psicologia profesional en latinoamerica: Roles cambiantes para una sociedad en proceso de tranformacion. Esenanza e Investigacion en Psicologia, 3(1), 5-20.

Ardila, R. (1978). Los 10 primeros anos de la Revista Latinoamericana de Psicologia. Revista Latinoamericana de Psicologia, 10, 321-326.

Ardila, R. (1978) Behavior modification in Latin America. In M. Hersen, R. M. Eisler, & P. M. Miller (Eds.), Progress in behavior modification, (Vol. 6, pp. 123-142). New York: Academic Press.

Ardila, R. (Ed.). (1978). La profesion del psicologo. Mexico: Trillas.

Ardila, R. (1978). El entrenamiento de los psicologos latinoamericanos: Analisis de los problemas y una propuesta de solucion. In R. Ardila (Ed.), La profesion del psicologo. Mexico: Trillas.

Ardila, R. (1978). Entrenamiento en psicologia clinica. In R. Ardila (Ed.), La profesion del psicologo. Mexico: Trillas.

Ardila, R. (1978). Conclusiones de la I Conferencia Latinoamericana sobre Entrenamiento en Psicologia. In R. Ardila (Ed.), La profesion del psicologo. Mexico: Trillas.

Ardila, R. (1980). Latin America. In J. Brozek & L. J. Pongratz (Eds.), Historiography of modern psychology. Toronto: C. J. Hogrefe.

Ardila, R. (1981). The evolution of psychology in Latin America. Spanish-Language Psychology, 1, 337-346.

Ardila, R. (1982). International Psychology. American Psychologist, 37, 323-329.

Ardila, R. (1982). La terapia del comportamiento en America Latina. Ensenanza e Investigacion en Psicologia, 8(1), 5-15.

Ardila, R. (1982). Psychology in Latin America today. Annual Review of Psychology, 33, 103-122.

Ardila, R. (1982). International developments in behavior therapy in Latin America. Journal of Behavior Therapy & Experimental Psychology, 13, 469-472.

Ardila, R. (1986). La Psicologia en america latina: Pasado, presente y futuro. Bogota: Siglo Veintinno, 209 pages.

Ardila, R. & Finley, G. E. (1975). Psychology in Latin America: A bibliography. Revista Interamericana de Psicologia/Interamerican Journal of Psychology, 9, Whole Nos. 3-4.

Argandona, M., & Kiev, A. (1972). Mental health in the developing world: A case study in Latin America. New York: Free Press.

Asociacion Psicoanalitica Argentina (1984). XV Congreso Psicoanalitico de America Latina. Revista de Psicoanalisis, 61(4,5).

Baranger, W., & Mom, J. M. (1984). Corrientes actuantes en el pensamiento psicoanalitico de America Latina. Revista de Psicoanalisis, 61, 589-608.

Barreto, C. A., Lacombe, F., Pelegrino, H., Lima, J., & Chebaby, W. (1984). Corrientes actuantes en el pensamiento psicoanalitico de America Latina. Revista de Psicoanalisis, 61, 625-632.

Barrientos, G. A. (1967). Publicaciones psicologicas profesionales en Espanol y Portugues. Revista Interamericana de Psicologia/Interamerican Journal of Psychology, 1, 172-174.

Beebe-Center, J. G., & McFarland, R. A. (1941). Psychology in South America. Psychological Bulletin, 38, 627-667.

Bermann, G. (1972). Psiquiatria comparada en America Latina. Revista de Neuro-psiquiatria, 35, 14-20.

Bertin, M. A. (1974). An overview of psychology in Latin America. Chicago: Office of Naval Research.

Campos Santelicas, A., Brenes, A., & Quevedo Reyes, S. (1980). Crisis, dependencia y contradicciones de la psicologia en America Latina. Revista Latinoamericana de Psicologia, 12, 11-27.

Castano, D. A., & Sanchez, G. (1978). Problemas de la importacion de conceptos de la psicologia industrial a paises en desarrollo. Revista Latinoamericana de Psicologia, 10, 71-82.

Castro Sanchez, R. (1980). Las implicaciones ideologicas y politicas de la psicologia. Santo Domingo: Author.

Clair, D. J. (1972). Hospitalizacion de pacientes mentales en suramerica. Revista Latinoamericana de Psicologia, 4, 117-128.

Colotla, V. A., & Ribes Inesta, E. (1981). Behavior analysis in Latin America: A historical overview. Spanish-Language Psychology, 1, 121-136.

Cortada de Kohan, N. (1978). El entrenamiento de psicologos en tecnicas de investigacion. In R. Ardila (Ed.), La profesion del psicologo. Mexico: Trillas.

Cruz, J. R. (1981). De Rappaport a Marx: Una posicion Dominicana. Actualidad en Psicologia, 3, 35-44.

D'Arrigo Busnello, E. (1980). Psiquiatria dos subdesenvolvidos ou psiquiatria subdesenvolvida? Boletin de la Oficina Panamericana de la Salud, 89, 322-327.

De La Torre Molina, C. (1983). La influencia de la psicologia Norteamericana en el desarrollo y crisis acutal de la psicologia clinica en America Latina. Revista del Hospital Psiquiatrico de La Habana, 24, 21-34.

Diaz Guerrero, R. (1978). La semantica general en la formacion del psicologo. In R. Ardila (Ed.), La profesion del psicologo. Mexico: Trillas.

Diaz Guerrero, R. (1971). La ensenanza de la investigacion en psicologia en
America Latina: Un paradigma. Revista Latinoamericana de Psicologia, 3, 5-
36.

Escovar, L. A. (1977). El psicologo social y el desarollo. Psicologia, 4,
367-377.

Finley, G. E. (1981). Aging in Latin America. Spanish-Language Psychology,
1, 223-248.

Fonseca, J. J. (1973). Los psicologos en el tercer mundo. Puebla, Mexico:
Universidad Autonoma de Puebla.

Fuenmayor, J., Marcano, S., Melia, J., Torres de Carvalho, A. T., & Valedon, C.
(1984). Corrientos actuantes en el pensamiento psicoanalitico
latinoamericano. Revista de Psicolanalisis, 61, 633-640.

Gallegos, X., & Colotla, V. A. (1980). A revised list of Spanish translations
of operant terminology. Journal of the Experimental Analysis of Behavior,
33, 409-414.

Goldstein, N., & Marucco, N. C., Saimovici, E., & Weissman, F. (1984).
Relexiones sobre las vicisitudes de las ideas psicoanaliticas en America
Latina. Revista de Psicoanalisis, 61, 903-912.

Gonzalez, J. M. (1978). Entrenamiento en psicologia: El punto de vista de un
estudiante. In R. Ardila (Ed.), La profesion del psicologo. Mexico: Trillas.

Gonazalez, R. (1976). Tendencias de la salud mental en America Latina.
Revista de Psicoanalisis, 22, 232-237.

Gonzalez, R. (1976). Salud mental en America Latina: Problemas y
perspectivas. Boletin de la Oficina Sanitaria Panamericana, 81, 93-108.

Hall, M. E. (1946). The present status of psychology in South America.
Psychological Bulletin, 43, 441-476.

Halpern, R. (1980). Early childhood programs in Latin America. Harvard
Educational Review, 50, 481-495.

Heineken, E. (1979). Zur lage der psychologie in Lateinamerika. Sonderdruck
aus Psychologie Rundschau, 30, 257-268.

Hereford, C. P. (1966). Current status of psychology in Latin America. Latin
America Research Review, 1, 97-109.

Holtzman, W. H. (1970). Los seminarios internacionales de psicologia de
Texas: Un experimento continuo de intercambio transcultural en psicologia.
Revista Interamericana de Psicologia/Interamerican Journal of Psychology, 4,
279-282.

Horas, P. A. (1978). Rol, posicion legal y formacion del psicologo
educacional. In R. Ardila (Ed.), La profesion del psicologo. Mexico:
Trillas.

Leon, C. (1972). Psychiatry in Latin America. British Journal of Psychiatry, 121, 121-136.

Leon, C. (1976). Perspectivas de la salud mental comunitaria en latinoamericana. Boletin de la Oficina Sanitaria Panamericana, 81, 122-138.

Leon, C. (1981). Reflexiones en torno a la salud mental comunitaria en nuestro medio. Revista Colombiana de Psiquiatria, 10, 91-105.

Leon, C. (1982-83). Perspectives on mental health care for Latin America. International Journal of Mental Health, 11, 84-97.

Leon, R. (1981). El primer congreso latinoamericano de psicologia (1950): Un evento olvidado. Revista Latinoamericana de Psicologia, 13, 345-359.

Leon, R. (1981). El aporte de Blumenfeld a la psicologia en habla castellana. Revista de Psicologia General y Aplicada, 36, 941-951.

Leon, R. (1982). Historiografia sudamericana de la psicologia: Una panoramica. Revista de Historia de la Psicologia, 3, 157-169.

Leon, R. (1982). Los psicoanalistas latinoamericanos y la difusion de sus trabajos en la revista Internationale Zeitschrift for Psychoanlyse: Un estudio bibliometrico. Revista Latinoamericana de Psicologia, 14, 171-182.

Litvinoff, N., & Gomel, S. K. (1975). El psicologo y su profesion. Buenos Aires: Nueva Vision.

Mainou Abad, V. (1980). Psicologia humanistica: Bibliografia castellana. Ensenanza e Investigacion en Psicologia, 6, 140-147.

Malgrat, C. M. (1978). La formacion del psicologo y politica nacional. In R. Ardila (Ed.), La profesion del psicologo. Mexico: Trillas.

Mansilla, A. (1973). El servicio de orientacion y algunos de los problemas de su organizacion en America del Sur. Revista Interamericana de Psicologia/Interamerican Journal of Psychology, 7, 91-101.

Mariategui, J. (1980). Hermilio Valdizan, la psiquiatria comparativa y la medicina folklorica. Acta Psiquiatrica y Psicologica de America Latina, 26, 96-106.

Marin, G. (Ed.). (1975). La psicologia social en Latinoamerica. Mexico: Trillas.

Marin, G. (1978). La psicologia social y el desarrollo de la America Latina. Boletin de la Asociacion Venzolana de Psicologia Social, 1(3), 1-12.

Marin, G. (1978). Entrenamiento del psicologo social en Latinoamerica. In R. Ardila (Ed.), La profesion del psicologo. Mexico: Trillas.

Marin, G. (1979). Inter-American Society of Psychology (SIP). In B. B. Wolman (Ed.), International directory of psychology. New York: Plenum Press.

Marin, G. (1979). Social psychology in Latin America: An annotated
bibliography for 1977. <u>JSAS catalogue of selected documents in psychology</u>,
<u>9</u>, 8, Ms. No. 1809.

Marin, G. (1981). Latin American research in social psychology: An annotated
bibliography for 1978-1979. <u>Basic and Applied Social Psychology</u>, <u>2</u>, 137-159.

Marin, G. (Ed.). (1981). <u>La psicologia social en Latinoamerica</u> (Vol. 2).
Mexico: Trillas.

Marin, G. (1983). The Latin American experience in applying social psychology
to community change. In F. Blackner (Ed.), <u>Social psychology and developing
countries</u>. Chichester, U.K.: Wiley.

Marin, G. (1984). Difusion internacional de la psicologia Iberoamericana.
<u>Papeles del Colegio de Psicologos</u>, <u>3</u>(16/17), 48-52.

Marin, G., & Pearlman, S. (1982). Drug use among Latin American youth: A
bibliography. <u>Spanish-Language Psychology</u>, <u>2</u>, 75-90.

Martin-Baro, I. (Ed.). (1976). <u>Problemas de psicologia social en America
Latina</u>. San Salvador: Universidad Centroamericana.

Martin-Baro, I. (1985). El papel del psicologo en el contexto
centroamericano. <u>Boletin de Psicologia</u>, <u>4</u>, 99-112.

Molina Aviles, J. (1983). El metodo en psicologia: Un punto de vista
dialectico. <u>Ensenanza e Investigacion en Psicologia</u>, <u>9</u>(2), 227-232.

Montero, M. (1980). La psicologia social y el desarrollo de comunidades en
America Latina. <u>Revista Latinoamericana de Psicologia</u>, <u>12</u>, 159-170.

Montesinos, J., Cuvo, A., & Preciado, J. (1983). Aspectos etico-legales de la
modificacion del comportamiento en America Latina. <u>Revista Latinoamericana
de Psicologia</u>, <u>15</u>, 295-309.

Navarro, M. (1979). Research on Latin American women. <u>Signs</u>, <u>5</u>, 111-120.

Negrete, J. C. (1976). El alcohol y las drogas como problema de salud en
America Latina. <u>Boletin de la Oficina Sanitaria Panamericana</u>, <u>81</u>, 158-175.

Ortega, M., & Munoz, C. (1984). Analisis de la situacion de la psicologia
industrial. <u>Revista Interamericana de Psicologia Ocupacional</u>, <u>3</u>, 59-62.

Padilla, A. M. (1980). Notes on the history of Hispanic psychology. <u>Hispanic
Journal of Behavioral Sciences</u>, <u>2</u>, 109-128.

Portillo, G. (1978). La nueva ciencia social latinoamericana y la teoria
dependentista. <u>Psicologia</u>, <u>5</u>, 125-131.

Ramirez, M. (1983). <u>Psychology of the Americas: Meztizo perspectives on
personality and mental health</u>. New York: Pergamon.

Rengel, J. (1979). Relexiones y proposiciones sobre algunos aspectos de la investigacion en las ciencias sociales de Venezuela. Psicologia, 6, 357-363.

Ribes, E. (1978). La formacion de profesionales e investigadores en psicologia con base en objetivos definidos conductulmente. In R. Ardila (Ed.), La profesion del psicologo. Mexico: Trillas.

Rimoldi, H. J. A. (1978). Educacion en la investigacion interdisciplinaria: El investigador y su labor. In R. Ardila (Ed.), La profesion del psicologo. Mexico: Trillas.

Roca, P. (1962). Educational research in countries other than the United States: An overview of educational research in Latin America. Review of Educational Research, 32(3), 247-249.

Rodrigues, A. (1978). A Associacao Latino-Americana de Psicologia Social (ALAPSO). Arquivos Brasileiros de Psicologia Aplicada, 30, 235-236.

Rodriques, A. (1981). Latin American social psychology: A review. Spanish-Language Psychology, 1, 39-60.

Roth, E. (1984). Hacia un modelo integrado en psicologia: Un aporte latinoamericano. Revista Latinoamericana de Psicologia, 16, 225-234.

Salazar, J. M. (1977). Vigencia y perspectivas de la psicologia social. Psicologia, 4, 3-14.

Salazar, J. M. (1979). Dependencia o cooperacion? La aplicacion de la psicologia social en latinoamerica. Psicologia, 6, 45-50.

Sanchez, L. J. (1974). Psicologos y psiquiatras. Revista Latinoamericana de Psicologia, 6, 83-103.

Sanguinetti Vargas, Y. (1981). La investigacion participativa en los procesos de desarrollo de America Latina. Revista de la Asociacion Latinoamericana de Psicologia Social, 1, 221-238.

Seguin, C. A. (1972). Hacia una psiquiatria Latinoamericana. Acta Psiquiatrica y Psicologia de America Latina, 18, 413-419.

Stanton, J. L., Chandran, R., & Hernandez, S. A. (1982). Marketing research problems in Latin American. Journal of the Market Research Society, 24, 124-139.

Talento, M., & Ribes Inesta, E. (1979). Algunas consideraciones sobre el papel social de la profesion psicologica. Psicologia, 6, 225-242.

Valdes Mier, M. A. (1981). Psiquiatria en los paises desarrollados y subdesarrollados: Estudio comparativo. Revista del Hospital Psiquiatrico de La Habana, 22(1), 37-47.

Vargas, A. (1978). Hacia un desarrollo de la psicologia industrial. In R. Ardila (Ed.), La profesion del psicologo. Mexico: Trillas.

Vinaccia, S. (1984). Historia de la terapia del comportamiento en latinoamerica. Aprendizaje y Comportamiento, 1, 11-20.

Vinaccia, S. (1984). Historia de la bioretroalimentacion en America Latina. Revista Latinoamericana de Psicologia, 16, 373-385.

Williams, M. T. (1974). Social psychology and Latin American studies. Latin American Research Review, 9, 141-153.

By Country

Argentina

Ardila, R. (1970). Jose Ingenieros, psychologist. Journal of the History of the Behavioral Sciences, 6, 41-47.

Ardila, R. (1979). La psicologia en la Argentina: Pasado, presente y futuro. Revista Latinoamericana de Psicologia, 11, 77-91.

Astigueta, F. D., & Bion, T. (1974). The Argentina School and psychoanalytic group psychotherapy. International Mental Health Research Newsletter, 16, 6-9.

Bricht, S., Calvo, I., Dimant, F., Pravaz, S., Calvo de Spolansky, M., Troya, E., Danis, J., Grego, B., Kaumann, I., Harari, R., Musso, E., Knobel, M., Malfe, R., Ostrov, L., & Palacios, I. (1973). El rol del psicologo. Buenos Aires: Edicion Nueva Vision.

Brignardello, L. (1974). La imagen de la profesion, proyeccion de autoimagen sexual-profesional. Revista Interamericana de Psicologia/Interamerican Journal of Psychology, 8, 247-253

Brignardello, L. (1975). Psicoterpias y psicoterapeutas en Argentina. Revista Interamericana de Psicologia/Interamerican Journal of Psychology, 9, 187-211.

Brignardello, L. (1983). Acerca de la psicologia social en la Argentina. Revista Latinoamericana de Psicologia, 15, 397-401.

Goldin, A. (Ed.). (1970). Mesa redonda sobre formacion del psicologo en la decada del 70. Revista Argentina de Psicologia, 6, 109-121.

Gottheid, R. (1969). Historia de la psicologia en la Argentina. Revista Latinoamericana de Psicologia, 1, 13-33.

Gottheid, R. (1969). Historia de la psicologia en la Argentina, Segunde parte. Revista Latinoamericana de Psicologia, 1, 183-198.

Horas, P. (1977). La imagen del la psicologia y del psicologo. Acta Psiquiatrica y Psicologia de America Latina, 23, 118-130.

Horas, P. A. (1981). Current status of psychology in Argentina. Spanish-Language Psychology, 1, 357-364.

Horas, P. A., de Barbenza, C. M., de Mikusinski, E. B., Montoya, O. A., de Pantano, J. C. (1977). La imagen del psicologo y de la psicologia. Acta Psiquiatrica y Psicologica de America Latina, 23, 118-131.

Knobel, M. (1975). Child psychology in Argentina. Journal of Clinical Child Psychology, 4(2), 7-9.

Litvinoff, N., & Gomel, S. K. (1975). El psicologo y su profesion. Buenos Aires: Nueva Vision.

Mikusinsky, E., Carugno, O., & Nassif, M. (1976). Imagen del psicologo clinico y del psiquiatra en la Argentina. Revista Latinoamericana de Psicologia, 8, 363-374.

Papini, M. R. (1976). Datos para una historia de la psicologia experimental Argentina (hasta 1930). Revista Latinoamericana de Psicologia, 8, 319-335.

Papini, M. R. (1978). La psicologia experimental Argentina durante el periodo 1930-1955. Revista Latinoamericana de Psicologia, 10, 227-258.

Papini, M. R. (1985). Notas sobre la psicologia experimental en la argentina: breve resena historiografica. Revista de Historia de la Psicologia, 6(3), 213-226.

Papini, M. E., & Mustaca, A. E. (1979). Experimental psychology in Argentina between 1956 and 1978. Revista Latinoamericana de Psicologia, 11, 349-361.

Piraces, A. (1976). Centro de Estudios de Psicologia Objetiva "I. P. Pavlov". Revista Latinoamericana de Psicologia, 8, 131-134.

Reca de Acosta, T. (1966). Argentine republic. In S. Ross, I. E. Alexander, & H. Basowitz (Eds.), International opportunities for advanced training and research in psychology (pp. 7-10). Washington: American Psychological Association.

Rimoldi, H. J. A. (1976) El Centro Interdisciplinario de Investigaciones en Psicologia Matematica y Experimental (CIIPME). Revista Latinoamericana de Psicologia, 8, 345-352.

Rimoldi, H. J. A. (1976) El Centro Interdisciplinario de Investigaciones en Psicologia Matematica y Experimental (CIIPME). Revista de Psicologia General y Aplicada, 31, 195-201.

Wolman, B. B. (1979). Argentina. In B. B. Wolman (Ed.), International directory of psychology. New York: Plenum.

Bolivia

Aguilar, G. (1983). Historia de la psicologia en Bolivia. Revista Latinoamericana de Psicologia, 15, 311-325.

Carnibella, P. J. (1979). Bolivia. In B. B. Wolman (Ed.), International directory of psychology. New York: Plenum.

Heinzen, A. D. (1983). Counselor training in Bolivia: Problems and possibilities. Personnel & Guidance Journal, 61, 501-504.

Perotto, P. C. (1975). Psicoterpia en Bolivia: Necesidad o despilfarro? Revista Interamericana de Psicologia/Interamerican Journal of Psychology, 9, 105-109.

Brazil

Angelini, A. (1965). Desarrollos recientes en la educacion y entrenamiento de psicologos en el Brasil. Archivos Panamenos de Psicologia, 1, 120-124.

Angelini, A. (1966). Brazil. In S. Ross, I. E. Alexander, & H. Basowitz (Eds.), International opportunities for advanced training and research in psychology (pp. 27-32). Washington: American Psychological Association.

Angelini, A. (1973). Applied psychology and problems of Brazil as a developing country. Revista Interamericana de Psicologia/Interamerican Journal of Psychology, 7, 65-75.

Angelini, A. (1975). Current aspects of the practice of psychology in Brazil. Cadernos de Pesquisa Aplicada, 3, 35-52.

Angelini, A. L. (1978). Analisis de la formacion en psicologia en Brasil en los ultimos anos. Boletin de la Sociedad de Psicologia de Uruguay, Whole no. 47, 33-38.

Angelini, A. L., & Seminerio, F. L. (1979). Brazil. In B. B. Wolman (Ed.), International directory of psychology. New York: Plenum.

Batitucci, M. D. (1978). Psicologia organizacional: Uma saida para uma profissao em crise no Brasil. Arquivos Brasileiros de Psicologia Aplicada, 30, 137-156.

Borges-Andrade, J. E., Bastos Cunha, M. H., & Costa, M. T. (1983). Descricao do psicologo do Distrito Federal: Perfil social e economico e formacao profissionao. Arquivos Brasileiros de Psicologia, 35, 85-117.

Caldas, Y. (1980). Formacao de psicologos no Brasil--IV. Arquivos Brasileiros de Psicologia, 32, 556-559.

Campos, F. (1973). A divisao de selecao (ISOP). Arquivos Brasileiros de Psicologia Aplicada, 25(1), 17-72.

Carvalho, A. M. (1982). A profissao em perspectiva. Psicologia, 8(2), 5-17.

Castilho, A. (1980). Impasses vividos pelos psicologos organizacionais. Arquivos Brasileiros de Psicologia, 32, 393-398.

Centro de Informacao e Pesquisa Ocupacional. (1974). A profissao do psicologo na Gunabara. Arquivos Brasileiros de Psicologia Aplicada, 26(4), 3-29.

Centro de Informacao e Pesquisa Ocupacional. (1978). Distribuicao dos cursos de formacao de psicologia existentes no Brasil. Arquivos Brasileiros de Psicologia Aplicada, 30, 37-40.

D'Amorim, M. A. (1980). Formacao de psicologos no Brasil--II. Arquivos Brasileiros de Psicologia, 32, 549-552.

Da Silva, A. R. (1973). A etica e a legislacao profissional. Arquivos Brasileiros de Psicologia Aplicada, 25(1), 171-172.

Da Silva, M. R. C. (1980). Problemas gerais do exercicio profissional. Arquivos Brasileiros de Psicologia, 32, 569-573.

De Almeida, A. R. (1977). Quem publicou mais e o que em psicologia: 1970-1974. Arquivos Brasileiros de Psicologia Aplicada, 29, 111-120.

De Almeida, A. R. (1978). Estereotipo do psicologo em quatro grupos profissionais: Um estudo preliminar. Arquivos Brasileiros de Psicologia Aplicada, 30, 61-67.

Earp, I. Z., Papaleo, W., Leite, M. G., & Bussoloti, M. (1980). Conceitos fundamentais e formas de atucao em psicologia educacional. Arquivos Brasileiros de Psicologia, 32, 154-165.

Engelmann, A (1971-72). University teaching of psychology in Brazil. Boletin de Psychologie, 25, 13-20.

Ferreira, M. C. R. (1985). The study of behavioral development in Brazil: Contemporary research, teaching, and practice. International Journal of Behavioral Development, 8, 139-151.

Figuereido, J. C., & Soares, O. R. A. (1973). A informacao ocupacional (ISOP). Arquivos Brasileiros de Psicologia Aplicada, 25(1), 73-82.

Filho, L. S. (1970). A psicologia no Brasil nos ultimos 25 anos. Rio de Janeiro: Fundacao Getulio Vargas.

Freitas, E. (1973). A divisao de orientacao (ISOP). Arquivos Brasileiros de Psicologia Aplicada, 25(1), 73-82.

Freitas, E. (1973). Origens e organizacao do ISOP. Arquivos Brasileiros de Psicologia Aplicada, 25(1), 7-16.

Galvao, L. D. (1976). Prehistory and history of the Brazilian Review of Psychoanalysis. Revista Brasileira de Psicanalise, 10, 7-11.

Gentil Filho, V. (1981). Reflexoes sobre a evolucao da psicofarmalogia clinica no Brasil e sua interacao com a politica editorial das principais revistas. Journal Brasileiro de Psiquiatria, 30, 393-396.

Ginsberg, A. (1983). Psychology as profession in Brazil: An example of full legal recognition. International Journal of Psychology, 18, 572-573.

Goldeberg, J. P. (1980). Problemas gerais do exercicio profissional--IV. Arquivos Brasileiros de Psicologia, 32, 580-583.

Gunther, H. (1978). Perspectivas e objetivos da psicologia no Nordeste. Arquivos Brasileiros de Psicologia Aplicada, 30, 57-60.

Lins de Albuquerque, T. (1980). Formacao de psicologos no Brasil--III. Arquivos Brasileiros de Psicologia, 32, 553-555.

Lourenco Filho, M. B. (1971). The historical vision of Lourenco Filho about psychology in Brazil. Arquivos Brasileiros de Psicologia Aplicada, 23, 113-158.

Katzenstein, B (1970). Indentidade profissional do psicologo clinico. Arquivos Brasileiros de Psicologia Aplicada, 22(2), 55-63.

Katzenstein-Schoenfeld, B., & Lourencao van Kolck, O. (1975). Clinical child psychology in Brazil. Journal of Clinical Cchild Psychology, 4(2), 11-14.

Landin, R., & Lemgruber, V. (1980). O trabalho do psicologo na favela. Arquivos Brasileiros de Psicologia Aplicada, 32, 584-587.

Lins, T. (1970). O psicologo clinico. Arquivos Brasileiros de Psicologia Aplicada, 22(2), 55-63.

Lourencao van Kolck, O. (1975). O exercicio de psicoterpia no Brasil. Revista Interamericana de Psicologia/Interamerican Journal of Psychology, 9, 111-123.

Lourencao van Kolck, O. & Barros, C. G. (1985). School psychology in Brazil. School Psychology International, 6, 145-150.

Monteiro, S. V. (1980). Problemas gerais do exercicio profissional-II. Arquivos Brasileiros de Psicologia, 32, 584-587.

Moreira, H., & Carmo, S. (1972). Algums aspectos da higiene mental no Brasil. Revista Interamericana de Psicologia/Interamerican Journal of Psychology, 6, 51-62.

Moura, W. (1980). Problemas gerais do exercicio profissional-II. Arquivos Brasileiros de Psicologia, 32, 574-576.

Pancaro, D. (1971). Music therapy activities in Brazil. Journal of Music Therapy, 8, 83-89.

Penna, A. G., & Schneider, E. (1973). Formacao e exercicio da profissao de psicologo. Arquivos Brasileiros de Psicologia Aplicada, 25(1), 163-169.

Penna, A. G. (1980). Formacao de psicologos no Brasil-I. Arquivos Brasileiros de Psicologia, 32, 545-548.

Podeitz, L. (1970). Impressions of Brazil. _Revista Interamericana de Psicologia/Interamerican Journal of Psychology_, _4_, 275-277.

Rodrigues, A. (1981). Identidade do psicologo social: Reflexoes sobre of problema no Brasil. _Revista da Sociedade de Psicologia do Rio Grande do Sul_, _7_, 14-17.

Rossetti-Ferreira, M. C. (1985). The study of behavioral development in Brazil: Contemporary research. _International Journal of Behavioral Development_, _8_, 139-151.

Saldanha, A. M. (1980). Estado atual da psicologia no Brasil. _Arquivos Brasileiros de Psicologia_, _32_, 5-12.

Schneider, E. (1971). A psicologia social no Brasil. _Arquivos Brasileiros de Psicologia Aaplicada_, _23_(4), 9-13.

Seminerio, F. L. (1973). A pesquisa (ISOP). _Arquivos Brasileiros de Psicologia Aplicada_, _25_(1), 93-98.

Seminerio, F. L. (1973). O ISOP aos 25 anos. _Arquivos Brasileiros de Psicologia Aplicada_, _25_(1), 109-123.

Seminerio, F. L. (1978). Pos-graduacao em psicologia. _Arquivos Brasileiros de Psicologia Aplicada_, _30_, 237-241.

Seminerio, F. L. (1980). Formacao de psicologos no Brasil--V. _Arquivos Brasileiros de Psicologia_, _32_, 560-567.

Serrano, A. I., & Carvalho, D. R. (1985). Brazil: Socio-economic crisis and psychiatry in a dependent country. _Issues in Radical Therapy_, _11_, 30-32.

Stubbe, H. (1979). Ethnopsychiatry in Brazil. _Social Psychiatry_, _14_, 187-195.

Stubbe, H. (1980). Psychotherapy in Brazil. _Social Psychiatry_, _14_, 187-195.

Teitelbaum, S., & Suarez de Puga, I. (1975). O campo de atuacao do psicologo escolar configurado atraves de una experiencia. _Arquivos Brasileiros de Psicologia Aplicada_, _27_, 70-76.

Thebaud, A. (1970). Aspirations of psychology students. _America Latina_, _13_, 3-29.

Vasconcelos, R. M. M. (1980). Problemas gerais do exercicio profissional-- III. _Arquivos Brasileiros de Psicologia_, _32_, 577-579.

Velloso, E. D. (1977). Psicologia clinica no Brasil na atualidade. _Arquivos Brasileiros de Psicologia Aplicada_, _29_, 3-17.

Velloso, E. D. (1982). Psicologia clinica no Brasil. _Arquivos Brasileiros de Psicologia_, _34_, 21-36.

Waisberg Bonow, I. (1971). Lourenco Filho in contemporary psychology. <u>Arquivos Brasileiros de Psicologia Aplicada</u>, <u>23</u>, 13-20.

Chile

Badal, M. P. (1980). En el centenario de la creacion del primer laboratorio de psicologia experimental. <u>Revista Chilena de Psicologia</u>, <u>3</u>, 15-19.

Bravo Valdivieso, L. (1969). La psicologia en Chile. <u>Revista Latinoamericana de Psicologia</u>, <u>1</u>, 95-104.

Dorna, A. (1982). La psicologia del comportamiento en Chile entre los anos 1970 y 1973. <u>Revista Latinoamericana de Psicologia</u>, <u>14</u>, 147-155.

Ortiz, L., & Fernandez, H. (1975). Informe sobre los psicologos y la psicoterapia en Chile. <u>Revista Interamericana de Psicologia/Interamerican Journal of Psychology</u>, <u>9</u>, 1-13.

Zuniga, R. B. (1975). The experimenting society and radical social reform: The role of the social scientist in Chile's Unidad Popular experience. <u>American Psychologist</u>, <u>30</u>, 99-115.

Wolman, B. B. (1979). Chile In B. B. Wolman (Ed.), <u>International directory of psychology</u>. New York: Plenum.

Colombia

Ardila, R. (1967). La psicologia en Colombia. <u>Revista Interamericana de Psicologia/Interamerican Journal of Psychology</u>, <u>1</u>, 239-251.

Ardila, R. (1970). Applied psychology in Colombia. <u>International Journal of Applied Psychology</u>, <u>19</u>, 155-160.

Ardila, R. (1970). Historical development of the Colombian Federation of Psychology. <u>International Journal of Psychology</u>, <u>5</u>, 143-145.

Ardila, R. (1971). Una psicologia para Colombia y para el siglo 20. <u>Revista de Psicologia</u>, <u>16</u>, 5-15.

Ardila, R. (1973). <u>Psicologia en Colombia: Desarrollo historico</u>. Mexico: Trillas.

Ardila, R. (1975). Roles of the clinical child psychologist in Colombia. <u>Journal of Clinical Child Psychology</u>, <u>4</u>(2), 17-19.

Ardila, R. (1975). La psicologia como ciencia y profesion en Colombia. <u>Acta Psiquiatrica y Psicologica de America Latina</u>, <u>21</u>, 215-220.

Ardila, R. (1975). La historia de la psicologia Colombiana y el plan quinquenal 1970-1975. <u>Revista Latinoamericana de Psicologia</u>, <u>7</u>, 435-446.

Ardila, R. (1975). Behavior therapy in Colombia. Newsletter of the Association for the Advancement of Behavior Therapy, 2(4), 5-6.

Ardila, R. (1976). Tendencias en la psicologia experimental Colombiana. Revista Latinoamericana de Psicologia, 8, 303-317.

Ardila, R. (1976). Necesidades de psicologos para Colombia. Revista Latinoamericana de Psicologia, 8, 135-138.

Ardila, R. (1979). Colombia. In B. B. Wolman (Ed.), International directory of psychology. New York: Plenum.

Ardila, R. (1985). El analisis experimental del comportamiento en Colombia. Paper presented at 20th Interamerican Congress on Psychology, Caracas, Venezuela.

Ardila, R., & Castro, L. (1973). The role of applied psychology in the national development program in Colombia. International Review of Applied Psychology, 22, 65-75.

Ardila, R., & Pereira, F. (1975). Psychotherapy in Colombia. Revista Interamericana de Psicologia/Interamerican Journal of Psychology, 9, 149-163.

De los Rios, H. (1984). La psicologia social aplicada: Ejemplos de experiencias en la Universidad del Valle. Boletin de la AVESPO, 7, 17-23.

Federacion Colombiana de Psicologia. (1974). Funciones, responsabilidades y codigo etico del psicologo. Revista Latinoamericana de Psicologia, 6, 263-278.

Gonzalez, J. M. (1977). Tests psicologicos en Colombia. Revista Latinoamericana de Psicologia, 9, 429-435.

Gonzalez, J. M. (1978). Psicologia profesional: Una revision de los trabajos realizados en Barranquilla. Gaceta Neuro-Psiquiatrica, 2, Whole no. 10, 76-83.

Republica de Colombia. (1984). Reglamentacion de la psicologia en Colombia. Revista Latinoamericana de Psicologia, 16, 332-336.

Roselli, H. (no date). Evolucion de la psiquiatria en Colombia. In A. Bateman, L. Duque Gomez, J. Jaramillo Uribe, F. A. Martinez, V. M. Patino, E. Perez Arbelaez, H. Rosselli, & A. Soriano (Eds.), Apuntes para la historia de la ciencia en Colombia. Bogota: Fondo Colombiano de Investigaciones Cientificas "Francisco Jose de Caldas".

Suarez, G. (1976). School psychology in Colombia. In C. D. Catterall (Ed.), Psychology in the schools in international perspective, Vol 1. Columbus: International School Psychology Steering Committee.

Sutter, C., & Morales, M. (1971). Present status of industrial psychology in Colombia. International Journal of Psychology, 6, 323-327.

Uribe, V. (1984). Psychiatry and therapeutic trends in Colombia. <u>American Journal of School Psychiatry</u>, <u>4</u>, 25-28.

Wilde, G. (1966). Colombia. In S. Ross, I. E. Alexander, & H. Basowitz (Eds.), <u>International opportunities for advanced training and research in psychology</u>. Washington: American Psychological Association. pp. 55-57.

Costa Rica

Acuna Sanabria, J., Claudet, P. T., Sanchez Ruphuy, R., Gallegos Chacon, A., & Gonzalez Murillo, G. (1979). <u>La psiquiatria y la psicologia en Costa Rica</u>. San Jose, Costa Rica: Editorial Estatal a Distancia.

Adis-Castro, G. (1966). Costa Rica. In S. Ross, I. E. Alexander, & H. Basowitz (Eds.), <u>International opportunities for advanced training and research in psychology</u> (pp. 61-63). Washington: American Psychological Association.

Adis-Castro, G. (1975). Psicoterapia en Costa Rica. <u>Revista Interamericana de Psicologia/Interamerican Journal of Psychology</u>, <u>9</u>, 23-28.

Thomas, P. (1970). Situacion de la psicologia en Costa Rica. <u>Revista Latinoamericana de Psicologia</u>, <u>2</u>, 11-17.

Thomas, P. (1975). La evolucion de la psicologia en Costa Rica. <u>Anuario de Psicologia</u>, <u>13</u>(2), 101-118.

Cuba

Bernal, G. (1985). A history of psychology in Cuba. <u>Journal of Community Psychology</u>, <u>13</u>, 222-235.

Bernal del Riesgo, A. (1955). 50 anos de psicologia en Cuba. <u>Revista Cubana de Psicologia</u>, <u>1</u>, 5-10.

Bustamante, J. A. (1966). Cuba. In S. Ross, I. E. Alexander, & H. Basowitz (Eds.), <u>International opportunities for advanced training and research in psychology</u> (pp. 64-66). Washington: American Psychological Association.

Bustamante, J. A. (1968). The development of psychology in Cuba. <u>Voprosky Psikhologii</u>, <u>14</u>, 156-160.

Calvo Montalvo, N. (1978). Por que estamos haciendo un thesaurus? <u>Boletin de Psicologia</u>, <u>1</u>, 13-17.

Camayd-Freixas, Y., & Uriarte, M., & Canas, J. (1981). Sistemas de salud mental comunitarios: La integracion de modelos cubanos y norteamericanos en servicio al inmigrante Hispano. <u>Psicologia</u>, <u>8</u>(1), 3-32.

Camayd-Freixas, Y. (1985). Psychiatric social epidemiology in Cuba I: Contextual and developmental considerations. Journal of Community Psychology, 13, 162-172.

Casana, A., Fuentes, M., Sorin, M., & Ojalvo, V. (1984). Estado actual y perspectivas de desarrollo de psicologia social en Cuba. Revista Cubana de Psicologia, 1, 17-53.

De La Torre Molina, C. (1983). Influencia de la psicologia norteamericana en el desarrollo y crisis actual de la psicologia clinica en America Latina. Revista del Hospital Psiquiatrico de La Habana, 24, 21-34.

Figueroa, F. (1978). The work of a psychologist. Cuba Review, 8(1), 36-37.

Garcia Averasturi, L. (1978). La psicologia en el sistema de salud de Cuba. Psicologia, 5, 445-461.

Garcia Averasturi, L. (1980). La psicologia de la salud en Cuba. Areito, 6(24), 16-19.

Garcia Averasturi, L. (1980). Psychology and health care in Cuba. American Psychologist, 35, 1090-1095.

Garcia Averasturi, L. (1985). Community health psychology in Cuba. Journal of Community Psychology, 13, 117-123.

Garcia Gallo, G. J. (1979). La psicologia: Ciencia en formacion (la gnoseologia, la logica y la metodologia marxista-leninista como fundamento teorico-practico de la psicologia). Psicologia, 6, 183-191.

Gilpin, M. (1978). Focus on mental health care. Cuba Review, 8(1), 31-32.

Guevara Valdes, J. J. (1984). El establecimiento y desarollo de las ideas psicologicas en Cuba. Revista Cubana de Psicologia, 1, 81-92.

Holland, J. G. (1980). Alternative social systems: An analysis of behavior change in China and Cuba. In D. Glenwick & L. Jason (Eds.), Behavioral Community Psychology (pp. 380-408). New York: Praeger.

Knapp Rodriquez, E. (1984). Algunas cuestiones de la psicologia clinica. Revista Cubana de Psicologia, 1, 145-151.

Losada, J. V. (1974). La psicologia en Cuba. Psicologia, 1, 47-51.

Lowenthal, A. S., Danson, C., & Lowenthal, B. B. (1985). Psychology and human services in Cuba: Personal perspectives. Journal of Community Psychology, 13, 105-116.

Marin, B. V. (1985). Community psychology in Cuba: A literature review. Journal of Community Psychology, 13, 138-154.

Marin, G. (1979). Cuba. In B. B. Wolman (Ed.), International directory of psychology. New York: Plenum.

Mitjans Martinez, A., & Febles Elejalde, M. (1983). La funcion social del psicologo en Cuba. <u>Revista del Hospital Psiquiatrico de La Habana</u>, <u>24</u>, 5-20.

Montijo, J. A., Ruiz, B. I., Aponte, H. L., & Monilor, D. (1985). The Puerto Rican and Cuban public health systems: A comparison. <u>Journal of Community Psychology</u>, <u>13</u>, 204-221.

Nikelly, A. (1980). The Cuban experience: Observations on mental health care. <u>Clinical Psychologist</u>, <u>33</u>, 13-14.

Somers, B. J. (1969). Psychology education and mental health services in Cuba in 1968. <u>American Psychologist</u>, <u>24</u>, 940-943.

Suarez Vera, D. (1978). El psicologo en la comunidad terapeutica. <u>Revista del Hospital Psiquiatrico de La Habana</u>, <u>19</u>, 95-101.

Vernon, W. H. D. (1944). Psychology in Cuba. <u>Psychological Bulletin</u>, <u>41</u>, 73-89.

Van Ginnekin, J. (1969). Letters from foreign lands: Cuba, the revolution and psychology. <u>Nederlands Tijdscrift voor de Psychologie en haar Grensgebieden</u>, <u>24</u>, 61-66.

Dominican Republic

Meija Ricart, T. (1975). La psicoterapia en la Republica Dominicana. <u>Revista Interamericana de Psicologia/Interamerican Journal of Psychology</u>, <u>9</u>, 125-129.

Equador

Elsitdie, J. L. (1975). Psychotherapy in Ecuador: Origin and trends. <u>Revista Interamericana de Psicologia/Interamerican Journal of Psychology</u>, <u>9</u>, 43-45.

Panay Claros, R. (1979). Ecuador. In B. B. Wolman (Ed.), <u>International directory of psychology</u>. New York: Plenum.

Seguin, C. A. (1966). Ecuador. In S. Ross, I. E. Alexander, & H. Basowitz (Eds.), <u>International opportunities for advanced training and research in psychology</u> (pp. 78-79). Washington: American Psychological Association.

El Salvador

Barrios Pena, J. (1966). El Salvador. In S. Ross, I. E. Alexander, & H. Basowitz (Eds.), <u>International opportunities for advanced training and research in psychology</u> (p. 80). Washington: American Psychological Association.

Cabrera, E. E. (1975). Formacion psicologia y psicoterapia en El Salvador. <u>Revista Interamericana de Psicologia/Interamerican Journal of Psychology</u>, <u>9</u>, 37-41.

Martin-Baro, I. (1982). Un psicologo social ante la guerra civil en El Salvador. <u>Revista de la Asociacion Latinoamericana de Psicologia Social</u>, <u>2</u>, 91-111.

Guatemala

Barrios Pena, J. (1966). Guatemala. In S. Ross, I. E. Alexander, & H. Basowitz (Eds.), <u>International opportunities for advanced training and research in psychology</u> (pp. 118-120). Washington: American Psychological Association.

Davis, L., & Morales Chinchilla, E. (1975). Psychotherapy in Guatemala. <u>Revista Interamericana de Psicologia/Interamerican Journal of Psychology</u>, <u>9</u>, 173-175.

Gilbert Almengor, O. (1975). La psicoterapia en Guatemala. <u>Revista Interamericana de Psicologia/Interamerican Journal of Psychology</u>, <u>9</u>, 169-172.

Honduras

Carleton Corrales, J. (1973). Como hacer mas efectivos los servicios de orientacion en Honduras. <u>Revista Interamericana de Psicologia/Interamerican Journal of Psychology</u>, <u>7</u>, 119-123.

Risso, W. L. (1972). Algunos aspectos de la salud mental en Honduras. <u>Revista Interamericana de Psicologia/Interamerican Journal of Psychology</u>, <u>6</u>, 71-74.

Mexico

Almeida, E., & Diaz Guerrero, R. (1980). El Instituto Nacional de Ciencias del Comportamiento y de la Actitud Publica. <u>Revista Latinoamericana de Psicologia</u>, <u>12</u>, 546-558.

Alumnos y Profesores del Departamento de Psicologia Social. (1981). Evaluacion general de la Facultad de Psicologia de la UNAM. <u>Revista de la Asociacion Latinoamericana de Psicologia Social</u>, <u>1</u>, 159-174.

Alvarez, B. (1977). Educational psychology in Mexico. In C. D. Catterall (Ed.), <u>Psychology in the schools in international perspective</u> (Vol. 2). Columbus: International School Psychology Steering Committee.

Alvarez, B. (1979). Psicologia educacional en Mexico. <u>Ensenanza e Investigacion en Psicologia</u>, <u>5</u>, 415-423.

Alvarez, G., & Ramirez, M. (1979). En busca del tiempo perdido. *Ensenanza e Investigacion en Psicologia*, 5, 386-391.

Belsasso, G. (1969). The history of psychiatry in Mexico. *Hospital & Community Psychiatry*, 20, 342-344.

Carbrera, F., & Diaz, J. E. (1980). Algunas consideraciones acerca de la ensenanza, investigacion y aplicacion de la psicologia en Mexico. *Ensenanza e Investigacion en Psicologia*, 6, 246-255.

Calderon Narvaez, G. (1970). Salud mental en Mexico: Antecedentes historicos y enfoques presentes. *Acta Psiquiatrica y Psicologia de America Latina*, 16, 234-239.

Colotla, V. A., & Jurado, S. (1983). Contributions to the history of psychology: XXXIV. Enrique O. Aragon, a pioneer in Mexican psychology. *Perceptual & Motor Skills*, 57, 1013-1014.

Colotla, V. A. (1984). Rafael Santamarina y los origenes de la psicometria en Mexico. *Revista de Historia de la Psicologia*, 5, 163-170.

Comite Local Mexicano. (1972). Informe preliminar elaborado por el Comite Local Mexicano en relacion con las actividades de salud mental del pais. *Revista Interamericana de Psicologia/Interamerican Journal of Psychology*, 6, 99-110.

Cueli, J., & Reidl, L. (1972). *Corrientes psicologicas en Mexico*. Mexico: Editorial Diogenes.

De la Fuente, R. (1984). Vision panoramica de las actividades del Instituto Mexicano de Psiquiatria (1983-1984). *Salud Mental*, 7(4), 4-9.

Diaz Guerrero, R., Morales Castillo, M. L., & Reyes Lagunes, I. (1975). El Institutio Nacional de Ciencias del Comportamiento y de la Actitud Publica. *Revista Latinoamericana de Psicologia*, 7, 461-467.

Diaz Guerrero, R. (1966). Mexico. In S. Ross, I. E. Alexander, & H. Basowitz (Eds.), *International opportunities for advanced training and research in psychology* (pp. 203-209). Washington: American Psychological Association.

Diaz Guerrero, R. (1976). Mexico. In V. S. Sexton & H. Misiak (Eds.) *Psychology around the world*. Monterey, CA: Brooks, Cole.

Diaz Guerrero, R. (1977). A Mexican psychology. *American Psychologist*, 33, 934-944.

Diaz Guerrero, R. (1979). Mexico. In B. B. Wolman (Ed.), *International directory of psychology*. New York: Plenum.

Diaz Guerrero, R. (1981). Momentos culminantes en la historia de la psicologia en Mexico. *Revista de Historia de la Psicologia*, 2, 125-142.

Diaz Guerrero, R. (1981). The National Institute for the Behavioral Sciences and Public Opinion of Mexico. *Spanish-Language Psychology*, 1, 347-356.

Diaz Guerrero, R. (1983). La psicologia de los pueblos. <u>Revista de Historia de la Psicologia</u>, <u>4</u>, 33-41.

Diaz Guerrero, R. (1984). Contemporary psychology in Mexico. <u>Annual Review of Psychology</u>, <u>35</u>, 83-112.

Diaz Guerrero, R. (1984). Luminarze historii psychologii w Meksyku. <u>Prezeglad Psychologiczny</u>, <u>27</u>, 13-26.

Diaz Guerrero, R. (1984). Transference of psychological knowledge and its impact on Mexico. <u>International Journal of Psychology</u>, <u>19</u>, 123-134.

Freixa I Baque, E. (1982). Etude comparative de l'image de la psychologie chez les etudiants en psychologie Belges, Espagnols, Francais, Mexicains et Quebecois. <u>International Journal of Psychology</u>, <u>17</u>, 475-499.

Gallegos, X., Colotla, V. A., & Jurado, S. (1985). Desarollo de la psicologia en Mexico. <u>Revista de Historia de la Psicologia</u>, <u>6</u>(3), 227-239.

Gomez del Campo, J. (1978). Formacion del psicologo profesional en la perspectiva de la psicologia humanista. <u>Ensenanza e Investigacion en Psicologia</u>, <u>3</u>(2), 70-81.

Lara Tapia, L. (1983). Resena historica de los antecendentes de la Facultad de Psicologia de la UNAM. <u>Ensenanza e Investigacion en Psicologia</u>, <u>9</u>(1), 162-183.

Lichtszajn, J. (1975). Psychotherapy in Mexico. <u>Revista Interamericana de Psicologia/Interamerican Journal of Psychology</u>, <u>9</u>, 29-36.

Lopez Sierra, A. J. (1982). La psicologia en Mexico: Necesidad de una politica educativa a nivel nacional. <u>Ensenanza e Investigacion en Psicologia</u>, <u>8</u>, 276-285.

Maldonado, I., & Chagoya, L. (1979). Family therapy in Mexico--1978. <u>International Journal of Family Therapy</u>, <u>1</u>, 100-101.

Marin-Foucher, M. (1975). Psychiatry in Mexico: Past and present. <u>Psychiatric Opinion</u>, <u>12</u>, 27-30.

Mekler, S. K. de (1975). Clinical child psychology in Mexico. <u>Journal of Clinical Child Psychology</u>, <u>4</u>(2), 44-45.

Mouret Polo, E. (1978). La formacion del psicologo Mexicano: problematica actual. <u>Ensenanza e Investigacion en Psicologia</u>, <u>3</u>(2), 50-59.

Mouret Polo, E., & Ribes Inesta, E. (1977). Panoramica de la ensenanza de la psicologia en Mexico. <u>Ensenanza e Investigacion en Psicologia</u>, <u>3</u>(2), 6-24.

Nieto Cardoso, E. (1975). La Universidad de Monterrey y su papel en la formacion de profesionales de alta calidad tecnica en psicologia a nivel de licenciatura. <u>Ensenanza e Investigacion en Psicologia</u>, <u>1</u>(1), 91-95.

Nunez, R. (1976). The profession of clinical psychology in Mexico. Clinical Psychology, 30, 2-3, 37.

Perez, F. (1979). El taller nacional para la definicion del perfil profesional del psicologo: Algunas implicaciones. Ensenanza e Investigacion en Psicologia, 5, 641-643.

Perez Cota, A. (1984). Algunos datos sobre el desarrollo de la psicologia en la Universidad de Las Americas. Ensenanza e Investigacion en Psicologia, 10(1), 121-126.

Ribes Inesta, E. (1968). Psychology in Mexico. American Psychologist, 23, 565-566.

Ribes Inesta, E. (1975). Recent developments in psychology in Mexico. American Psychologist, 30, 774-776.

Ribes Inesta, E. (1975). El Consejo Nacional para la Ensenanza e Investigacion en Psicologia. Ensenanza e Investigacion en Psicologia, 1(1), 85-90.

Ribes, E., et al. (1980). Ensenanza, ejercicio e investigacion de la psicologia: Un modelo integral. Mexico: Trillas.

Rodriguez de Arizimendi, G. (1971-1972). University teaching of psychology in Mexico. Bulletin de Psychologie, 25, 38-44.

Segrera, A. S. (1983). Desarrollo del enfoque centrado en la persona en Mexico de 1972 a 1982. Ensenanza e Investigacion en Psicologia, 9(2), 289-294.

Scott, R. L. (1983). A course surveying the discipline of psychology from a Mexican perspective. Teaching of Psychology, 10, 171-172.

Nicaragua

Boehmer de Selva, R. (1975). Psicoterapia en Nicaragua: Una realidad? Revista Interamericana de Psicologia/Interamerican Journal of Psychology, 9, 181-185.

Fonseca Pasos, E. (1975). Estado de la psicologia en Nicaragua. Revista Interamericana de Psicologia/Interamerican Journal of Psychology, 9, 177-179.

Pasos, E. F. (1975). El estado de la psicologia en Nicaragua. Revista Interamericana de Psicologia/Interamerican Journal of Psychology, 9, 177-179.

Sipe, R. B. (1985). Sandinista psychology and contra terrorism: An eyewitness report on Nicaragua Libre. Issues in Radical Therapy, 11, 16-19, 50-52.

Whitford, J. (1985). Apuntes sobre algunos aspectos de la historia de la psicologia en Nicaragua. Managua: Author.

Panama

Cano, M. E., Mon, M. P., Delgado, R., Polo, O. R., Sera, L., Setton, L. S., & Lopes, R. (1984). Estado actual de la psicologia en Panama. La Antigua, 141-174.

Escovar, L. A., & Cano, M. E. (1977). School psychology in Panama. In C. D. Catterall (Ed.). Psychology in the schools in international perspective (Vol. 2). Columbus: International School Psychology Steering Committee.

Malgrat, C. M. (1966). Panama. In S. Ross, I. E. Alexander, & H. Basowitz (Eds.), International opportunities for advanced training and research in psychology (pp. 232-233). Washington: American Psychological Association.

Malgrat, C. M. (1975). La psicoterapia en Panama. Revista Interamericana de Psicologia/Interamerican Journal of Psychology, 9, 55-56.

Wolman, B. B. (1979). Panama. In B. B. Wolman (Ed.), International directory of psychology. New York: Plenum.

Paraguay

Franco Costa, J. A. (1975). Psicoterapia en Paraguay. Revista Interamericana de Psicologia/Interamerican Journal of Psychology, 9, 57-58.

La Fuente Flecha, C. L. (1979). Paraguay. In B. B. Wolman (Ed.), International directory of psychology. New York: Plenum.

Reca de Acosta, T. (1966). Paraguay. In S. Ross, I. E. Alexander, & H. Basowitz (Eds.), International opportunities for advanced training and research in psychology (pp. 234-235). Washington: American Psychological Association.

Peru

Alarcon, R. (1968). Panorama de la psicologia en el Peru. Lima: Universidad de San Marcos.

Alarcon, R. (1975). El psicologo y la psicoterapia en el Peru. Revista Interamericana de Psicologia/Interamerican Journal of Psychology, 9, 47-54.

Alarcon, R. (1980). Desarollo y estado actual de la psicologia en el Peru. Revista Latinoamericana de Psicologia, 12, 205-235.

Alarcon, R., Infante, J., Ponce, C., & Bibolini, A. (1975). La investigacion psicologica en el Peru. Lima: Sociedad Peruana de Psicologia.

Amoros, V. (1980). Acerca del psicologo clinico. Revista Interamericana de Psicologia/Interamerican Journal of Psychology, 12, 363-369.

Burgos de Chendke, I. (1985). La investigacion psicologia y el nino peruano. Revista Latinoamericana de Psicologia 17(2), 173-179.

Feijoo Portal de Cunti, G. (1980). Hechos e ideas de la psicologia en San Marcos. Revista de Psicologia, 1, 33-39.

Leon, F. R. (1982). La investigacion psicologica del trabajo y la organizaciones en el Peru: 1956-1981. Socialismo y Participacion, Whole no. 19, 61-71.

Leon, F. R. (1985). La investigacion basica, transcultural, y aplicada en la psicologia Peruana contemporanea. Informativo de la Asociacion Peruana para el Fomento de las Ciencias Sociales, Whole no. 4.

Leon, R. (1981). El aporte de Blumenfeld a la psicologia en habla castellana. Revista de Psicologia General y Aplicada, 36, 941-954.

Leon, R. (1982). Dos psicologos Peruanos: Walter Blumenfeld y Honorio Delgado. Acta Psiquiatrica y Psicologia de America Latina, 28, 310-318.

Leon, R. (1983). Un pionero de la psicologia en America Latina: Walter Blumenfeld. Revista Latinoamericana de Psicologia, 15, 433-452.

Sequin, C. A. (1966). Peru. In S. Ross, I. E. Alexander, & H. Basowitz (Eds.), International opportunities for advanced training and research in psychology (pp. 236-237). Washington: American Psychological Association.

Sequin, C. A. (1979). Psiquiatrica folklorica. Lima: Ermar.

Silva Tuesta, M. (1972). Bibliografia de Carlos Alberto Sequin: 1931-1972. Acta Psiquiatrica y Psicologica de America Latina, 18, 420-424.

Silva Tuesta, M. (1979). Conversaciones con Sequin. Lima: Mosca Azul Editores.

Sociedad Peruana de Psicologia. (1980). Codigo de etica profesional. Revista Latinoamericana de Psicologia, 12, 381-390.

Wolman, B. B. (1979). Peru. In B. B. Wolman (Ed.), International directory of psychology. New York: Plenum.

Puerto Rico

Montijo, J. A., Ruiz, B. I., Aponte, H. L., & Monilor, D. (1985). The Puerto Rican and Cuban public health systems: A comparison. Journal of Community Psychology, 13, 204-221.

Nurse Allende, L. (1984). La psicometria en Puerto Rico: Un analisis sobre la adecuacion e inadecuacion de las pruebas de inteligencia. Homines, 8, 401-412.

Rivera Medina, E., Cintron, C., & Bauermeister, J. (1978). Developing a community psychology training program in Puerto Rico. <u>Journal of Community Psychology</u>, <u>6</u>, 316-319.

Rivera Ramos, A. N. (1985). <u>La mujer Puertorriquena: Investigaciones psico-sociales</u>. San Juan: Centro para el Estudio y Desarrollo de la Personalidad Puertorriquena.

Rosada, G. (1977). Psychology in Puerto Rico. In C. D. Catterall (Ed.), <u>Psychology in the schools in international perspective</u> (Vol. 2). Columbus: International School Psychology Steering Committee.

Valez Diaz, A., & Martinez Monfort, A. (1975). Psychotherapy in Puerto Rico: The state of an art and a profession. <u>Revista Interamericana de Psicologia/Interamerican Journal of Psychology</u>, <u>9</u>, 131-137.

Uruguay

Ekroth, G. (1983). Estado actual del analisis y modificacion del comportamiento en Uruguay. <u>Revista Latinoamericana de Psicologia</u>, <u>15</u>, 455-456.

Reca de Acosta, T. (1966). Uruguay. In S. Ross, I. E. Alexander, & H. Basowitz (Eds.), <u>International opportunities for advanced training and research in psychology</u> (pp. 363-364). Washington: American Psychological Association.

Tuana, E. J. (1975). Estado actual de la psicoterapia en el Uruguay. <u>Revista Interamericana de Psicologia/Interamerican Journal of Psychology</u>, <u>9</u>, 139-147.

Wolman, B. B. (1979). Uruguay. In B. B. Wolman (Ed.), <u>International directory of psychology</u>. New York: Plenum.

Venezuela

Bustamante, M. J. (1975). Psychologists who practice psychotherapy in Venezuela. <u>Revista Interamericana de Psicologia/Interamerican Journal of Psychology</u>, <u>9</u>, 167-168.

Casado, E. (1975). La orientacion en Venezuela: Problemas del liderazgo tecnico-administrativo. <u>Psicologia</u>, <u>2</u>(3), 41-45.

Colegio de Psicologos. (1981). Codigo de etica profesional del psicologo de Venezuela. <u>Psicologia</u>, <u>2</u>(3), 41-45.

Del Olmo, F. (1966). Venezuela. In S. Ross, I. E. Alexander, & H. Basowitz (Eds.), <u>International opportunities for advanced training and research in psychology</u> (pp. 365-367). Washington: American Psychological Association.

Feldman, N., & Feldman, M. (1981). Reading and learning disabilities in Venezuela. In L. Tarnopol & M. Tarnopol (Eds.), Comparative reading and learning difficulties. (pp. 497-517). New York: Lexington Books.

Instituto de Psicologia. (1981). Contribuciones recientes a la psicologia en Venezuela. Caracas: Universidad Central de Venezuela.

Ocando, A., & Montero, M. (1981). Ensenanza de la psicologia comunitaria en Venezuela. Boletin de la AVESPO, 4(1), 8-11.

Orantes, A. (1981). La psicologia educativa en nuestro medio: Problemas y perspectivas. Psicologia, 8, 179-199.

Orantes, A. (1984). La investigacion educativa en Venezuela: Leyenda negra o dorada? Investigaciones Educativas Venezolanas, 4(4), 18-25.

Pinto, S., Noguera, C., Bravo, E., & Prieto, C. (1978). Revision critica y analitica de la tendencia de la investigacion en pre-escolar durante el periodo 1966-1977 en Venezuela. El pre-escolar en Venezuela. (pp. 581-618). Caracas: Fundacion Eugenio Mendoza.

Pittaluga, C. (1975). Comentario relativo al ejercicio de la psicologia en Venezuela. Revista Interamericana de Psicologia/Interamerican Journal of Psychology, 9, 165-166.

Salazar, J. M., Casalta, H., Colina, I., Munoz, C., Noguera, C., Orantes, A., Ortega, M. C., Sanchez, E., Santoro, E., & Villegas, J. (1978). Una experiencia en la ensenanza de la investigacion en psicologia a nivel de pregrado. Psicologia, 5, 51-66.

Salazar, J. M. (1982). Research on nationalism in Venezuela: An example of an approach to applying social psychology. Spanish-Language Psychology, 2, 185-192.

Salazar, J. M. (1984). The use and impact of psychology in Venezuela: Two examples. International Journal of Psychology, 19, 113-122.

Sanchez, E. (1983). Psychology in Venezuela. Spanish-Language Psychology, 3, 57-62.

Sanchez, E., Wiesenfeld, E., & Cronick, K. (1983). Environmental psychology in Venezuela. Journal of Environmental Psychology, 3, 161-172.

Wiesenfeld, E., & Sanchez, E. (1983). Tecnologia social: Analisis de algunos casos. Boletin de la AVESPO, 6, 3-11.

Wolman, B. B. (1979). Venezuela. In B. B. Wolman (Ed.), International directory of psychology. New York: Plenum.

10

General Resources

In this chapter we provide a bibliography (annotated where possible) of publications that provide readers with general information on work beyond their national borders, and on becoming sensitive to the cultural differences between the United States and Latin America. This listing is not comprehensive but does include some of the best known and most recent publications. These sources of information can be seen as stepping stones for preparing to work, study, or simply travel outside of your own country.

To facilitate purchase of the various sources listed here, we have tried to include the ISBN numbers. These numbers should be particularly helpful since many of the publishing houses are small and relatively obscure.

Scientific Issues

Hoopes, D. S. (1985). Global guide to international education. Yarmouth, ME: Intercultural Press.

A guide to programs, universities, and institutions interested in international education, including exchange programs, information sources, publishers, organizations, periodicals, etc.

Ross, S., Alexander, I. E., & Basowitz, H. (1966). International opportunities for advanced training and reserach in psychology. Washington: American Psychological Association. Out of print.

An outdated survey of psychology around the world. Useful as an historical source of information in order to contrast current status of psychology in Latin America and in other parts of the world.

UNESCO. (1982). World directory of social science institutions. Paris: UNESCO. (ISBN: 92-3-002007-9)

A trilingual (English, French, Spanish) directory of institutions doing research in the social sciences throughout the world, including 18 Latin American countries. The directory is based on UNESCO's data bank of institutions that voluntarily provided the information included in the directory and includes descriptions of staff, funding patterns, research facilities, publications, etc. Updated periodically.

UNESCO, (1982). <u>World list of social science periodicals</u>. Paris: UNESCO. (ISBN: 92-3-002-058-3)

A trilingual (English, French, Spanish) directory of journals publishing in the social sciences around the world. The listing of Latin American journals is not comprehensive.

Finley, G. E. (1979). Collaborative issues in cross-national research. <u>International Journal of Intercultural Relations</u>, <u>3</u>, 5-13.

Grow, M. (1979). <u>Scholar's guide to Washington, DC for Latin American and Caribbean studies</u>. Washington: Smithsonian Institution Press. (ISBN: 0-87474-486-5)

A detailed and comprehensive listing of information sources in Washington, DC, for those interested in studying or learning about Latin America and the Caribbean. The book contains complete listings of libraries, archives, and museums dedicated to or with substantial holdings on Latin America as well as listings of associations, cultural exchange organizations, publications, bookstores, research centers, and academic programs.

Lowenstein, J., & Taylor, M. L. (Eds.). (1976). <u>Study in the American Republics Area</u>. NY: Institute of International Education. (ISBN: 0-87206-080-2)

A somewhat outdated directory of universities and areas of instruction for the various countries in the Americas. It includes a very useful overview of education in each country, listings of special programs for international students, addresses of the various institutions, volunteer and exchange programs, and sources of additional information. Information on psychology is outdated.

Shuter, R. (1985). <u>World researchers and research in intercultural communication</u>. Wauwatosa, WI: Culture Publications.

A fairly comprehensive listing of 400 scientists with names, addresses, research interests and selected publications of individuals interested in culture and its influence on behavior from around the world. Includes indices by academic area and by country of residence.

Intercultural Learning

Amado, G. (1932). <u>Espiritu do nosso tempo</u>. Rio de Janeiro: Ariel.

Aramoni, A. (1961). <u>Psicoanalisis de la dinamica de un pueblo</u>. Mexico: Universidad Nacional Autonoma de Mexico.

Arens, W., & Montague, S. P. (Eds.). <u>The American dimension</u>. Sherman Oaks, CA: Alfed Publishing. (ISBN: 0-88284-119-X)

A collection of articles from sociology and cultural anthropology that describe United States culture and some of its objects (e.g., MacDonald's restaurants; bagels; graffitti; etc.).

Arguedas, A. (1937). <u>Pueblo enfermo: Contribuciones de la psicologia de los pueblos hispanoamericanos</u>. Caracas: Monte Avila. Originally published in Spain in 1910.

Arguedas, J. M. (1975). <u>Formacion de una cultura nacional indoamericana</u>. Mexico: Siglo XXI. (ISBN: 968-23-0694-9)

Asante, M. K., Newmark, E., & Blake, C. A. (1979). <u>Handbook of intercultural communication</u>. Beverly Hills, CA: Sage. (ISBN: 0-8039-0954-3)

A collection of essays dealing with communication across cultures. Includes theoretical considerations, conceptual frameworks, research on culture, and applications in industry.

Austin, C. N. (1983). <u>Cross-cultural reentry: An annotated bibliography</u>. Abilene, TX: Abilene Christian University Press. (ISBN: 0-915547-00-7)

Biesanz, R., Biesanz, K. Z., & Biesanz, M. H. (1979). <u>Los costarricences</u>. San Jose: Editorial Universidad Estatal a Distancia. (Also available in English as <u>The Costa Ricans</u>. (1982). Englewood Cliffs, NJ: Prentice Hall.)

Bochner, S. (Ed.). (1982). <u>Cultures in contact</u>. New York: Pergamon. (ISBN: 0-08-025805-0).

An easily readable collection of research studies dealing with cross-cultural experiences including uses of language, misattributions, culture shock, and tourism.

Briceno Valero, A. (1905). <u>Factores etnicos de la raza hispanoamericana</u>. Caracas: Tipografia del Centro Industrial.

Brislin, R. W. (1981) <u>Cross-cultural encounters</u>. New York: Pergamon. (ISBN: 0-08-026313-5)

A social psychologist's analysis of the process of facing a new culture.

Brislin, R. W., Cushner, K., Cherrie, C., & Yong, M. (1986). <u>Intercultural interactions: A practical guide</u>. Beverly Hills, CA: Sage. (ISBN: 0-8039-2558-1)

A cultural assimilator designed to help individuals become familiar with cultural differences in various countries. The book is highly interactive, easy to read, and an excellent guide for understanding cultural differences.

Bruce, J. (1953). <u>Those perplexing Argentines</u>. New York: Longmans, Green.

Butler, N. M. (1939). <u>El norteamericano tal como es</u>. Buenos Aires: J. Perotti.

Casse, P. (1982). _Training for the multicultural manager_. Washington: SIETAR. (ISBN: 0-933934-09-2)

A collection of workshop materials for use in training executives to become culturally sensitive. Put together by a well known cultural trainer.

Casse, P. (1979). _Training for the cross-cultural mind_. Washington: SIETAR. (ISBN: 0-933-934-06-08)

Workshop materials for intercultural training. Many can be used by a person interested in increasing cultural sensitivity.

Cerwin, H. (1947). _These are the Mexicans_. New York: Reynal & Hitchcock.

Chesanow, N. (1985). _The world-class executive_. New York: Rawson Associates. (ISBN: 0-89256-258-7)

A culture-learning guide directed at the business executive with useful suggestions for how to deal with cultural differences. One chapter is entitled "Latins: The other Americans."

Clissold, S. (1966). _Latin America: A cultural outline_. New York: Harper & Row.

Condon, J. C. (1980). _Interact: Guidelines for Mexican and North Americans_. Chicago: Intercultural Press. (ISBN: 0-933662-13-0).

Condon, J. C. (1985). _Good neighbors: Communicating with the Mexicans_. Chicago: Intercultural Press. (ISBN: 0-933662-60-2)

A short and highly informative book on the cultural differences between the United States and Mexico. Areas covered include collectivism, sex roles, ways of speaking, time orientation, management techniques, etc. Many of the suggestions are generalizable to other Latin American countries.

Cooper, C. S. (1918). _Understanding South America_. New York: G. H. Doran.

Copeland, L. & Griggs, L. (1985). _Going international: How to make friends and deal effectively in the global marketplace_. New York: Random House. (ISBN: 0-394-54450-1)

A guide to developing a business strategy and the required cultural sensitivity in order to function properly in a new culture. A short guide to various countries is included together with some suggestions for women.

Cordero, J. A. (1980). _El ser de la nacionalidad costariccense_. San Jose, Costa Rica: Editorial Universidad Estatal a Distancia.

An historical perspective on how Costa Rica became a nation and a distinct group of people with attitudes and values all of their own.

Cuadra, P. A. (1969). _El nicaraguense_. Madrid: Editorial de Cultura Hispanica.

Dias, C. G. & Chebabi, W. L. (1985). Negritud y psicoanalisis en Brasil. _Revista de Psicoanalisis_, 42(5), 987-1017.

Discusses the unconscious emotional conflicts of Afro-Brazilians resulting from inherent contradictions between African and European cultures.

Diaz-Guerrero, R. (1982). _Psicologia del mexicano_. Mexico: Trillas.

A collection of publications by this well-known Mexican psychologist that identify personality and socio-psychological characteristics of Mexicans. An English version of a previous edition (1971) is available from the University of Texas Press.

Dokecki, P. R. (1982). Liberation: Movement in theology, theme in community psychology. _Journal of Community Psychology_, 10, 185-196. See also follow-up article by Canavan in same journal, Volume 11, pp. 83-90.

An analysis of liberation theology and its implications for community psychology in First and Third World countries.

Dominguez, J. A. (1939). _Los norteamericanos son asi_. Mayaquez, Puerto Rico: Mayaquez Publishing Company.

Dzikowska, E. (1973). _Hombre: Reportaze z Wenezueli, Peru, Boliwii, Chile, i Brazylii_. Warsaw: Ministerstwa Obrony Narodowej.

Espinoza Tamayo, A. (1918). _Psicologia y sociologia del pueblo ecuatoriano_. Guayaquil: Imprenta Municipal.

Fabragat Cuneo, R. (1980). _Caracter sudamericano_. Mexico: Universidad Nacional Autonoma de Mexico.

Fisher, G. (1980). _International negotiation: A cross-cultural perspective_. Chicago: Intercultural Press. (ISBN: 0-933662-24-6)

A guide on the effects of cultural differences in business negotiations. Considers individual differences, styles, national character, and the problems of translators.

Frank, W. (1942). _Ustedes y nosotros_. Buenos Aires: Losada.

Fromm, E., & Maccoby, M. (1970). _Social character in a Mexican village_. Englewood Cliffs, NJ: Prentice-Hall. (available in Spanish by Fondo de Cultura Economica, Mexico, 1982).

A well-known psychoanalytic study of Mexican villagers that may provide some interesting details to those wishing to live or to do research in small towns in Mexico.

Gissi Bustos, J. (1982). Identidad, "caracter social," y cultura latinoamericana: Hacia una psicologia social dialectica. _Estudios Sociales_, Whole no. 33, 141-171.

Godoy, H. (1976). _El caracter Chileno_. Santiago: Editorial Universitaria.

An historical and sociological analysis of Chileans by a well-known Chilean sociologist. The book includes sections describing the people of Chile as early as the time of the Spanish conquest as well as some more recent authors and ideas.

Gonzalez Pineda, F. (1961). El mexicano: Psicologia de su destructividad. Mexico: Editorial Pax.

Gorden, R. (1974). Living in Latin America: A case study in cross-cultural communication. Skokie, IL: National Textbook Company.

A book written by a sociologist based on interviews with Colombians and U.S. citizens covering problems in communication (e.g., use of certain rooms in the house, role relationships) as well as expectancies by members of both cultures. Information here probably can be generalized to all of Latin America.

Grossman, H. (1984). Educating Hispanic Students: Cultural implications for instruction, classroom management, counseling and assessment. Springfield, IL: Charles C. Thomas. (ISBN: 0-398-05057-0)

An empirically derived book full of suggestions for culturally appropriate behavior in the school setting. Many of the issues dealt with in the book are applicable to other settings as well as to Latin Americans.

Guinchard, M. T. (1972). Le macho et les sud-Americaines. Paris: Denoel-Gonthier.

Hall, E. T. (1959). The silent language. Garden City, NY: Anchor. (ISBN: 0-358-05549-8)

This and the following two books are classics in the field written by a well-known anthropologist.

Hall, E. T. (1969). The hidden dimension. Garden City, NY: Anchor. (ISBN: 0-385-08476-5)

Hall, E. T. (1983). The dance of life: The other dimension of time. Garden City, NY: Anchor. (ISBN: 0-385-15964-1)

An interesting analysis of cultural differences in time perception, orientation, and use. Particularly relevant to Latin America.

Harris, P. R., & Moran, R. T. (1979). Managing cultural differences. Houston: Gulf Publishing Company. (ISBN: 0-87201-160-7)

A book directed at business people that provides suggestions for how to deal with cultural differences. Special emphasis is given to managing individuals from different cultures, culture shock, organizational culture, etc. Some sections are dedicated to Latin America.

Harrison, P. A. (1983). Behaving Brazilian. Rowley, MA: Newbury House Publishers. (ISBN: 0-88377-315)

A comprehensive guide to the behavior and attitudes of Brazilians. Many of the incidents and most of the information is generalizable to other countries in Latin America. A good source of cultural information on topics such as conversation patterns, foods, doing business in Brazil, family life, gestures, etc.

Hess, J. D. (1980). From the other's point of view. Scottdale, PA: Herald.

Descriptions of Latin American countries and the role the United States has played in their politics and economic development.

Hofstede, G. (1980). Culture's consequences. Beverly Hills, CA: Sage. (ISBN: 0-8039-1444-X)

An interesting book on cultural differences between countries that hypothesizes four major dimensions for differentiating countries. Various Latin American countries are studied.

Holtzman, W. H., Diaz-Guerrero, R., & Swartz, J. D. (1975). Personality development in two cultures. Austin, TX: University of Texas Press. (ISBN: 0-292-77512-1)

Descriptions of a series of studies comparing Mexico and the United States. May provide some insights into Mexican personality.

Imaz, J. L. (1984). Sobre la identidad iberoamericana. Buenos Aires: Sudamericana.

Kepler, J. Z., Kepler, P. J., Gaither, O. D., & Gaither, M. L. (1983). Americans abroad: A handbook for living and working overseas. New York, NY: Praeger. (ISBN: 0-030605-98-9)

A guide for individual planning for living abroad, including specific questions and general issues to consider before, during, and after relocation. The book is based on interviews with expatriates and should prove useful for those considering living and working in a new country. Topics covered include health care, safety, legal matters, readjustment, with separate chapters for living in certain European and Pacific-basin cities.

Keyserling, H. de (1932). Meditations sudamericaines. Paris: Librairie Stock.

Kolhs, L. R. (1979). Developing intercultural awareness. Washington: Intercultural Press, Inc. (ISBN: 0-933-934-07-6)

Kolhs, L. R. (1979). Survival kit for overseas living. Yarmouth, ME: Intercultural Press. (ISBN: 0-933662-04-1)

A concise but very useful manual directed at the individual facing overseas living. The book explains our stereotypes and preconceptions and helps the indvidual prepare for new environments and for dealing with a new culture.

Landis, D., & Brislin, R. W. (1983). _Handbook of intercultural training_. 3 Vol. New York: Pergamon. (ISBN: 0-08-027533-8)

A collection of articles on culture-training, approaches, implications, theoretical background, and case studies. Of great academic and practical interest.

Lanier, A. R. (1981). _Living in the U.S.A._ Chicago: Intercultural Press. (ISBN: 0-933662-10-6)

A book intended for overseas visitors that may help us see ourselves as others see us.

Leite, D. M. (1976). _O carater nacional brasileiro_. Sao Paulo: Livraria Pioneira Editora.

A pioneering--and now classic--book on national character from a well-known Brazilian psychologist. Little empirical detail but the ideas are important and useful.

Mafud, J. (1965). _Psicologia de la viveza criolla: Contribuciones de la realidad social argentina y americana_. Buenos Aires: Americalee.

Magii, C. (1963). _El Uruguay y su gente_. Montevideo: E. Alpa.

Marin, G., & Triandis, H. C. (1985). Allocentrism as an important characteristic of the behavior of Latin Americans and Hispanics. In R. Diaz-Guerrero (Ed.), _Cross-cultural and national studies in social psychology_ (pp. 85-104). Amsterdam: Elsevier.

An empirical demonstration of the significance of the family and the individual's reference group in the social behavior of Hispanics and Latin Americans. Emphasis is given to familism, the cultural role of simpatia, positive social interactions, and other important components of allocentrism/collectivism.

Marinovic, M. (1978). _Sicologia del chileno: Estudio exploratorio de la personalidad nacional realizado a traves del arte_. Santiago: Editorial Aconcagua.

Martin-Baro, I. (1972). Presupuestos psicosociales de una caracterologia para nuestros paises. _ECA. Estudios Centroamericanos, 27_, 763-786.

Martinez Estrada, E. (1946). _Radiografia de la pampa_. Buenos Aires: Losada.

Marquez, J. (1966). _Anatomia del gringo: Impresiones de un sudamericano_. Bogota: Tercer Mundo.

Matta, R. (1979). _Carnavais, Malandros e Herois: Para uma sociologia do dilem brasileiro_. Rio de Janeiro: Zahar.

Mayers, M. K. (1982). _A look at Latin American lifestyles_. Dallas: International Museum of Cultures. (ISBN: 0-88312-170-0)

A brief but useful book that describes Latin American culture and its main differences with U.S. culture. Areas covered include social status, manliness, marriage, the family, the church, the military, values, and economic life.

Olien, M. D. (1973). Latin America: Contemporary peoples and their cultural traditions. New York: Holt, Rinehart & Winston.

Patin, E. (1950). Observaciones acerca de nuestra psicologia popular. Ciudad Trujillo: Editorial Montalvo.

Parker Pen Company. (1985). Do's and taboo's around the world. Elmsford, NY: Benjamin Co. (ISBN: 0-87502-164-6)

A compilation of appropriate and inappropriate behavior in various countries or areas of the world regarding protocol and etiquette, hand gestures, gift giving, and so forth. General cultural characteristics of a number of countries are also included that will make life easier for a tourist or sojourner.

Paz, O. (1961). The labyrinth of solitude. New York: Grove. (ISBN: 0-394-17242-6)

A classic that tries to define the life and thought of Mexico--and by extension Latin America.

Peattie, L. R. (1968). The view from the barrio. Ann Arbor: The University Press.

An anthropological view of a neighborhood of a planned city in Venezuela. It describes the problems of migration and adaptation to new environments of poor, somewhat unskilled laborers in Latin America.

Perez Amuchastegui, A. J. (1965). Mentalidades argentinas. Buenos Aires: Editorial Universitaria de Buenos Aires.

Piet-Pelon, N., & Hornby, B. (1985). In another dimension: A guide for women who live overseas. Yarmouth, ME: Intercultural Press. (ISBN: 0-933662-58-0)

A helpful guide for women faced with the challenge of living overseas alone or with their families. The book contains a number of suggestions for how to deal with problems that arise with travel preparations and with settling in, as well as issues that are specific to women (e.g., machismo, gender role interactions, etc.).

Quintero Rivera, A. G. (1979). Identidad nacional y clase social. Rio Piedras, PR: Huracan.

Radler, D. H. (1964). El gringo: La imagen Yanqui en America Latina. Bogota: Tercer Mundo.

Ramirez, S. (1977). El mexicano: Psicologia de sus motivaciones. Mexico: Grijalbo. (ISBN: 968-419-029-8)

A well-known (in it's tenth edition) psychoanalytic study of Mexicans covering topics as diverse as sexual behavior and similarities among Mexican painters.

Rangel, C. (1977). Del buen salvaje al buen revolucionario. Caracas: Monte Avila.

Reyes Nevarez, S. (1952). El amor y la amistad en el mexicano. Mexico: Porrua y Obregon.

Riding, A. (1984). Distant neighbors: A portrait of the Mexicans. New York: Knopf. (ISBN: 0-394-50005-9). Available in Spanish as Vecinos distantes: Un retrato de los mexicanos. Mexico: Joaquin Mortiz-Planeta, 1985. (ISBN: 968-0491-X)

A fairly up-to-date description of Mexico as a country: Its history, politics, people, general culture, and characteristics of the behavior and attitudes of Mexicans in the 1980s.

Rivera, J. (1978). Latin America: A sociocultural interpretation. New York: Irvington.

Rodriquez, J. H. (1967). The Brazilians: Their character and aspirations. Austin, TX: University of Texas Press.

Sanchez-Perez, J. M. (1970). Lo hispanico: Nuevo concepto de Hispanidad. Mexico: Costa-Amic.

Santamaria, A. (1985). El machismo y sus indentificaciones. Revista de Psicoanalisis, 42(5), 1127-1144.

Discusses Mexican male chauvanism (machismo) in relation to national identity.

Seda Bonilla, E. (1976). Ensayo sobre cultura y personalidad. Revista de Ciencias Sociales, 20, 91-121.

Silvert, K. H. (1977). Essays in understanding Latin America. Philadelphia: Institute for the Study of Human Issues. (ISBN: 0-915980-02-9)

A political scientist's view of Latin America in the 1970s.

Schmidt, H. C. (1978). The roots of lo mexicano: Self and society in Mexican thought. College Station, TX: Texas A&M University Press.

Smith, E. C., & Luce, L. F. (Eds.). (1979). Toward internationalism. Rowley, MA: Newbury House. (ISBN: 0-88377-123-3)

A good collection of essays on intercultural interactions including such classics as "The people of Nacirema."

Smith, T. L. (1970). Studies of Latin American societies. New York: Anchor.

A collection of the sociological works by Smith on Latin America dealing with development, population, social structure, and social change.

Stewart, E. C. (1972). _American cultural patterns_. Yarmouth, ME: Intercultural Press.

An excellent and well-documented book on U.S. culture and the attitudes and values of U.S. Americans. Excellent source of information on how others perceive the "typical American."

Thompson, W. (1952). _The Mexican mind: A study of national psychology_. Boston: Little, Brown & Co.

Triandis, H. C., Marin, G., Lisansky, J., & Betancourt, H. (1984). Simpatia as a cultural script of Hispanics. _Journal of Personality and Social Psychology_, _47_, 1363-1375.

Proposes the empirically derived behavioral script of simpatia Hispanics and Latin Americans. Important implications for intergroup contact are mentioned.

Tumin, M., & Feldman, A. (1971). _Social class and social change in Puerto Rico_. New York: Bobbs-Merrill.

Vetter, C. T. (1983). _Citizen ambassadors: Guidelines for responding to questions asked about America_. Provo, UT: Brigham Young University.

A good preview of the attitudes and concerns people outside the United States have about the United States, its people, its government, its policies, its values.

Wagner, R. V. (1979). Teaching in South America: Some generalities. _Teaching of Psychology_, _6_, 1131-1135.

Ward, T. (1984). _Living overseas: A book of preparations_. New York: The Free Press. (ISBN: 0-02-933960-X)

A helpful book that describes the various problems overseas travellers and emigres are likely to encounter and helps them develop appropriate coping techniques. Information and guidelines are included for topics such as learning a new culture, acquiring new coping skills, dealing with job stresses, planning the move, returning, health, etc.

Wekman, S. (1977). _Bringing up children overseas: A guide for families_. New York: Basic Books.

A useful guide full of suggestions for families that move abroad with growing children.

Williams, M. T. (1974). Social class and Latin American studies. _Latin American Research Review_, _9_, 141-153.

Zea, L. (1974). _Dependencia y liberacion en la cultura latinoamericana_. Mexico: Editorial Joaquin Mortiz.

Altbach, P. G., & Nystrom, B. (1970). Higher education in developing countries. Cambridge, MA: Harvard University Press.

A listing of over 2,000 books and articles on higher education in all developing countries.

Blat Gimeno, J. (1983). Education in Latin America and the Caribbean: Trends and prospects. 1970-2000. Paris: UNESCO. (ISBN: 92-3-101908-2)

Proceedings of a UNESCO conference on educational plans in the various Latin American countries.

Boaventura, E. (1971). Universidade em mudanca: Problemas de estructura e de funcionamento da educacion superior. Bahia: Imprensa Oficial.

A discussion of changes in higher education in Brazil and the influence of the French and U.S. educational systems in the reforms that took place between 1966 and 1969.

Kertesz, S. D. (Ed.). (1971). The task of universities in a changing world. Notre Dame, IN: Notre Dame Press.

Includes articles on the internal struggles and on inter-university relations in various countries of the world including Latin America.

Aitken, D. J. (Ed.). (1983). International handbook of universities. London: MacMillan.

Published by MacMillan for the International Association of Universities, this annual guide includes information provided by 5,000 universities about their academic and administrative structures, admissions requirements, degrees and diplomas, enrollment, and staff.

King, R. G., Guerra, R., Kline, D., & McGinn, N. F. (1971). The provincial universities of Mexico: An analysis of growth and development. New York, NY: Praeger.

An assessment of the quantitative and qualitative characteristics of the various provincial universities in Mexico.

Lemke, D. A. (Ed.). (1970). Educational systems in the Americas. New York, NY: American Press.

Chapters on Argentina, Brazil, Chile, Colombia, Costa Rica, Mexico, Uruguay, and Venezuela are included.

Page, G. T., & Thomas, J. B. (Eds.). (1980). International directory of education. Cambridge, MA: MIT Press.

A guide to educational terms utilized throughout the world for all educational levels (preschool to postgraduate).

Ross, S. R. (1970). <u>Latin America in transition: Problems in training and research</u>. Albany, NY: State University of New York University.

UNESCO. (1982). <u>World guide to higher education</u>. Epping, England: Bowker Press and Paris: UNESCO. (ISBN: 92-3-101914-7)

A fairly up-to-date survey of educational systems, degrees, profiles, and descriptions of the educational systems in most countries of the world including 19 in Latin America. Each country's description includes a useful glossary of degree titles and the time required to obtain them.

von Klemperer, L. (1973). <u>International education: A directory of resource materials on comparative education and study in another country</u>. Garrett Park, MD: Garrett Park Press. (ISBN: 0-912048-09-3)

A list of publications dealing with education in all areas of the world. Most recent citation is for 1973.

Waggoner, G. R., & Ashton Waggoner, B. (1971). <u>Education in Central America</u>. Lawrence, KS: University Press of Kansas.

Presents a descriptive summary of educational institutions in Central America including cooperative efforts among the six nations.

<u>The World of learning</u>. (1987). London: Europa Publications. (ISBN 0-9466653-28-3).

A comprehensive directory of educational, cultural, and scientific institutions throughout the world. Names, addresses, and other information on over 25,000 colleges, universities, libraries, art galleries, learned societies, and research institutes, with the names of 150,000 individuals active in them. Also includes over 400 international educational, scientific, and cultural organizations. Revised annually.

Job Search Strategies and Directories

Berman, S. (1983). <u>Your career in the international field</u>. New York: Arco. (ISBN: 0-668055-073)

Cahn Connotillo, B. (Ed.). (1984). <u>Teaching abroad</u>. New York: Institute of International Education. (ISBN: 0-87206-124-8)

Casewit, C. W. (1984). <u>Foreign jobs: The most popular countries</u>. New York: Monarch Press. (ISBN: 0-668060-15-8)

Cohen, M. A. (1984). <u>Volunteer!: The comprehensive guide to voluntary service in the U.S. and abroad</u>. Yarmouth, ME: Intercultural Press. (ISBN: 0-933662-56-4)

A fairly complete guide to opportunities for volunteer work for people of all ages both in the United States and in other countries. There are no specific listings for psychologists but there are a number of opportunities for professionals interested in health, social services, etc.

Fischer, G. E. (1982). <u>All you ever wanted to know about overseas employment but didn't know who to ask</u>. Irvine, CA: Author.

Kocher, E. (1984). <u>International jobs: Where they are, how to get them</u>. Reading, MA: Addison-Wesley. (ISBN: 0-201116-61-8)

Parsons, K. O. (1983). <u>Strategies for getting an overseas job</u>. Babylon, NY: Pilot Books. (ISBN: 0-875761-05-4)

Powell, J. N. (1983). <u>The Prentice-Hall global employment guide</u>. Englewood Cliffs, NJ: Prentice-Hall. (ISBN: 0-136966-66-7)

<u>Work Abroad</u>. A monthly newsletter listing employment opportunities outside the United States. Published by Mr. Information, 2515 Rainier South, Suite 307, Seattle, WA 98144.

World Trade Academy Press. (1985). <u>Looking for Employment in Foreign Countries</u>. New York: Author. (ISBN: 0-8360-0026-9)

The World Trade Academy Press, Suite 509, 50 East 42nd. St., New York, NY 10017, telephone: (212) 697-4999, also publishes lists and directories of U.S. firms operating in foreign countries, as well as other material useful to the international job seeker.

Educational Exchange

Chapter 8 of this guide is devoted to sources of support for educational and scientific exchange. The chapter includes a section on institutional and bibliographic resources, as well as a special section devoted to exchanges of teachers.

Guides for Travelers and Emigrés

Because of the nature of the information contained here, this section is not organized in strict bibliographical format. Rather, it is presented as a listing of resources that could be helpful for someone contemplating a visit or a move abroad.

<u>Americas</u>. A bimonthly magazine that showcases the arts, the people, and the geography of the Americas. Excellent for getting a pictorial preview of Latin America and for understanding the culture and the arts. Published in English and Spanish by the Organization of American States. To subscribe write to the following address: P.O. Box 973, Farmingdale, NY 11737.

<u>Background Notes of the Countries of the World</u>. Washington, DC: U.S. Government Printing Office. Short, factual pamphlets written by the State

Department that describe basic characteristics of various countries around the world (people, history, political conditions, economy, foreign relations, etc.).   The booklets may be obtained at a U.S. Government Printing Office Bookstore or by writing the Superintendent of Documents, U.S. Government Printing Office, Washington, DC 20402.   The following Notes are available for Latin America:

Country	GPO Stock Number
Argentina	044-000-92574-5
Bolivia	044-000-92644-0
Brazil	044-000-92732-2
Chile	044-000-92586-9
Colombia	044-000-92723-3
Costa Rica	044-000-92724-1
Cuba	044-000-92200-7
Dominican Republic	044-000-92660-1
Ecuador	044-000-92682-2
El Salvador	044-000-92619-9
Guatemala	044-000-92640-7
Honduras	044-000-92697-1
Mexico	044-000-92629-6
Nicaragua	044-000-92735-7
Panama	044-000-92678-4
Paraguay	044-000-92708-0
Peru	044-000-92720-9
Venezuela	044-000-92667-9

The budget traveller's guide to Latin America. (1981). New York: E. P. Dutton. Basic information on low-cost travel in Latin America.

Culturegrams. Center for International and Area Studies, Brigham Young University, Provo, Utah. These are four-page pamphlets that describe basic characteristics of a given country and its people. The information is well selected and should prove useful to those unfamiliar with a country. They are very inexpensive (approximately 50 cents each) and can be obtained by writing to the following address: Publication Services, Center for International and Area Studies, Brigham Young University, Box 61, Faculty Office Building, Provo, UT 84602. Culturgrams are available for the following Latin American countries:

Argentina	Honduras
Bolivia	Mexico
Brazil	Nicaragua
Chile	Panama
Colombia	Paraguay
Costa Rica	Peru
Ecuador	Puerto Rico
El Salvador	Uruguay
Guatemala	Venezuela

Embassies, Consulates, and National Tourist Offices. One should not discount
the possibility of obtaining useful information from embassies, consulates, and
national tourist offices of the countries of the region.

The <u>Diplomatic List</u> provides the addresses, phone numbers, and staff lists
of the foreign embassies in Washington. This booklet is U.S. Department of
State publication 7894, and may be obtained from the Superintendent of
Documents, U.S. Government Printing Office, Washington, DC 20402.

Consulates are likely to have detailed information on educational and
scientific subjects but are, of course, useful for obtaining visas and the
like. <u>Foreign Consular Offices in the United States</u> is U.S. State Department
publication 7846 and is available from the Superintendent of Documents at the
address given in the preceeding paragraph.

All countries of the Americas maintain offices abroad that aim to promote
tourism and travel. In the United States, these offices are generally located
in New York, Washington (generally within the embassy), Miami, or Los Angeles.

Epstein, J. (1977). <u>Along the gringo trail</u>. Berkeley, CA: And/Or Press.
(ISBN: 0-915904-25-X). A culture-sensitive travel guide to Latin America.
Great suggestions for seeing Latin America as the locals do and for travelling
on a tight budget.

<u>Foreign Area Handbooks/Country Studies</u>. Washington, DC: U.S. Government
Printing Office. This is a collection of books that describe a country's
social, economic, political, and military characteristics. History and
cultural origins are also described in detail. Each book is written by an
interdisciplinary team and tries to present an accurate picture of what the
country is like; however, some of the books are somewhat outdated. The books
may be obtained at a U.S. Government Printing Office Bookstore or by writing
the Superintendent of Documents, Washington, DC 20402. The following books are
usually available:

Country	GPO Stock Number
Argentina (1974)	008-020-00536-3
Bolivia (1974)	008-020-00506-1
Brazil (1983)	008-020-00975-0
Chile (1982)	008-020-00930-0
Colombia (1977)	008-020-00647-5
Costa Rica (1984)	008-020-01009-0
Cuba (1976)	008-020-00626-2
Dominican Republic (1973)	008-020-00484-7
Ecuador (1973)	008-020-00449-9
El Salvador (1971)	008-020-00367-1
Guatemala (1984)	008-020-00987-3
Honduras (1984)	008-020-00997-1
Mexico (1975)	008-020-00585-1
Nicaragua (1982)	008-020-00932-6
Panama (1981)	008-020-00868-1
Paraguay (1972)	008-020-00402-2
Peru (1981)	008-020-00869-9
Uruguay (1971)	008-020-00361-1
Venezuela (1977)	008-020-00676-9

Hillman, S. M., & Hillman, R. S. (1980). Travelling healthy: A complete guide to medical services in 23 countries. New York: Penguin. A complete guide on how to prepare for health emergencies in countries other than the United States.

The International American A monthly newsletter for U.S. expatriates. Useful information for those living abroad as well as for those contemplating a long-term stay outside the United States. For subscriptions write to the following address: 201 East 36 Street, New York, NY 10016.

Latin American Monitor. A new company that publishes a series of regional newsletters, annual country reports, and topical reports on current events and issues in Latin America. The regional newsletters are sold by (costly) subscription in looseleaf form. Primarily designed to provide up-to-date political and economic information for business executives and government agencies. Address: 342 York Road, London SW18 ISS, England, telephone: (1)820-9748

McKay, V. (1982). Moving abroad: A guide to international living. Hong Kong: Author. (ISBN: 962-7060-01-1) An excellent guide to the immeasurable details one must take care of when moving from one country to another. The book discusses the major issues that need to be considered (e.g., health, education, children, two-career families) before moving, and also the myriad details that must be attended to in making a move (renting a house, taxes, travelling papers, banking, attorneys, packing, etc.).

Pocket Guides. American Forces Information Service. Very short booklets intended for U.S. service personnel who find themselves in a foreign country. Each pocket-sized booklet includes descriptions of the people, the government, day-to-day living conditions, and other details. The booklets may be obtained at a U.S. Government Printing Office Bookstore or by writing the Superintendent of Documents, Washington, DC 20402. Panama and Puerto Rico are the only Latin American countries currently included in the series.

Update. Overseas Briefing Associates. Short booklets with basic information on various countries of use to the business person as well as to the scientist interested in visiting or working in a given country. The series is available from Intercultural Press at the following address: P.O. Box 768, Yarmouth, ME 04096. The following guides are available for Latin America:

> Lanier, A. R. (1980). Mexico.
> Lanier, A. R. (1981). Venezuela.
> Lanier, A. R. (1982) Brazil.